Power of Attorney

THE ONE-STOP GUIDE

Exemption ID#
UCC Contract Trust Account #
CUSIP #
Issue Date:
Value $
(FRB routing#)
(Surety Bond#)
By:

Maturity Date:

Power of Attorney

THE ONE-STOP GUIDE

All you need to know: granting it, using it or relying on it

Sandra McDonald

SOUVENIR
PRESS

First published in Great Britain in 2021 by
Souvenir Press,
an imprint of Profile Books Ltd
29 Cloth Fair
London
ECIA 7JQ
www.profilebooks.co.uk

10 9 8 7 6 5 4 3 2 1

Typeset in Dante by MacGuru Ltd
Printed and bound in Great Britain by
CPI Group (UK) Ltd, Croydon, CR0 4YY

A CIP catalogue record for this book is available from the British Library.

ISBN 978 1 78816 463 4
eISBN 978 1 78283 663 6

To the memory of my father, Steven Brian Leach

Contents

Introduction

For fourteen years I was the Public Guardian for Scotland. It's a title that has the ring of something with great power: I was once asked 'does it come with a cape?'. And though it does not, the role is one that does come with great responsibility. This is because it is the Public Guardian's job to support and supervise those who administer the affairs of people who are no longer able to do so themselves. Most people in this position have a Power of Attorney (PoA).

A PoA comes into play at a point in life that can be challenging for all involved. The document is one way of being legally authorised to manage the money and property, or health and welfare, of a person when they lose the mental ability to do so personally. The person themselves grants the PoA while they are still able, choosing someone, called an attorney, to whom they give that legal responsibility. When the time comes for a PoA to be enacted, whether through accident, old age or illness, there are so many factors involved that it is important to have support and guidance.

Acting as an attorney, especially for a loved one, can seem quite a natural thing to do – so much so that the demands of the role are often overlooked. During my time as Public Guardian, working with others at the Office of the Public Guardian (OPG), I spoke with thousands of people acting as attorney. Very many of them would relay tales of woe. It was common to hear such comments as: 'No one told me this before,' 'If I'd have known what it involved I wouldn't have done it,' 'It's not worth the paper it's written on,' 'No one takes any notice of my authority' or 'I have rows with everyone'. It was evident to me that being an attorney was not as simple as people assumed.

It was with some trepidation, therefore, that I agreed to be appointed as attorney to my own parents – but you don't say no, do you? They supported you, so you do the same for them. Sadly, some years later my father went on to develop dementia. It didn't matter that I was the Public Guardian and worked regularly with families in this position; this was my dad, and I was suffering, just like any daughter, watching the deterioration of her beloved parent.

For the first few years of his illness my family supported Dad to make his own decisions, but as things progressed it became necessary to start acting formally – using the PoA. Thank goodness he had had the foresight to do this.

After some months of acting as his attorney I became conscious that I'd had none of the issues that, in my professional life, I was still hearing so many complaints about. I spent time considering why this was and concluded that it was because I was empowered: I knew what I could and couldn't do as attorney, what I was and was not entitled to, and how to assert my authority, to whom and when. For me the PoA was the efficient and powerful document that Dad had intended it to be. This started the drive I now have to put every attorney in that same empowered position.

I realised this empowerment came from having knowledge and being prepared, so I started to look at what information was available. There was (is) a lot of information, but it obviously wasn't working. Why not? I asked a number of people, from those acting as attorney to those thinking of granting a PoA, and their responses were consistent: 'Yes, there is a lot of information, but it's too much, you don't know what applies to you and what doesn't. There is so much that it's overwhelming and confusing, so you end up ignoring it.' Rather than finding anything useful in the mass of information, someone told me that *'you learn by the school of hard knocks'* – I found this so poignant that it has stayed with me.

So, if there is so much information out there that it creates confusion, why am I adding to it with this book? Well, I have deliberately gone for a comprehensive, 'one-stop' guide that gives you all you need to know in one text and saves you having to trawl through the rest.

This book is not just for attorneys. You may have picked it up because you're thinking about making a PoA and are considering all the key questions, like whom do you give it to? What powers *can* you give, and when is the right time to assign them? The book will guide you through all the dilemmas. The range of ideas it offers will ensure that you grant a PoA which allows your attorney to use it as the effective document you want it to be.

A PoA is best done as a planned exercise. Too frequently I hear from relatives who tell me their loved one always intended to do a PoA but never got round to it. Things then become much more complicated; your loved ones, at what may well be the most traumatic time in their life, have to go to court to apply for the court's approval to manage things for you; this is emotionally testing, as well as financially burdensome, and comes with ongoing supervision and reporting. So if you are thinking of making a PoA, I can only urge you to do so as soon as possible – this book will guide you through the process as well as the considerations.

The granting (making) of a PoA, and role of being an attorney, can come at one of the most stressful times of a person's life. There will be many other things you are also needing to think about; you'll be juggling lots of other responsibilities at the same time.

You don't have to question whether I, as an independent advisor, 'have an angle', or think, 'She would say that, wouldn't she, because she's trying to get my business.' This book gives an honest portrayal of what I have learnt, both as Public Guardian and personally as attorney to my father. It is not an academic text, but there will be some 'science bits': I have tried to explain the legal concepts you need to know in easy-to-understand terms. If you are thinking of granting a PoA, the book allows you to consider all of the relevant issues ahead and be fully informed; and if you are operating as an attorney, it aims to empower you to use the PoA as the effective document it should be. If I can get you to that position, then I will see it as the legacy of my career and some real positivity will have come out of my own personal experience as an attorney. I hope you find it valuable.

How to use this book

It is important for me to stress at the outset that this book relates entirely to ongoing PoAs, ones which are specifically intended to remain in place beyond any loss of mental capacity of the granter. I specify this because there is another kind of PoA, often referred to as an 'ordinary' or 'general' PoA, which gives legal authority for someone to act on another's behalf if, for whatever reason, the person is not able to do so themselves for a *defined period*. For example, if someone is planning an extended holiday and may be out of contact for some time but has business affairs that they wish maintained in their absence, they may nominate someone else to act for them by way of an ordinary or general PoA. This type of PoA is *not* valid if the person loses mental capacity. If you have one of these types of PoA, you will still need to grant an ongoing type if you wish your attorney to support you or act on your behalf should you lose capacity.

The book is divided into chapters, some of which are quite obviously directed to a particular group, whether donors/granters of PoAs, or attorneys themselves. For example, Chapters 2–5 (which consider the powers that can be included in a PoA, how to choose an attorney and how to grant a PoA) will be particularly useful for a potential donor/granter of a PoA; Chapter 6 onwards will be of specific interest to attorneys, or others who are supporting an incapable person; and Chapter 13 talks to those working with attorneys. That said, I have structured the book in this way in order to give valuable information across a range of topics relating to PoAs, and I would strongly recommend that you read all the chapters, including those which do not appear on the surface to relate to you. For example, Chapter 7 details the rights that an attorney must respect, but it is highly relevant to donors/granters as well as to anyone working with an attorney. It is important to understand the context and application of PoAs and to appreciate the role of other people in this network: an attorney should know what a donor/granter has had to consider, and a donor/granter will find it helpful to know what an attorney will have to do, as will those working with attorneys.

The book is structured in a roughly chronological way, so that each chapter corresponds to a moment in the PoA journey. It is my hope that you will read the whole book and find all sections interesting and of value.

There are case studies throughout. If I refer to a name at the end of the example, this is an actual case, used with permission. Cases which are not attributed to an individual are drawn from an amalgamation of various cases, in order to anonymise. If you read such a case and think, 'This is me, how dare she use my case without permission,' please be assured that it is not your case – maybe you can gain some comfort from knowing it is a common scenario.

Now, a brief word about how this book applies across the UK. The UK comprises three jurisdictions, i.e. three different legal systems (England and Wales, Scotland and Northern Ireland); each of these jurisdictions has its own law on PoA. This is further complicated by the fact that, at the time of writing, Northern Ireland is in what may be called a transitional period, with a new law drafted but not yet in force. To avoid creating too much confusion by referring to current and new law in Northern Ireland, I focus on the new law – the law as it will be in the long term. Where the jurisdictions differ, I will refer to them separately. If I don't draw any specific distinction, then what I'm talking about refers to them all.

Throughout the book a reference to 'he' or 'him' applies equally to 'she', 'her' or 'other' and vice versa, while a reference to the singular applies equally to the plural: for example, a reference to 'an attorney' also applies to 'attorneys' if there is more than one attorney appointed.

Happy reading, and I sincerely hope you find material of real value.

Common terminologies

> 'When I was listening to people talking about PoA I was confused by lots of words I didn't understand.' (Stuart, sixty)

To help put in context what can be a confusing legal topic I'm going to start with some common terminologies At the back of the book there is a full list of abbreviations and terms, but below I've given the meaning of the most common terms you will come across in the book, and when dealing with PoA in practice.

Power of Attorney

Both the document *and* the person who operates it are referred to as the Power of Attorney – which can sometimes be confusing. In this book, if I'm talking about the document I'll refer to the Power of Attorney, or PoA, and if I'm referring to the person operating the PoA I'll simply say 'attorney'.

PoA

I have already used the commonly accepted and recognised abbreviation 'PoA' for Power of Attorney.

> *Tip: If someone is talking to you about 'the Power of Attorney' it is worth double-checking whether they mean the person or the document, as it's not always clear. I once had a lengthy conversation with an attorney, which seemed to become more confusing the longer we went on, until it became clear that when I was referring to the PoA they thought I was talking about them, when in fact I was talking about the document.*

LPA

In many other texts you will see the abbreviation LPA, which refers to the lasting Power of Attorney (in England and Wales and Northern Ireland). As the terminology differs throughout the UK, for ease in this book I mainly use the more generic term PoA, as most of what I'm talking about applies to either type of PoA (finance and property or health and welfare) and in any of the jurisdictions.

MCA and AWI

MCA is the Mental Capacity Act 2005, which is the law governing PoA in England and Wales, or the Mental Capacity (Northern Ireland) Act 2016, which will become the equivalent law in Northern Ireland.

AWI is the Adults with Incapacity (Scotland) Act 2000, the equivalent law in Scotland.

Donor/granter

In England, Wales and Northern Ireland, the 'donor' is the person who has decided that if they ever lose the mental capacity to make decisions for themselves, they want to donate this power, this responsibility, to a trusted person. They give this authority to another by way of the PoA document.

In Scotland this person is referred to as the 'granter' (of the PoA), because they grant the authority to another.

'P' or 'adult'

In England, Wales and Northern Ireland, once the donor of the PoA has lost capacity they may be referred to as 'P', and in Scotland they may be referred to as 'the adult'. I don't use either of these terms in this book but I include them here so that, if you see references to 'P' or 'the adult' in other texts or documents, you will know to whom this is referring. I don't care for either of these terms as, to me, they dehumanise the individual. Consequently, throughout this book I refer in full to 'the person who lacks capacity', 'the person with incapacity' or 'the person' or, 'the individual'.

OPG

The abbreviation OPG occurs regularly. This stands for the Office of the Public Guardian. The Public Guardian, who is the head of the OPG, is a statutory position, i.e. one created by law. The Public Guardian has a range of responsibilities related to the care and support of incapable persons, but in respect of PoAs, for ease, let me describe the role as one of regulation. There is a Public Guardian and OPG for England and Wales and a separate Public Guardian and OPG for Scotland. There will be an equivalent office and office holder in Northern Ireland in due course.

In/capacity

There are various ways of describing a lack, or loss, of mental capacity, which include 'mental incapacity', or just 'incapacity', 'lack of cognitive ability', 'cognitive impairment', or 'volitional impairment'. You will see them used seemingly interchangeably in various texts. Some authors have a preference for one over the other; for ease and simplicity I shall refer to 'capacity' or 'incapacity'. Capacity denotes that a person has the mental ability to decide matters for themselves, and incapacity that they lack, or have lost, this ability.

Chapter 1

What is a Power of Attorney and why is it important?

Just to reiterate, this book relates entirely to PoAs that last, or continue, beyond incapacity. If you have a general PoA, which allows someone to make decisions for you now, should you be indisposed, this comes to an end on incapacity; you will need to do a lasting version if you wish someone to support you should you lose capacity.

Even though we should all be planning a PoA in advance, in reality we often end up dealing with the subject in a period of high stress, with many different factors calling on our attention, which can leave us confused and on a steep learning curve at a demanding time.

In this introductory chapter we will look at what a PoA is, why it is important, consider some of the myths that exist about it and explore what happens if you don't have one when you need it. The following chapters will set out what powers you can include in a PoA, how to decide on your attorneys and of course how you actually go about making one. But first, let us be clear we know what a PoA is.

What is a PoA?

You may be reading this book and know exactly what a PoA is, but it is always important to start with a definition.

A PoA is a legal document which a person creates, while mentally able to do so, in order to grant, or mandate, to someone else the power to manage their affairs should they no longer have the mental capacity to do so themselves. There are some things which a PoA must contain to make it legal, which we will come to in due course, but it does not have to be in a set format, there is no set length, and there are no set powers it has to grant: these powers are the decision of the granter. In other words, while there are certain parts of the PoA that are obligatory in order to make it legally binding, there is also flexibility that allows you to personalise the document to your own situation.

A PoA can offer powers relating to finances, property, health and welfare matters. These are all things that we might usually look after ourselves but, in the case of our incapacity, would need someone else to take care of. Examples of financial decisions include paying bills and sorting out household finances. Property powers allow a person to do things necessary to look after your house and other property. Examples of welfare decisions include agreeing care and social activities. There is much more detail about the powers that a PoA can give, what these mean and how they can be used in the following chapters.

The people given the authority of a PoA are called attorneys. While the PoA document is important, it is nothing without the attorney who will take on its responsibilities. Therefore, choosing an attorney is a key decision when making a PoA and is crucial in ensuring that a PoA is effective. An attorney will be acting on the donor/granter's behalf and needs to be able to stand up for that person's rights; an attorney can challenge anyone who, or situation which, seems to be taking advantage of the donor/granter's vulnerability. With this in mind, it is clear that an attorney should be chosen for their abilities: it is not always a case of picking one's closest relative or best friend. It's a decision to consider carefully: Chapter 3 goes into this in more detail.

With the right wording and the right attorney, a PoA is a protection: it allows the maker and their affairs to be safeguarded if they can no longer do this themselves. Knowing there is a robust PoA in place, well in advance of when it needs to be used, gives everyone peace of mind.

Types of PoA

There are two specific types of PoA.

1. *Lasting or continuing Power of Attorney – property and finance*

A lasting Power of Attorney for Property and Financial Affairs (in England and Wales), or for Property and Affairs (in Northern Ireland), is the name of the PoA which gives authority to enable someone to assist a person with their financial and property affairs. As the name suggests, the authority 'lasts' should the person lose mental capacity (ability).

In Scotland, this document is called a continuing Power of Attorney, but it gives the same financial and property authority which 'continues' beyond any loss of mental capacity.

> *You live in your own home, but bills need to be paid to keep your electricity on so you can cook, be warm and have light, and you must have your telephone connected, in case you need to get in touch with people in an emergency. But you are ageing and don't have much energy these days, and are getting weary of sorting all these things out; you are not as confident as you used to be. A PoA which gives authority for your attorney to manage your financial affairs would allow them to sort out these things for you, with your permission.*

For ease, I tend to refer to this type of PoA simply as a financial PoA, but this term does apply to property too.

2. Lasting Power of Attorney – health and welfare

There is also an option to give authority to someone to support you with making decisions about your health and welfare, or to make such decisions on your behalf if you are no longer able to make them yourself.

In England and Wales this type of PoA is also called a lasting Power of Attorney, but with the addition of the words 'health and welfare'. You may hear this referred to as a PoA for personal welfare, or a PoA for health and care decisions. These are all the same thing: a PoA under which you give someone authority over matters relating to your person, as opposed to your property or finances. Likewise, in Northern Ireland this type of PoA is called a lasting Power of Attorney for Care, Treatment and Personal Welfare; in Scotland it is a Welfare Power of Attorney. These are marginally different terminologies, but they all mean the same thing.

You are living in your own home but get confused: you get muddled with the time, thinking it is daytime when it's night; you forget to get dressed some days, and often forget to eat. It would be helpful to have carers come in several times a day to make sure you are up, dressed, have a regular meal and are tucked up in bed at night. Your health and welfare attorney can make these arrangements for you if you are no longer able to arrange this personally.

There is much more detail in Chapter 2 about each of these types of PoA, what powers they can offer, what the powers mean and how they can be used. For now, you need to know that these options exist, and that they serve distinct purposes.

In Scotland, the two types of powers, financial and welfare, can be combined into one document, referred to as a combined PoA.

Finally, a brief note about age. You don't need a PoA to make decisions in the interest of a child. Since PoAs are intended to confer the rights of an adult, they must be made between adults. In England and Wales, that means you have to be aged eighteen or over to grant either type of PoA; in Scotland and Northern Ireland you have to be aged sixteen or over.

Before we look at what powers you may wish to include and how to decide on who will administer them on your behalf, I just want to touch on some of the myths which surround PoAs.

Myths about PoA

There are some myths about PoA which make people think, 'Yes, a PoA is important, but I don't need to do one because ...'. If you fall into one of the groups below and think this makes a PoA unnecessary in your case, I hope I can persuade you to consider a PoA nonetheless.

My partner will just deal with things

There is a myth that if you are in a partnership, especially a formally recognised relationship like a marriage, then your partner will just manage things for you if you can no longer do so.

This is not true. Your partner, even a lifelong partner, cannot make decisions for you if you do not have capacity to do so personally, unless they have lawful authority. This authority can only come from a PoA. If you want your partner to deal with things for you, you will have to discuss it with them and create a formal PoA authorising them to act for you.

My children will look after me

There may be an assumption that, as you age, your children will just do things on your behalf. As with a partner, your children have no authority to act on your behalf unless they have your formal lawful permission, by way of an appropriate PoA.

I don't have enough money to warrant a PoA

A PoA is not just for wealthy people. If you don't have much money it can be even more important that you give direction about how what you do have is to be managed. You do this by way of appointing an attorney.

Also, remember that a PoA is not just about managing finances: it can authorise others to support you with, or make on your behalf, decisions about health and welfare.

I don't own any property

The word 'property' in a property and finance PoA refers to anything you own, not just bricks and mortar. So, you may live in rented accommodation, but you will still own things that are dear to you, maybe family jewellery, your computer, pictures, photographs, furniture, even your social media accounts and email. These are all your property; no one will have any say over them, should you lose capacity, unless you have granted them due authority by way of a property and finance PoA.

I have a will

Another myth is that a PoA is unnecessary if you have made a will. A will and a PoA are entirely different: a will expresses your wishes for the administration of your affairs after you have died, while a PoA details the arrangements you wish to be made while you are still alive, should you no longer be able to look after things for yourself. So, even if you do have a will, do not overlook a PoA.

I'm only young

There is a tendency to regard PoAs as being only for older people. We do not want to think about losing our mental capacity when we're young, but life-changing tragedies can happen. Even young people should have a PoA in place.

> *'I hadn't even thought about a PoA until my good friend got a severe head injury in a motorbike accident. His mum was telling me how difficult things were for her sorting out his flat, his bank account, his payments; she had to go to the court to get approval to look after her own son, she was so upset. She told me: do your family a favour, get yourself a PoA.' (Jamie, twenty-seven)*

It tempts fate

Some people are anxious that to do a PoA will mean that a loss of mental capacity is inevitable. An accident or illness which creates a loss of capacity is no more likely just because you have a PoA; what it does mean is that if this accident or illness arises you are much better protected than without it. Think of it like insurance; hopefully you never need it, but if you do it is so much better to be covered than face the hardships of not having it.

It costs too much

A PoA is not free, but you may be able to get assistance with the cost; also there are a range of ways to create one, from hiring lawyers to buying DIY forms, which come at different costs. It's understandable to worry about how much a PoA will cost, this should never be a reason for not doing one; you only have to do it once and it will cost much more, and not just financially, if you don't have one when it's needed. I talk more about costs in Chapter 4.

Why is a PoA important?

Having now looked at what a PoA is and busted some of the myths about it, I hope you can see why you should be thinking about making one, irrespective of your situation. However, if you are still in doubt, it's important to note that if you lose your mental capacity, whether gradually or suddenly, and want the person of your choice to support you, manage your affairs and make decisions on your behalf, then this is only possible if they have your prior authority by way of a PoA.

Many of us imagine that our loved ones will step in if we are ever in a situation where we can't speak for ourselves, but your partner cannot make decisions about your finances if you are in a coma; nor can your children decide what to do with your house if you have dementia. The only way your loved ones can make these sorts of decisions for you is if they have your lawful authority, which is done by way of a PoA. Lack of PoA can leave loved ones in quite a predicament when a person loses mental capacity and has not authorised someone to act on their behalf; as well as worrying about them, loved ones will have to go to court to get an order to administer matters. This can be avoided if a PoA is already in place.

A PoA offers peace of mind for you and attorney. It offers a sense of security and certainly relieves a lot of the burden that would otherwise be placed on family members.

In order to illustrate how useful a PoA can be, it may be helpful to consider more specifically some of the difficulties that can arise when people *don't* have a PoA in place. When reading this next section, it is worth thinking about what might happen for you and your loved ones if you were ever in these situations.

Property and finance

> *'I thought because my husband and I had a joint bank account and joint mortgage we didn't need to bother with a financial PoA.'* (Georgina, sixty-eight, retired librarian)

If you are each permitted to use a joint account individually, then for day-to-day matters there generally isn't a problem, but difficulties can arise when you need to do something more – for example, if you wish to close the account. In this case, you may both need to give permission for the closure. Problems arise if one of you is no longer able to give this permission. Georgina and her husband are two separate individuals who share an account. If Georgina wanted to close it, for example to move the money from it to pay for care fees for her husband, she wouldn't be able to do so unless he can also consent to this. What if he could not offer this consent? The account cannot be closed, or changed in any way, on the say-so of only one of the account holders. The consent of the husband in this example would come from his attorney, who could be his wife Georgina. You need to think of Georgina the wife and Georgina the attorney as two distinct people. In her position as the wife, Georgina cannot close the account, even as one of the joint account holders; but she can do so in her capacity as attorney (assuming the PoA gives her this authority, more of which later).

So even people who may have been married for a lengthy

period, with joint finances, need to have the authority of a PoA if they are to make decisions on behalf of their partner if the partner is no longer able to express their own view.

Similarly, if you have a joint mortgage you are classed as two distinct individuals who share the responsibility for the mortgage. Imagine that you wish to make adaptations to your house, perhaps to allow a loved one to be cared for at home for as long as possible, but your mortgage provider requires both of you to sign the necessary application. Permission to make the adaptations may be declined if one of you is not able to give the necessary signatures and undertakings. Again, Georgina would need authority from her husband's PoA to permit her to sign the application on his behalf.

These are just a couple of examples showing why a property and finance PoA is so important even if you are in a long-term relationship, and even more important if you have shared property and assets. A PoA sets out your wishes for your future and empowers your attorney accordingly.

Of course, these problems can be even more acute if the finances are not in a shared account. There is a very poignant video on the website of mypowerofattorney.org.uk that tells the story of a husband and wife, Irene and Jim. Jim met with a sudden accident which left him, for a period at least, mentally incapacitated. He was in the process of funding their daughter's wedding; he had the money in a separate savings account, but with the same bank where he and Irene had a joint current account. The final payment for the wedding venue was due; Irene assumed she would be able to take this from the savings account, but as this account was in Jim's name and she did not have his PoA she was not permitted to access it. As she couldn't make the final payment any other way, the venue cancelled on them. Just imagine: as well as enduring the emotion of her husband being critically ill, Irene was now faced with the loss of her daughter's wedding plans – all for want of a PoA. This case illustrates the unforeseen knock-on effect that can occur and shows why it's a good idea to have a PoA set up as early as possible.

These examples focused on property and finance PoAs, but difficulties can also arise if there isn't a health and welfare PoA in place.

Health and welfare

When reading this next section, consider – would this be me? Who's going to speak up for me and my needs if I don't have a health and welfare attorney? What position does it leave my relatives in?

> 'My wife knows my views, so would just make decisions about my health and welfare, like she always does, if I wasn't able to do so.' (Harry, seventy-two, retired joiner)

As has been stated, not even a long-term partner can make decisions on your behalf unless they have lawful permission, by way of, in this case, a health and welfare PoA. Even if your loved ones know your wishes, they won't automatically be listened to unless they have the lawful position of being your attorney.

The most common complaint I hear from non-attorneys, in respect of health matters, is that the medical/nursing team refused to engage with them because their patient's condition is confidential, and without due permission the family have no right to know the details. Families feel they are given placatory and basic information only; they often say that all they get is

'He's comfortable.' They become very frustrated, and naturally extremely upset, with having no meaningful information about what is happening with their loved one.

I hear, too, from families who are ignored by the medical team; the family knew very well what the individual would have wanted, but the medical team ignored those views and did something else, as they are lawfully permitted to do, because it was their duty of care to their patient.

To use Irene and Jim, we know now that Irene didn't have Jim's finance PoA but neither did she have his health and welfare PoA. When she phoned the hospital in the morning to see how he'd been overnight all she was told was 'He remains critical but stable.' When she asked what this meant she was told: 'We can't discuss details of a patient's condition without their permission.'

Irene knew full well that Jim would have been fine with her having all his medical details, and he certainly would not have wanted to add to her emotional upset with this sense that she was 'in the dark'; but unless the hospital staff had Jim's lawful permission to offer his medical information to Irene, by way of her being his health and welfare attorney, Jim's medical information remained a matter of confidentiality.

Another common example is families who, because no family member has a health and welfare PoA, feel 'at the mercy' of the social-care team, who make long-term care decisions for the individual without consulting the family, or overrule the family's decision.

It is important that I put this in context: the majority of clinical staff recognise the value which family members bring to the overall well-being and care of their patient, and willingly involve them. This may make you think that a health and welfare PoA is not necessary. However, having one gives you the comfort of knowing that your loved ones will be included in important decisions, and that it isn't left to chance or the goodwill of doctors and nurses. If there was a difference of opinion between what the clinical team felt was right for you and what your family knew you would prefer, with your PoA your family would have a legal position to advocate for you.

Thus, having a health and welfare PoA can ensure you feel empowered and avoid feeling helpless or frustrated in these situations.

> *'The health and welfare PoA meant we had Dad's back; it did mean standing our ground on occasions, but we knew we had the authority.' (Jeremy, forty-seven, office worker)*

Jeremy's father, aged seventy-seven, lived alone; he was getting increasingly frail but was fiercely independent. He was now facing the removal of his leg. The family felt that the loss of his limb would be the beginning of the end for their dad, with increasing physical dependence and a corresponding loss of emotional independence. The doctors had explained how serious things were, and that in their view amputation was the preferred treatment option. The family knew that their dad would not want this and would have pushed the boundaries, even if this meant risking death; so, as his health and welfare attorneys, they pushed the boundaries on his behalf. They had a few extremely dicey days, but in the end their dad rallied and improved, with his leg intact. He's now back home, seventy-nine and enjoying the best health he's had for a good while. He's just won his first bowling tournament.

Jeremy's view was that they knew they had stood their ground and weren't that popular, but they felt in a position of authority: they were advocating for their father as he would have done for himself had he been able, and, they believe, as he would have wanted them to do on his behalf when he gave them the power as attorneys. They are so thankful that their dad had granted them the health and welfare PoA when he did.

What happens if you don't have a PoA (either type)?

As has been shown, there are a range of difficulties which families face if they don't have a PoA. To summarise, if something happens to you and you lose capacity without a PoA in place, your family may:

- be excluded from decisions being made by the medical or social teams about what should happen to you
- be excluded from representing your views on any health and welfare matters
- not be able to access money that may be required
- not be able to administer your property on your behalf (remember, property in its widest sense).

If a position arises where property, finance or health and welfare authority is required but there is no PoA in place, a court process is required. The court does not grant a PoA, as this can only be 'gifted' by the person concerned. The court would appoint a deputy or guardian.

Going to court: deputyship/guardianship

'My husband's major stroke, at the age of fifty-four, changed our life for ever, within seconds. I became so, so, thankful we had been advised to do a PoA for health and welfare as well as property and finance. Life was difficult enough, in every way – too many ways for me to tell you about – but the health and welfare PoA made things much easier. I can't imagine how it would have been to have to go to court to get authority to care for my own husband. I was stressed out enough. I would urge anyone to get a health and welfare PoA, as well as a property and finance one, done, now.' (Jenny, attorney)

The court process in England and Wales will, if the judge agrees, result in the appointment of a deputy – this may be a property and finance deputy, or a health and welfare deputy, or both.

In Scotland, if the sheriff authorises it, a guardian will be appointed – this may be a financial guardian, or a welfare guardian, or both.

The person appointed as deputy or guardian could be the person the donor/granter would have appointed; you might therefore question the need for a PoA. However, there is no guarantee that the judge will agree to appoint the person the donor/granter would have appointed and, even if they do, the role of being a deputy/guardian is much more burdensome than that of being an attorney, as the following section illustrates.

Deputies and guardians are supervised (an attorney is not). This means that the deputy/guardian is accountable for their actions. In England and Wales this is to the Public Guardian; in Scotland a financial guardian is supervised by, or accountable to, the Public Guardian for Scotland and a welfare guardian is supervised by the relevant local authority (council). In Northern Ireland the appointee is supervised by the Office of Care and Protection. A Public Guardian will be appointed in Northern Ireland in due course and will become the official to whom a deputy becomes accountable.

The following example illustrates the burden that some people can feel under the supervision which comes from a court-appointed role. This also comes with costs.

'My husband and I didn't have PoAs. I had to go to court to get appointed to look after my husband; it took months, and we couldn't do anything in that time. Our solicitor was great, but even he seemed to be getting frustrated by it all. I went to the court; I felt on trial, even though the sheriff was lovely. I got appointed (as guardian, as it is called), but I couldn't cope with all that was required. I couldn't get my reports right; the Public Guardian tried to help, but I just couldn't manage it. In the end I was reported back to court; that felt terrible, like I was a bad person, when all I'd been doing was my best, and trying my hardest. The sheriff removed me as guardian. I was very upset but at the same time it felt like a weight had been lifted off my shoulders. He gave the job to my solicitor, which made me feel better. My solicitor involved me and respected me as Alf's wife. In the end I could see that I should never have been appointed as guardian – I had too much to do looking after Alf. It all worked out for the best in the end, but better still would have been if we had had PoAs, because then the guardianship wouldn't have been necessary in the first place. Needless to say, I've now got a PoA and I won't put our daughter in the same position if anything happens to me.'
(Anon., guardian)

A PoA does not have the same costs associated with it. There will usually be moderate set-up costs, but the attorney does not have to do the same reporting to the authorities, which is detailed and onerous and has associated ongoing costs. There is more detail about costs of a PoA is Chapter 4.

> *'The costs of guardianship were like a dripping tap, non-stop hand in pocket.' (Guardian)*

This completes the introductory information; hopefully you're now persuaded about the value of a PoA, and in which case are thinking, 'How do I make one?' There are a whole range of things to consider: for example, who do you want as your attorney, what powers should you give them, and how much does it cost? You'll find detailed answers to these questions, as well as information on things you probably didn't even think about, in the chapters which follow.

Chapter 2

Deciding what powers to offer in a Power of Attorney

Once you have decided that you are going to grant a PoA, the very next question is usually: whom shall I pick as my attorney?

However, before deciding on the person, you need to know what you want that person to do – in other words, what powers you want to grant in your PoA. This may influence your choice of attorney.

Since the document is flexible, there are no obligatory powers: a PoA document is intended to empower the attorney as far as you want. What you set down in writing will form the scope of their ability to act on your behalf, and so it is worth giving serious consideration to what you want the PoA to contain. You can create a list within the document that covers things point by point, or assign all powers with a catch-all term.

This chapter will consider the powers that you can offer, how you grant these and when they can start. We will also look in specific detail at the powers which generate the more common concerns.

What powers can you offer?

'Powers' is the technical name given to the authority you grant in your PoA to your attorney; so, for example, if you want your attorney to pay for your day-to-day expenses if you can no longer do so yourself, you would grant 'power' to your attorney to manage your day-to-day finances. Another way of saying it would be: your attorney would have power to manage your day-to-day finances.

> *'For me, being advised to think ahead about what powers I may wish to grant was good advice; it really helped me get things clear in my head before getting going.' (Caroline, sixty, teacher)*

You can grant a PoA offering property and financial powers, and/or one offering health and welfare powers. Here are some examples of the powers that may be included.

Typical property and finance powers may cover such things as:

- banking matters
- pension and benefit matters
- legal matters
- tax affairs
- access to financial information and passwords
- payment of household expenses
- insurance matters
- buying, selling, leasing or renting property
- taking out or offering loans
- sorting our debts
- setting up a trust
- paying for medical care and residential care costs
- making gifts
- paying for holidays

- paying for cars
- paying for specialist advice
- reimbursement to the attorney for out-of-pocket expenses.

Property powers, as the name suggests, allows someone to manage your property, which includes not just your house but anything else you own.

Typical health and welfare powers may cover such things as:

- deciding on your care
- deciding where you live
- disclosure of confidential medical information
- consent to, or refusal of, medical treatments
- legal action regarding welfare matters
- deciding on what you wear, eat, your personal appearance
- decisions regarding social and cultural activities
- deciding who can, or cannot, visit you
- agreeing work, education or training
- holidays for you
- reimbursement to the attorney for out-of-pocket expenses.

You can change the powers at a later date, if you are still capable; so you could add in a new power that has become necessary, but at the outset you should include powers that you think it is reasonably foreseeable that your attorney may need.

If you are doing the PoA yourself, make sure you put property and finance powers into the lasting or continuing PoA and welfare powers into the health and welfare version. If the PoA contains the wrong powers, they won't have any effect: for example, if you put a welfare power into a financial PoA, the welfare power that you have given will not count.

There is no set order to listing the powers; people tend to start with the more common things and move on to those that will occur less regularly. For example, begin with routine management of money and lower down the list refer to sale of the house; but it doesn't matter if sale of the house is the first item – as long as this is in the property and financial PoA it will have effect.

If you are doing the PoA yourself you may wonder how to word the powers. It's not possible for me to be explicit as everybody's situation is unique to them. My advice is to give as much detail as you can. The most common difficulty with DIY PoAs is ambiguously worded powers that end up being unusable because what is intended is not clear. On occasion, this can result in the attorney having to seek the judgment of the court.

Powers are strictly interpreted, which means that when it comes to legal interpretation of the powers you have granted there is no possibility of deducing implied powers. So you should be clear and specific as to what powers you are assigning, and how you perceive them.

For example: in the first list, one of the bullet points refers to the power to 'buying, selling, leasing or renting property'. Property is not just a house, so let us assume you have a nice piece of jewellery which you wish your daughter to have; a power to sell property means this item of jewellery could be sold by your attorney at his or her discretion. So you may wish to say: 'buying, selling, leasing or renting property in accordance with my wishes', then make sure these are clear by way of a Statement of Wishes and Feelings (which we will discuss elsewhere). This will prevent your attorney from selling items that you do not wish to be sold.

Here is another example: you may be happy for your attorney to buy things as required, but not happy for them to sell any of your property. In this case you would need to exclude the word 'selling'. Take 'paying for holidays' – this phrasing is vague. What do you wish to be included here? Is it just paying for holidays for you, or are you happy to pay for a carer to accompany you if necessary? What about other family members?

There are no set words or rules – it is your choice as to what you want to include; but please bear in mind my comment about strict interpretation, so be as clear and specific as you can.

If you are unsure what granting powers over any of these matters means, or what is the best wording for you, or what or whether something is right in your circumstances, you should take legal advice.

Some specific powers to think about

You should think carefully about all of the powers you are vesting in another person, but there are some which are worthy of particular mention.

Welfare power to decide where you live, temporarily or permanently

The power does not have to be, or may not be, worded exactly like this; it can be any wording which gives authority to your attorney to make decisions about your accommodation. It is a welfare power, so it would not appear if you are only considering a financial PoA.

This power gives your attorney authority to make decisions about your future accommodation, should this be required: for example, deciding whether you need to go into care and, if so, which care home. Most people would prefer to remain at home and be cared for by their loved ones; but sometimes, with the best will in the world, as an illness progresses, this is just not possible: it can become unsafe for both you and your loved one for you to remain at home. If and when it becomes necessary, does your attorney have your permission to place you in care, even if this goes against your then adamant wishes?

As well as thinking about what you want when it comes to care, you need too to consider what happens if you are in care and want to leave. Once in care, some people have what seems an almost innate determination to leave, even though this may be to go to a former home that they recall from many years ago, or to return to a partner they have forgotten is now deceased. It is hard for a person at this stage of their illness to appreciate that to remain in care is actually the safest and most appropriate place for them. An unwillingness to go into care or a determination to leave may create a situation in which you are considered to be deprived of your liberty (freedom to do what you wish), or that your liberty is significantly restricted.

A person cannot be deprived of their liberty without there being a lawful authorisation for this. To offer a little more detail here, the proposals for England and Wales which allow someone to be deprived of their liberty in certain circumstances are called liberty protection safeguards and are currently scheduled to commence in spring 2022. There is a process to be followed, for which certain health and care professionals are authorised; as part of the process the professionals must consult with a person's family and/or advocates and take account of the person's own wishes. These liberty protection safeguards replace, and simplify, the current system, called deprivation of liberty safeguards. To avoid confusion, I don't intend to talk about the current process; and in any case it will soon be outdated.

The liberty protection safeguards for Northern Ireland will be very similar. It is likely that in due course there will be a process for Scotland, but at the time of writing this is very much in the decision-making stages.

You may wonder, therefore, what need there is for any reference to this in your PoA, if the process (to deprive you of your liberty if this became necessary) is authorised by health and care professionals. The PoA expresses your wishes, which have to be taken into account, as well as recognising the authority of your attorney to advocate for you, which is also part of the process.

There are no guarantees, but generally it is felt prudent to have some wording in your PoA which touches on potential deprivation of liberty situations rather than nothing at all; some wording to this effect will validate your attorney's involvement in these decisions.

You will gather from this that the law in this area is ever evolving, so rather than be more specific here my advice to you is to be aware that you will need to give this situation particular consideration. If you are using an advisor, ask them about this; they should cover it with you, prepare ahead and give it some thought. If you are drafting the document for yourself, please make sure you research this ahead. The OPG websites, associated guidance and Codes of Practice will offer information; an internet search for 'liberty protection safeguards', 'deprivation of liberty safeguards' or similar wording will bring up several sites which will give you up-to-date information.

Welfare power to decide with whom you consort

The next power that is worthy of particular consideration is the power to decide with whom you consort. Again, the power does not have to be, or may not be, worded exactly like this; it is any wording which gives authority to your attorney to make decisions about whom you can see. Consort is just a fancy way of saying whom you can and cannot have contact with. The issue of who can and cannot visit you can be problematic, so it is worth giving specific instructions to your attorney.

> *'My children adore their granddad, my father-in-law, and vice versa; they got such comfort from him when they lost their dad and I think, likewise, he got comfort from them in dealing with the loss of his son. My father-in-law has gone on to develop dementia, and his daughter, who has always been difficult, is using her welfare PoA to stop my children from visiting their granddad, I don't know why. I see how desperately this is affecting my children; I can't find words to explain why they can't see their Papa and I can only imagine how he must be missing them too, and not being able to understand why they have seemingly abandoned him. I have taken legal advice to try and get the actions of my sister-in-law overruled. It's proving lengthy and costly but it'll be worth it. The lawyers keep talking about what my father-in-law's wishes would be; it would have been easier for me to prove this if there had been something in writing about him still wanting to see his grandchildren.' (Anon.)*

This example proves how situations can change. You should give instructions as to what you would wish to happen in future. You can do this by way of a Statement of Wishes and Feelings, which is covered in Chapter 5. It is particularly important to make your feelings known if you have complicated family dynamics. Estranged children, second marriages, stepfamilies, half-siblings, blended families and adoptive and foster situations are more prone to create contact disputes.

From this and the following example you will see that, no matter what your situation is, it is helpful to give some detail on who you would, or would not, wish to see, rather than leaving this to the discretion of the attorney.

> '*My father and brother fell out about twenty years ago because of my brother's unacceptable behaviour. He assaulted Dad so badly one evening that he ended up in intensive care. This ended their relationship: my father would say he disowned my brother, my brother would say he estranged himself – whatever, my brother hasn't spoken to any of us in all that time and there seemed no inclination, by any of us, to reconcile the situation. But I'm now in a quandary: my brother has materialised out of the blue and is demanding to see Dad (who is dying). It feels like this would appease my brother's conscience before Dad dies, but what would Dad want? It would have helped if we had spoken about it. If only I had asked Dad, if the worst came to the worst: would he wish to see his son? But I don't know. Should I let him see Dad, or not? Will it hurt Dad to see him, or hurt him more to think his son didn't care even when on his deathbed? Deep down, would he really want reconciliation? Is it safe to let my brother in? I don't know his views on his relationship with Dad. What do I do?' (Anon.)*

There is a school of thought which says no one should have power to decide who visits you. You can see that if the daughter in the first example had not had this power, she would not have been able to prevent the grandchildren visiting, which you may regard as advantageous; but contrast this with the second example. If the daughter there had not had that power, the estranged son could have visited: a person who has abused the incapable person could not be prevented from contact with him without a formal legal process. Granting this power, or not, is very much personal preference. I include it here so you can deliberate this in advance.

Power to access social media

Your social media account(s) is/are your private business; accessing these can be problematic if and when anything happens to you, unless you have granted permission by way of your PoA. As your social media accounts are your 'property', the powers authorising someone else to make decisions about these would need to be included in a lasting or continuing PoA, which covers financial and property matters.

Two immediate things to think about here are: if no one has access to your social media account, how are your contacts notified of your new situation, your loss of capacity, or offered any updates? And for many, a more important consideration is access to photographs and special memories which are held in your account. Any photographs which are saved in your account are yours; accessing these in the absence of your express permission is difficult, even if it is a photo of the person who wants access, maybe with you on a special occasion, or a picture of your shared children.

Power to access digital data, including passwords

A similar difficulty can arise with access to online accounts that you have; online banking, but also other online accounts like shopping or debit payment ones. If you wish your attorney to manage these accounts for you, even if it is only to close them, then you will need to ensure they have the necessary permissions.

Use of CCTV

CCTV systems are available for home use and are increasingly used in care homes. In care homes they tend to be confined to communal areas, but what if these were to be used in private areas, for example residents' own rooms, bedrooms and bathrooms?

The use of CCTV generates mixed views, and the idea of CCTV in private areas polarises opinion. Some see CCTV as a valuable protection or safety net; these people are reassured by knowing someone could check a camera and make sure they were OK. The opposite view is that CCTV is an intrusion of privacy and so an invasion of one's rights.

You should make your views known to your attorney and also consider whether you wish to include express instruction in your PoA. Are you happy for your attorney to install CCTV in your home? What if this was in your private room in a care home? If it is in your home for your safety, do you wish to advise your attorney of any rules on its use?

> 'When my son first suggested that I have CCTV in my home I was against it; I didn't want him checking on my comings and goings, even though I've got nothing to hide, but as my health has deteriorated I now see why he suggested it. I think it is a good idea that my son and daughter can just double-check I've not fallen downstairs, but I've said they can only install it downstairs, not in my bedroom or bathroom, and that they can only check it twice a day at around 8.30 a.m. to make sure I'm up and OK and again at about 11 p.m. to make sure I'm in bed OK (if they don't see me downstairs they can assume this). They only have my permission to check it in between if they have genuine reason to believe there may be an emergency.'
> (Maud, eighty-six)

Payment power

This relates to any lay attorneys you may appoint, i.e. family and friends.

Generally, attorneys are permitted to be reimbursed for their out-of-pocket expenditure, e.g. petrol costs or train fares. If you are happy to approve reimbursement of such costs, you should make it clear what your wishes are; for example, does this apply to every visit to you, or a limited number? For petrol costs, what pence-per-mile rate do you find acceptable? The general rule of thumb is that an attorney may be reimbursed out-of-pocket expenditure for two visits per year, and only in addition to this if they are required to visit you specifically in their capacity as your attorney.

If you are wanting your attorney to receive some payment, think about any limits or restrictions on when, or for what, they can take payment. Would you wish a cap on the amount of payment they can take, say, in any one year?

So spend some time thinking about this and talk to your solicitor, if you are using one, about your wishes.

Please note that this section does not apply to a professional appointment, i.e. if you are asking your solicitor to be your attorney: in his professional capacity, he is entitled to charge for his services – but should advise you at what rate.

Voting

This power requires less decision-making on your part, but I have included it as there are various dimensions to it which you may need to take into consideration, depending on your circumstances.

If you need your attorney to vote for you – for example, as part of a group you are involved with, on who should be elected as chair of a local committee – you can grant your attorney the power to vote on your behalf.

However, granting voting power does not give your attorney power to vote on your behalf in a political election. You do not lose your right to vote when you lose mental capacity, but when it comes to the actual voting *you* need to be able to express your vote choice; another person, even with your permission by way of your PoA, cannot decide what your vote choice would have been, no matter how well they know you and even if they know that you have always voted a certain way. Someone can support you to express your vote choice, or even enact your choice for you if you are no longer able to do so personally, but the key is that it has to be your choice, made at the time of voting. Your local electoral registration office will be able to advise you if you need more detail on this.

If you need to vote in a business capacity, e.g. as director of a company, you should take advice from your company lawyers about how to protect this right. You as an individual and you as the company director are distinct people (even if the company is your own company and you are a sole trader). A PoA grants powers to your attorney over your personal affairs, but this will not necessarily be sufficient to allow them to act as a business proxy for you.

Unlawful powers

There are some powers that you are not permitted to offer to your attorney.

Examples are:

- the power for your attorney to appoint a successor (i.e. your attorney cannot decide for themselves who should act for you if they can no longer do so)
- the power to agree for you to marry
- the power for your attorney to consent for you to have sexual relations
- the power for your attorney to consent, or refuse, for you to have treatment for a mental disorder.

The reason why you're not permitted to give these powers to someone else is because (apart from the last one) they are so personal and go to the heart of what you must decide for yourself that it is considered inappropriate for an attorney to be permitted to decide for you. The last power is covered by other law: the Mental Health Acts in the respective countries.

If you do include these powers, be it accidentally or deliberately, your attorney would not be permitted to rely on them.

It is perhaps worth mentioning here that health and care professionals have authority, under the law, to mandate treatments, where the treatment is, in their opinion, required and is consistent with their duty of care to act in the best interests of their patient. The wishes of, or likely wishes of, the patient as well as the views of the family should be taken into account. In the main, a consensus view as to the best way forward is reached; but we do occasionally hear of cases, which are often in the court by this point, where the family and medical professionals have diametrically opposed opinions which they cannot reconcile.

The provision of support with decision-making

This is not a power as such, but you may wish to include within your PoA a reference to your attorney supporting you with your decision-making. Chapter 7 offers information, predominately to attorneys, about the requirement to support an incapable person with their decision-making. Even though this is a requirement, there can still be a tendency for attorneys to overlook this step and go straight to making decisions on your behalf. If you have made express reference in your PoA to requiring your attorneys to support you with your decision-making, your attorneys must ensure that they offer you this support.

The legal principles

There are certain legal principles which all attorneys are obliged, by law, to respect. In Chapter 9 we will consider these in detail, but it's worth saying here that, if followed, the principles will lead to the proper administration of the PoA.

However, many attorneys are not aware of the principles; to draw these to their attention, and so to ensure they know they are obliged to act in accordance with them, you may wish to make express reference to the principles in your PoA and ask your attorney to abide by them.

Use of your PoA abroad

If you make regular journeys between two countries and anticipate that this would remain the case even if you lost capacity, I would advise you to seek legal guidance on the best way to protect yourself in both countries. Do not assume that one PoA will cover all eventualities.

The Code of Practice

The Code of Practice has not yet been mentioned. There is a Code of Practice for England and Wales and a separate Code for Scotland. A Code of Practice is in development for Northern Ireland. The codes provide guidance to anyone who is working with and/or caring for people (specifically adults) who may lack capacity.

The MCA (England and Wales) requires an attorney to have 'regard to' relevant guidance in the Code of Practice, but neither Act, the MCA nor AWI (Scotland), imposes a legal duty on anyone to 'comply' with the code – it should be viewed as guidance rather than instruction. But if a person has not followed relevant guidance contained in the code, they may be expected to give good reasons why they have departed from it. You can find the codes on the respective Public Guardian's website.

That concludes the review of those powers to which I would recommend you give additional consideration; although of course you should think carefully about *all* the powers you are thinking of including. Before we leave the issue of powers, we should look at how you grant the powers you have decided on.

The granting of powers

In England and Wales and Northern Ireland, the standard approach is for the attorney to be granted all powers, unless you expressly wish to exclude anything. It is important therefore that you have thought about what, if anything, you may wish to exclude. The list of typical powers on p. 302 will assist you with this.

In Scotland, the standard format is inclusion of powers, i.e. that you list all the powers you wish to give to your attorney. It is important that you think about what powers you want to offer, as to leave something out may hamper the effective operation of the PoA at a later stage. Again, the list of possible powers at the back of the book will help you with this.

As the standard format in Scotland is inclusion of expressed powers, in order to avoid your omission of something it is usual to include what is referred to as a 'plenary power'. A plenary power is a 'catch-all' type of power: it goes ahead of the list of specific powers and will say something like, 'power to do every-thing I would have been able to do myself including but not limited to ...' and then the list would start.

You can decide whether, or not, you wish to include a plenary power. If a plenary power is included, you have effectively then granted all powers to your attorney. It is important that you know this. By way of example, let us say you do not want to allow your attorney to be able to sell your house, so you deliberately leave this power off the list of specific powers, but you include a plenary power which says: 'everything I would have been entitled to do myself'. This would then give the power to the attorney to sell your house, because selling your house is something you yourself would have been entitled to do.

There is one final thing for you to think about in relation to powers: when you wish them to start. You have some options here.

When can the powers start?

The 'rules' on when the PoA starts depend on whether one is talking about the welfare or the financial powers, even if these are combined in the same document (which is possible in Scotland).

Welfare powers

Welfare powers cannot start unless or until you become incapable of making the decision in question. In Scotland, by law, you have to consider how you wish your incapacity to be determined – and a statement to this effect must be in the PoA, otherwise it cannot be registered. There are really only two options: you can be considered incapable when your attorney reasonably believes this to be the case, or when professional opinion assesses this to be the case. If you choose this latter option, it is better to be specific about what professional opinion you prefer: medical or legal.

Financial powers

Financial powers can start as soon as the document has been

registered with the Office of the Public Guardian (OPG). It can be helpful for financial powers to commence sooner than incapacity, as this allows people to assist you with practical matters if you are finding them difficult.

> *'I'm with it "up there" but I get so tired these days, and I get flummoxed by all the terms and conditions these companies spout at you on the telephone; it's great that my PoA allows my daughter just to deal with these things for me. I tell her what I want and she sorts it out.' (Sarah, seventy-seven, granter of PoA)*

Deferral of financial powers

If you would prefer that the financial powers did not start straight away, then you have two options: you can add to the document a clause which defers its commencement; you would state what 'trigger' would then bring the powers into effect – which would usually be when your attorney believes you to be incapable, or when medical or legal opinion assesses this to be the case. In doing this you place the financial powers on the same footing as the welfare powers.

The other option for deferring financial powers is not to register the PoA with the OPG unless or until the powers are needed. The main risk here is that, when the time comes for your attorney to register your PoA, it is not registerable for some reason, and you have by then lost capacity and cannot correct whatever the flaw is. This means that your attorney will not be able to take up post and will have to apply to the court to become your deputy / guardian – with all the supervision, and costs, associated with this.

> *'My father decided to defer the registration of his PoA, I'm not sure why; but when it came to it, the solicitor who had done it for him had made a mistake with the signatures and it was not able to be registered. I had to apply to the court to become his deputy. This took a while; I felt like I was having to prove myself and I hated having to report to the OPG each year, let alone the cost of this, when none of it was what my dad had intended – indeed, he had tried to avoid this. I considered whether to sue the solicitor, as it seemed to be his fault that I was in this position, but I know Dad would not have wanted this, so I just had to "suck it up".' (Karen, sixty-five, deputy/frustrated attorney)*

In Scotland, although the welfare and financial powers can be combined in the same document, they can start at different times, so you don't have to defer financial powers to bring them in line with welfare or do separate PoAs.

My final piece of advice in this chapter is: take your time. Granting a PoA is critical to ensuring your future affairs are in order, but it should be something that is done with full and proper consideration. For most people there is no immediate rush, and diligent planning is recommended. Do not make a spur-of-the-minute decision on any of the decisions to be made. If something crops up which you have not thought about, it is fine to halt the process while you have a ponder, speak to a friend, look things up – whatever is your preference. So I'll close by saying: don't feel pressured, research things, ask around. Only go ahead once you feel you have a clear idea of what you want, for you, in your circumstances. But don't leave it until it's too late.

Chapter 3

How to decide on your attorney

Now you have decided what powers you wish to offer in your PoA, we will consider in this chapter who may be the best person for you to appoint to administer these powers. We will look at whom you can appoint and what sort of factors may influence your decision. If you wish to appoint more than one person, we will look at what authority you may wish to offer them in relation to each other. We will close by considering whether you wish there to be a replacement person nominated in the event of one of your attorneys no longer being able to act and whether you would prefer your attorneys to be supervised.

Whom to appoint?

Once you have decided what powers you want to assign, you can now think about whom to appoint. There are a few stipulations, by law, which limit your choice of attorney, so we'll get these out of the way first.

In England and Wales and Northern Ireland your attorney must be aged eighteen or over, and aged sixteen or over in Scotland. An attorney cannot manage financial powers if they are bankrupt (but they can have health and welfare powers). Health and welfare powers can only be granted to an individual (i.e. a named person), but financial powers can be granted to an entity (e.g. a trust corporation or firm of solicitors.)

Beyond this, you can appoint whomever you wish as your attorney. Here are some questions that may help you decide, with some discussion to follow.

- Whom do I *want* to appoint? (Which may be entirely different from whom I think I should, or must, appoint.)
- Do I genuinely trust the people I'm thinking of?
- What powers do I want to give to each?
- Do I really know what the role of attorney involves, so that I'm aware of what I'm asking of them? Will the people I'm thinking of be able to do what is required – for example, will they be able to manage my financial affairs?
- Do they get along?
- If they don't live nearby, are they OK with online banking etc.?
- Will they be able to get to see me to check on things?
- Will they be able to 'fight my corner' if necessary?
- Do they need anybody else to be appointed with them, so they have assistance in the role, or a reassuring hand?
- Are the people I'm thinking of going to be willing to do this for me?

Let's look at these factors in more detail.

First, pick the person you want: picking a person you trust is critical. There are some people who choose an attorney because they think they should, but they don't really want that person and sometimes don't even really trust that person. Please do not feel any pressure to pick a particular person. It should be your free choice.

When choosing an attorney, consider the person's skills, personality or abilities – and not their relationship to you. Do not feel you have to have, or should have, your next of kin, or your eldest child, just because they have that relationship to you.

> 'I had just assumed it "went down the line" and it was great to know I could pick who I wanted. It gave me the courage to go to someone I wanted, not who I thought I should have.' (Valerie, sixty-one, retired)

You may wish to opt for a good friend rather than a family member, or even a professional such as your family solicitor, because you feel they would be better able to fulfil the role. You might think they could do this more dispassionately than a family member, or you don't want to place the burden of responsibility on your children. You can even have a combination of family, friend and professional – it is entirely your choice.

Considering the powers that you want to grant will help your decision on whom to appoint; a particular person may be better for one role than another. For example, the person you have in mind may not be confident with making financial decisions, but they may be very well placed to advise on your care needs.

If you are granting both finance and welfare powers, you may prefer to have one person do finance and another do the welfare side. This is fine; you do not need to assign all powers to the same person or people.

The person doesn't have to live nearby; with digital banking it is easy for the attorney to operate at a distance, as long as the distance doesn't mean they don't know you and your circumstances or needs.

That said, the attorney must be willing to travel from time to time as there may be matters they have to attend to in person; generally the attorney should see you twice a year to make sure everything is 'panning out' the way they assume to be the case.

> *'My daughters live in America, but I see them about four times a year. They know me well and I would wish them to be my attorneys, but I had assumed they couldn't be because they weren't local; so I was pleased to hear that even though they live abroad I could still nominate them as my attorneys.' (Gillian, fifty-nine)*

You will see that whom you appoint is entirely up to you, but you should not underestimate the responsibility of being an attorney. You should read from Chapter 6 on so you know what the role truly involves. Pick a person you trust, who will make the best attorney for you and who is able to support you in the way that is required.

Finally, it is of course courteous to ask your proposed attorney if they are willing to undertake this role: don't just assume. And certainly, don't let them find out only when they receive the paperwork – it doesn't make for a good start! You should make time to have a serious conversation with whomever you hope to appoint about the responsibilities involved in being an attorney. And you must be prepared for them to refuse if they feel unable to take on that role. As with anything connected to PoAs, it is best to do this well in advance, so that everyone is equally prepared.

You may by now have a couple of people in mind; is there a limit on how many attorneys you can appoint?

How many attorneys can I, or should I, appoint?

This is entirely up to you. You can appoint either one person, or many people, in the same PoA document.

Appointing a sole attorney (one person) can be limiting. For example, if the person is of a similar age to yourself, then they may not be physically or mentally able to take on the role if and when the time comes, or they may have to give up the role earlier than is ideal. If this happens, and you no longer have mental capacity yourself, you will not be able to nominate somebody else. This means that you would be effectively left without a PoA. Another person would then have to appointed under a court order (see Chapter 1).

> 'I probably would have just appointed my wife; it seemed the natural thing to do, so it was helpful to be prompted to think about appointing my two children as well, and now I'm glad I did as my wife has developed dementia so she wouldn't have been able to be my attorney anyway.' (Stan, ninety-two)

For this reason, it can sometimes be helpful to have more than one attorney. There is no limit on the number, but the more you have the more complicated it can get; two or three is a good number.

The most important thing to consider when deciding to appoint more than one attorney is that they must have a good and trusting relationship with each other. You may not wish to show favouritism by selecting one child over another, and so grant the PoA to both, even though they do not speak to each other. This is a recipe for disaster. If the attorneys don't speak to each other, distrust one another, or if they are actively at logger-heads, they will never be able to make the PoA work effectively. Even if you hope that appointing them both may reconcile them, the challenges of the role are likely to be overwhelming.

If this is your family situation, then you really do need to have the courage to pick the person who will be the best attorney, which may be neither of your children. Opting for a friend over either child is often seen as a good compromise in such situations.

You may wish a generational mix, e.g. a partner and an adult child; some people like a gender mix, as they have a different relationship with their son than with their daughter and think both will have something to contribute.

You can appoint different people for the different types of PoAs: for example, you could appoint your adult daughter as your financial attorney and your partner as your health and welfare attorney. This is quite a common mix, as your partner may be more familiar with your likes, dislikes and preferences on things, whereas your adult child may be more confident with managing official paperwork and dealing with authorities. Alternatively, you may prefer to have both adult child and partner as attorneys for both types of PoA – the choice is yours.

No matter whom you are considering, in all cases it is important for attorneys to work well together, and for their primary concern to be your welfare and wishes, not grievances with each other.

If you are thinking of appointing multiple attorneys, what authority may you give them in relation to each other?

Authority of attorneys

Assuming you have decided to appoint a number of attorneys, you need to consider the authority you are going to give them respective to each other. Your options here are joint, joint and individual, or a mix. What's the difference?

Joint

If you wish both, or all, of your attorneys to work together on all matters you would appoint them jointly. It can offer comfort and reassurance to know that your attorneys have to operate jointly, are sharing the responsibilities, must reach agreement and have an equal say. It means you are not giving any one person control, and considerations can be discussed based on their individual knowledge of you as a person – they will hold each other to account. However, this option does have its downsides. One is that it can be inconvenient for attorneys to have to work jointly, especially if they live some distance apart.

Another key consideration is that with a joint appointment, the attorneys come as a unit, so if one of them is no longer able, or willing, to be the attorney then the PoA is void.

To offer more explanation, let us say you appoint A and B jointly; but subsequently A can no longer fulfil the role, even if this is after he has started acting as an attorney. The joint appointment of A *and* B means they are a single unit, thus it does not permit B to act on his own; so in the absence of A, B cannot act either, leaving you with no one, so your PoA becomes void.

Although this example only uses two attorneys, the same would happen if you appointed three or more attorneys to work jointly, and one could no longer fulfil the role: no matter the number of attorneys, with a joint appointment they are appointed as a single unit. 'All for one and one for all,' as it were.

If you do not wish the PoA to be void if one of the attorneys can no longer fulfil the role then you should appoint them jointly and individually (see below), or ensure you nominate a replacement (see below).

Joint and individual

If you are happy for your attorneys to work individually, you can appoint them jointly and individually. You may hear this referred to as appointing attorneys jointly and severally.

> *'I live in Stockport, my daughter lives in Scotland and my son lives in Surrey. They both have their own family responsibilities and work full-time, so it was going to be hard for them to act jointly; fortunately, they get along well and I trust both of them implicitly, so it made much more sense that they be appointed with joint and individual responsibility. Now either one of them can manage things for me, whichever one it is easier for, depending on what it is.' (Muriel, ninety-one, donor of PoA)*

This example demonstrates the main advantage of joint and individual appointments: the convenience for attorneys. As each attorney can act independently of the other, the relationship must be one of trust – not only between you and your attorneys, but between the individuals themselves.

Appointing your attorneys with joint and individual authority applies across the board: each attorney has authority to act individually on all matters. If you wish your attorneys to work together on some things, for example whether and when you go into care, or if there are certain decisions that you wish made by a particular attorney, or some of your attorneys, or a minimum number of attorneys (rather than any of them, individually, at any time), then you need to appoint them with mixed authority (see below).

Attorneys who are appointed with the authority to act individually are required to communicate and agree a decision with each other before one of them takes the action. That said, there is no guarantee this will happen. Although you may give authority for attorneys to act individually, they have legally what is called joint and several liability. What this means is that if one of them makes a decision or takes an action which the other (or others) knows nothing about, this other person can still be held liable.

If you do not make it clear what authority you are giving your attorneys respective to each other, then it is likely that this will be defaulted, for example by banks, to joint authority. Consequently, if joint and individual is your preference, make sure this is clear.

A mixture of joint and joint and individual

You may wish to appoint your attorneys with a mixture of joint and joint and individual. This option may be suitable if you are happy for your attorneys to take everyday decisions alone but want them to make important decisions together, such as selling a house.

You need to make it clear in the PoA on what matters you wish them to work jointly; for all the remaining matters it is assumed that they are permitted to work individually.

We talked earlier about joint attorneys being appointed as a unit. You need to bear this in mind here too. For the decisions on which you wish your attorneys to work jointly they are appointed as a single entity; if one attorney is not able to act, for whatever reason, your remaining attorneys won't be able to make any of the joint decisions.

For example: you appoint A and B jointly and individually for all matters except for the sale of your house, on which you wish A and B to work jointly. Attorney A gets dementia and can no longer act. B can continue as your attorney for everything except the sale of your house, as on this he is a single unit with A and the loss of A means the loss of B too for this one aspect.

> *Tip: If you are putting in specific requests about what attorneys must work on together, then make sure your wishes are clear. A lack of clarity on how attorneys must act, and over which matters, is one of the main reasons why PoAs don't, or maybe even can't, end up being used the way the donor/granter intended. It's one of the main reasons why attorneys have to seek the advice of the court.*

If you are using an advisor, tell them what your wishes are, and they can ensure that the drafting gives effect to your intentions. If you are doing the PoA yourself, you may want to ask someone you trust, who is not connected with the situation, to read the PoA in order to test what their interpretation of your wishes is. If they can't work it out, then, potentially, anyone who needs to rely on it in the future may also struggle. This may mean your PoA won't, or can't, be used in the way you intended.

Attorneys' relationship

We touched above on attorneys who have a poor relationship with each other. You may think that appointing them jointly will be a solution, and that it will compel them to work together. My many years of experience tell me that it won't. The effective operation of the PoA will fail. Perhaps you think allowing them to work jointly and individually will be the solution. Sadly, this doesn't work either: each tends to 'go it alone', without first discussing and agreeing with the other. Often they end up pulling in opposite directions, sometimes even deliberately, so as to aggravate the other person. Attorneys in this situation are easily consumed by their own relationship dynamics and overlook that you should be the focus of their concentration.

If this is your family situation, you are by no means alone, but you really do have to have the courage to pick the person who will be the best attorney. This may be neither of your children.

Having decided on your attorneys and what authority you want them to have, you now need to think about whether you wish to nominate a replacement person who could become your attorney in the event that one of your original attorneys is no longer able to act.

Replacement/substitute attorneys

'Replacement' is the MCA terminology (England and Wales and Northern Ireland); in Scotland the AWI uses the term 'substitute'. For ease I'll just use the word replacement, but it applies equally to all territories.

As the name suggests, replacements replace the original attorney if they are no longer able to act. It is a permanent replacement: the replacement cannot just bob in and out for temporary periods. If you want people to share the role, then refer back to the different types of authority that you can grant (such as joint and individual).

A replacement attorney can be hugely advantageous and avoid your whole PoA coming to an end if you only have one attorney and that person can no longer act.

Contrast the scenarios below.

Peter and his wife Maureen appointed each other as their respective attorneys. Neither nominated a replacement. Peter lost capacity, Maureen was managing things for him under his PoA, but a short time later Maureen herself began to lose capacity and could no longer manage – but Peter, with his loss of capacity, could not act as Maureen's attorney. Both of these PoAs were now unusable. Their daughter had to go to the court to apply to be deputy (guardian in Scotland) to manage the estate of both parents, with the costs and onerous undertakings being a deputy involves.   ➔

> *Peter and his wife Maureen appointed each other as their respective attorneys; they both nominated their daughter Louise as a replacement. Peter lost capacity, Maureen was managing things for him, but a short time later Maureen herself began to lose capacity and could no longer manage – but Peter, with his loss of capacity, could not act as Maureen's attorney. Louise took up appointment as replacement for both her mother and father and things carried on seamlessly.*

You need to take care to ensure you get your replacement appointed in a way which achieves what you want to achieve. The next scenario offers an illustration of when this failed.

> *Peter appointed his wife Maureen and daughter Louise, jointly, as his attorneys. He nominated Louise's son, his grandson, Matthew, as a replacement. He was thinking that if a time came when Maureen felt it was too much for her, then Matthew could be Maureen's replacement and Louise and Matthew could act together.*
>
> *Peter lost capacity, so Maureen and Louise were acting as his attorneys. Maureen went on to lose her own capacity, so could no longer act as Peter's attorney, but, as she was appointed jointly with Louise, they were appointed as a single unit. This meant that Louise could no longer continue acting for her father either. Matthew became sole attorney to his grandfather, sidelining Louise.*

You can imagine that this would create a lot of family tension – which would be compounded if Maureen had done a 'mirror PoA' appointing Peter and Louise jointly, as Louise would have been sidelined from this PoA too when her mother lost capacity.

Here's another example of when things don't go as intended.

> Peter appointed Maureen and Louise as his attorneys. They could act separately on day-to-day things, but he wanted them to make any decisions about the house jointly. He'd put this in because it was Maureen's house too and he didn't want Louise to make this decision without consulting Maureen. Louise's son, Matthew, was nominated as a replacement.
>
> Peter lost capacity, so Maureen and Louise were acting as his attorneys. Maureen went on to lose her own capacity, so could no longer act as Peter's attorney. Matthew came in as Maureen's replacement and was working with Louise on day-to-day things. All seemed to be working well, until a time came when they needed to think about selling the house. Louise then found out that she could not make this decision. She had been appointed jointly with Maureen on this, but as Maureen was no longer able to make the decision this took Louise out too. Only Matthew, as the replacement, could make the decision and take any required action.

You can imagine how appalled Louise would be by this: it was surely not what her father would have intended. Matthew was only twenty-two and, legally, was now the sole 'owner' of this decision. Surely not.

The correct appointment can work effectively, though, as this next example illustrates.

> Peter had appointed Maureen and Louise jointly and individually and nominated Matthew as a replacement for either one, to also work jointly and individually with the remaining person, and indicated that if there was a time when there was only a sole attorney he was happy for this person to act alone.
>
> We know that Peter, then Maureen, lost capacity. Matthew came in as replacement on both PoAs, and carried on acting with his mum, Louise, to support his grandparents; as had been the intention.

You will see from this that getting the appointment of the replacement correct is key to achieving what you intend.

In these examples there was only one person nominated as a replacement, but you can nominate more than one person as a replacement if you wish. If there is more than one, they will all come in at the same time, as one unit, unless you offer specific instruction otherwise.

So, if you nominate C and D as replacements, you may wish to stipulate C as a replacement, then, if necessary, D as a replacement, which would allow C and D to take up post individually, at separate times.

You may wish one to take over from a specific original attorney: for example C is to replace A, D is to replace B,

You can change the authority that they have. For example, you may have been happy for your original attorneys to act individually (jointly and individually), but you wish your replacements to work jointly.

All of these things are possible, but they require clear instruction. It is not the remit of this book to offer legal advice as to how best to word things, and in any event everyone's situation will be a little different. My advice therefore is:

- Be clear what you wish to achieve when appointing a replacement. What is it that you want from the final outcome? Who should be acting, with whom, with what respective authority and over what matters?

- Know what it means to appoint your attorneys jointly, jointly and individually, or with a mixture of joint and individual.

- If you are using a solicitor, tell them exactly what it is you wish to achieve from the appointment of a replacement: they will ensure the document is drafted to give effect to this.

- If you are using a DIY version, you may wish to take legal advice to check whether your wording of the appointment of a replacement will achieve what you intend (although you may find it hard to get a lawyer to comment on one aspect only when they have not advised on the totality).

This whole replacement business can sound fraught with complications, and you may be thinking, 'I'll just not bother'; so let me reiterate that a replacement can ensure your PoA remains valid, and avoid an even more complicated procedure through the courts. So please don't be dissuaded from nominating a replacement, but use the advice above to ensure you get the person appointed, and for your PoA to continue to work, as you intend.

Supervision of your attorneys

Before we leave this chapter on attorneys, there is one more thing to think about, and that is whether or not you want to put a provision in your PoA for your attorney to have to report to someone.

I mentioned that when there is no PoA already in place, deputies or guardians appointed by a court to manage the care and/or affairs of an incapable person will be supervised by the Public Guardian, or the relevant local authority. They have to report to the authorities on decisions they are making, or plan to make, for your health, welfare and care as well as how they intend to, or have, managed your financial or property affairs.

A PoA is not supervised in this way. Your right to choose, while capable, the person you trust to support you, and as may be required to act on your behalf, is respected and so the authorities do not oversee the actions of this appointee, your attorney. This means that, once you are incapable, the decisions rest entirely with your attorney as to what is the right care for you and what are the right steps to take regarding your finances and property. You can, however, ask an independent and impartial third party to 'oversee' the actions of your attorney. This can be helpful, especially where there is fracture in the family. In my experience, attorneys who are reporting to an independent party usually describe it as a positive experience, feeling reassured that an independent observer is involved. If you decide this is something you want, your attorney should be encouraged to see it as a protection for them rather than an intrusion.

If you wish to have such an overseer, it is up to you whom you choose. It can be another family member, if not all are appointed as attorneys, or it can be a close friend, or even a professional person, for example your solicitor or accountant – although of course there would be a charge for their services.

The England and Wales PoA system (more of which in the next chapter) accommodates the appointment of such an overseer. You should give direction on how often you would want the attorney and the 'overseer' to converse (monthly, quarterly, annually) and any other instructions which may assist this relationship. In Scotland you will need to make a specific point of mentioning that you would wish to have X act as overseer for your PoA as the concept of an overseer is less recognised.

Hopefully, by now you have a clear idea of whom you wish to appoint, as well as what powers you intend to give them. You are now ready to think about the options you have for making a PoA. We will look at these in the next chapter.

Chapter 4

How to make a Power of Attorney

By now, you should understand what a PoA is, and how it can protect your rights to dignity and self-determination even when you are incapacitated by old age, illness or accident. You've considered what powers you'd include in your PoA, and who you might like to act as your attorney (with all the other considerations that involves). But when and how do you actually make a PoA?

You can create a PoA at any stage of life, whether you have young children or feel young yourself, whether you have just got a new job, or are thinking of retiring. A PoA is an insurance for anyone. With this in mind, in this chapter we turn our attention to the question of creating a PoA: we will consider the options you have, the advantages and limitations of those various options, as well as the costs. I'm also going to address one of the questions that I get asked most frequently: 'How do I make my PoA watertight?' By the end of this chapter, along with the information in Chapters 2 and 3, you will have all the information you need to create your PoA by yourself, or to discuss it with a professional, whichever is your preference.

How do I make a PoA?

There are a number of options for creating a PoA: some people may search online and find various DIY templates, and be very comfortable completing these; others will prefer a solicitor to draw it up for them. I will take you through the options so you can decide which is right for you. I cover the costs of the various options in the next section.

DIY kits

DIY PoA kits can be purchased from high-street stationers. They are easily recognised, usually in A4 clear sealed envelopes, in the same section as you may find other DIY legal templates; or you can order them online – just search for 'Power of Attorney kit'. The kit will contain instruction sheets that 'walk you through' what is required. Because these are designed to help anybody, they can only offer generic information, and won't necessarily answer your more specific questions. This means that the outcome is usually a pro-forma style of PoA, which will cover many issues but may not include all of the things you find you need for your particular circumstances.

The kits contain forms for the different territories in the UK. The form for England and Wales is usually on the top; the temptation can be to start with what comes first, so it is not uncommon for a person in Scotland to complete the wrong form. Please make sure you have the right form to hand.

> Tip: 'If you're doing a Scottish PoA and using a DIY pack, make sure you use the Scottish version; I'm a researcher and I filled the wrong form in.' (Kirsten, fifty-six)

Please read all the information in the kit carefully BEFORE starting to fill in the form, again making sure you are reading the information relevant to your territory. Ideally, you should supplement this information with some personal research so that you are clear what you want to include before you begin – a good place to start is with the first three chapters of this book! Specifically, you should have a sense of what powers you would like to include. The information in the packs offers you all the instructions you need to complete the PoA form and tells you what to do afterwards, for example by way of witnesses co-signing the PoA. As always, take your time and go step by step.

Before the PoA can be used it needs to be registered with the respective Office of the Public Guardian (OPG). The kit will give you information on how to do this. Errors in completion of the PoA document can lead to the registration of your PoA being rejected; you will have the PoA returned to you and you will need to correct the problem then re-submit the document, for which a supplementary charge is made in England and Wales and can be made in Scotland. This is why I emphasise the importance of taking your time, reading everything carefully and following all instructions.

> '*I made a silly error and the registration was rejected. I had to make a correction and resubmit it with an additional fee; an expensive, silly error.' (Catherine, sixty-three, retired)*

Online services: England and Wales

The Public Guardian in England and Wales offers an online PoA application for those doing a PoA for use in England or Wales. Access is via the GOV.UK site at www.lastingpowerofattorney. service.gov.uk/home – or you can just search online for 'Public Guardian Power of Attorney online form'. This service is a popular way of creating a PoA, and is generally considered easy to use: there are clear instructions on the website's home page, and once you have set up an account you are taken stage by stage through the process.

The general view is that the online form is more intuitive and easier to follow than the paper forms, and so there is less chance of errors which might prevent registration; but these can still arise, so the advice is, as with other DIY options: read the accompanying information BEFORE filling in the form, and ideally supplement this with personal research. Take your time, read each question carefully and do exactly as advised.

Other online services

There is no Public Guardian online service in Scotland or Northern Ireland. In these territories, if you wish to use an online service you will need to use one of the other providers; use 'online power of attorney' as your search criteria to find them. I have heard mixed views about how easy these other online versions are to use, as well as the outcomes they offer. Some people say they are easy to follow and have no problem with them; other people regret using them. I discuss below how to decide on the best option for you.

If you are using one of the online providers, as ever, the advice about reading all the information they provide first and doing your research is the same.

Online services: Scotland

The Scottish government are planning to place a series of example PoAs on their website, with associated guidance, which allow you to create and complete a PoA for registration in Scotland. In order to select the right example for your circumstances you will need to have decided what kind of PoA you want (in Scotland, the choice is between continuing and welfare), how many attorneys you want, whether you want a substitute and how you wish your attorneys to be appointed – all of which we have considered in the previous chapters. Once you have selected the right example for your preferences, you should copy and paste it to your own computer and fill in the required sections from there, rather than completing an online form. You'll then need to print the form and send it by post. Again, there is guidance accompanying it which offers you all the help you need to complete it and tells you what to do then.

The Public Guardian in Scotland has a function which allows you to submit your PoA electronically; their website offers more information about how you do this. This service replaces postage of the hard copy forms, which are scanned and sent electronically; it does not allow for online completion of the PoA itself.

Professional advisor

There are a range of professional advisors who offer PoA services, the most obvious being solicitors, but other professionals, for example financial advisors, paralegals, will writers and accountants, perform this service too. As with any professional whom you engage, you should shop around, do your homework on what they offer, what they charge, and how satisfied their other clients are etc. Some non-solicitor professional advisors will only offer a property and finance PoA service; if you wish to have a health and welfare PoA, check that this can also be done by the professional or company you are thinking of using.

Although a professional advisor doesn't have to be a lawyer, many people do choose to use a solicitor. Just because you are using a professional advisor doesn't mean you should go to this meeting waiting for them to tell you what to do. You should still do your homework ahead so you know what you want to talk to your solicitor about; the result will be a document that is tailored to your circumstances, having had the benefit of legal advice to 'test' your thinking and assumptions; there may be better options for your situation than whatever you had assumed to be the case.

So, given there is such a range of options for getting a PoA, how do you decide which is the right one for you?

Which option? How to decide

Only you can know your own situation, and what will suit you best. But of course, all of the options have pros and cons which are worth considering while you make your decision.

A solicitor will offer you legal advice, which can be a reassurance, will do all the drafting, and will provide you with a PoA specifically tailored for your situation. Aside from expense (more on that next), one downside people report is the number of appointments required, which can be inconvenient and means the process can take several weeks from start to finish.

A DIY/online version can make you feel you have more control because you are doing the drafting yourself. It can be quicker and more convenient as you can do it from your front room. The downsides people report are anxiety about whether they are doing it right, and how long it takes to check and double-check; and that it only offers them a generic template, which sometimes doesn't seem to fit exactly what they want.

You can see from this that both approaches are in essence two sides of a coin: the advantages of one are the disadvantages of the other; they both have things to commend them and things to take into consideration.

It can help to read advice given in newspapers, magazines, money columns etc.; but read with caution if it is information offered by a provider – if they are an online provider, of course they are going to say an online PoA is easy, quick and cheap;

likewise, a solicitor is going to promote the importance of legal advice for a legal document.

It really is a matter of personal preference. There are many people who are very happy with the online/DIY method, and equally many people who are very happy with having had professional advice, and the opposite, in both cases. The best advice is to consider your own circumstances and ask around: what have other family members done, what have friends done, what made them decide to go the way they did, what would they recommend, or not, with the benefit of hindsight; then go with the route that feels right for you in your situation.

Costs

In deciding which option to go with, you are likely to think about costs. Indeed, 'What will it cost me?' is one of the first questions people tend to ask me about PoAs: you may be concerned about the cost of legal fees, or simply wondering whether this is something you can afford right now. As well as the monetary costs, it is also important to consider the non-financial costs.

Professional advisor

Since solicitors are generally regarded as the most expensive of the options, let's begin with this. There are many solicitors who do PoA work, and many offer preliminary advice free of charge; you should ask about this. Their fee thereafter will depend on various things, for example how complicated your affairs are, what their hourly rate is, or whether they are doing other things for you at the same time (e.g. a house sale or a will). You should, however, be given an indication upfront of the anticipated fee for the level of work that appears to be necessary; if things turn out to be more complex than was first anticipated, the solicitor should update you about the impact of this on the fee. Most people say the solicitor's estimate was accurate. This returns us to the importance of doing your research in advance: since time is money with this option, being prepared reduces the amount of time your solicitor will need to spend explaining your options and their pros and cons, and so saves you money.

Possibly because so many solicitors do PoA work, their fees are generally competitively priced, so do shop around: meet more than one solicitor for a consultation if you wish, look at reviews, ask family and friends for their opinion on what they got for what they paid. If you have taken advantage of a free consultation, then consider how approachable you found the solicitor, how knowledgeable they seemed, and how much reassurance and comfort you took from them. These are all factors that can influence you to go with one solicitor over another, and sometimes can be more important than the cost. If you have taken advantage of a free consultation, do not feel obliged to use that person if, for whatever reason, you didn't gel with them.

In Scotland, if you decide to use a solicitor, which most people do, you may be eligible for legal aid (by way of something called 'advice and assistance'), which will offer you some financial assistance in getting a PoA. This is means-tested – which means the level of financial assistance is proportionate to the amount of money you have (your overall asset base), so you may qualify for 100 per cent funding, 0 per cent, or anything in between. You can see if you qualify for assistance, and if so, how much support you may get, by going to the Scottish Legal Aid Board's website and inserting information about your circumstances. If you are eligible for some financial support, make sure the solicitor that you choose takes legally aided clients, because not all do. If you don't want to bother with what seems like the hassle of checking the Scottish Legal Aid Board's website, then you can also just ask your solicitor if you would qualify. Do not feel any embarrassment in asking this question; solicitors are very used to such discussions.

Legal aid for a PoA is less likely to be available in England and Wales, but there is no harm in checking with the advisor you've elected to use. The cost of doing a PoA via a non-legal professional, for example a financial advisor or will writer, may be less but the same advice applies, which is to check out what they offer, for what they charge, if there is anything they do not cover and how satisfied their other clients are.

Registering with the Office of the Public Guardian

In addition to the professional advisor's fee, you will have to pay a fee for registration of the PoA with the OPG. You can check the cost by visiting the relevant OPG website (contact details are at the back of the book), but at the time of writing, in England and Wales this is £82 for a property and finance PoA and £82 for a health and welfare version. In Scotland the fee is £81; but as both property and finance and health and welfare can be included in a combined document, this is a single fee.

Online

If you are choosing to complete your PoA using an online service you should check if there is a cost, and if so what this is; some of the providers, for example the Public Guardian's site in England and Wales, offer free access for your completion. Those that are provided commercially will tend to charge, perhaps around £100.

In Scotland there is an additional fee to consider. A capacity assessment has to accompany a PoA, and this can only be completed by a lawyer or a doctor. If you are using a solicitor, then they can do this as part of the overall PoA service; if you have decided on an online version you will typically approach your family doctor for the capacity assessment. Double-check first that your doctor is willing to offer such an assessment, as not all do. Your doctor may charge you, as this service, for the purposes of a PoA, is not covered under the NHS; it is in essence a private service. You can check the likely fee on the British Medical Association website, but again it can be in the region of £100.

If you are using an online service, in any of the territories, you will also have to add on the cost of registration with the OPG, explained above.

DIY

You may be considering a DIY paper version, which at the time of writing can be bought for around £10. You will need to pay the OPG registration fee mentioned above, and in Scotland you may also have to pay for the capacity certificate that is required, also mentioned above. You will see from this that, despite the initial price tag, you should not automatically assume that a DIY version is a better option financially.

Non-financial costs

One of the non-financial costs with an online/DIY version is the amount of thought that has to go into getting it right. A DIY/online version tends to be more intellectually taxing, as you have to think about what needs to be put where, whether you have completed it correctly, and whether it provides what you want. For some people, this increases stress.

Confidence is a related issue and can add to anxiety if you are unsure whether you have completed things properly. Clear step-by-step guidance is offered by the providers, but even the smartest people and the simplest guides can still go wrong. The level of concentration that is required, for some people, in completing an online/DIY version is both trying and tiring.

People also comment on the time it takes to do a DIY version, paper or online. The application itself may not take long, but they talk about the thinking time, the checking and double-checking, which all adds up. I suspect these factors and the ones in the paragraphs above are, in reality, interrelated, and arise because the process is one of completing a legal document oneself, which is critical to get it right; but it's on a subject that is not within most people's comfort zone.

With an online/DIY version you should also bear in mind that if you get something wrong in the drafting, it can work out more costly in the end to 'unpick' any mistakes. These non-financial costs which people report with the DIY options do not arise if you have a professional advisor to draw up the document; this offers comfort, confidence and reassurance; also, if a professional gets something wrong in the drafting it costs you nothing, as she is covered by her professional insurance.

The final cost which it is important to mention is that of not doing a PoA. As we have seen, a loved one cannot act on your behalf unless they have your authority; if, without a PoA, this subsequently becomes necessary, then your loved one, even a spouse of many years, will need to go to the court to obtain authority to administer your affairs. The court process (and ongoing supervision) comes with costs which are usually far in excess of those of a PoA; it is onerous and can create a significant emotional burden for your loved ones.

You will see from this that the costs of the various options, when taken as a whole, financial and non-financial costs, tend to be much of a muchness. To close this section, therefore, I'll just reiterate that there is no right or wrong way to obtain your PoA: some people are very confident with using an online facility and are very satisfied with the outcome, and others are very satisfied with using a professional advisor; by contrast, there are people who wished they'd used an advisor and others who wished they'd just done it themselves – so it really is a matter of personal preference.

Whichever option you decide on, you will want to make sure your PoA is as robust as possible. We will consider this next.

How do I make my PoA watertight?

As mentioned at the outset of this chapter, this is a question I get asked regularly. I suspect that behind it is often the fear that you may leave a loophole, or mis-word a power, that gives the attorney an opportunity to misuse the document. Sadly, we do hear of cases where an attorney has taken advantage of their position; we want to ensure that our PoA is robust so this doesn't happen to us.

First, though, I need to put the cases of abuse in perspective; the vast majority of attorneys bend over backwards to do a sterling job, so please don't let the proportionately small number of cases where things go wrong put you off making a PoA. You are far more likely to be exploited without the protection of a PoA, so you are better with one than without one; but I can understand the desire to ensure that the PoA that is granted is robust.

Of course you trust the person to whom you are granting the PoA, but nonetheless want to make sure your PoA is as secure as possible and free from the risk of abuse. The next section draws on the advice given in the previous chapters to consider what makes a strong PoA.

Do your homework

You are already on the road to making your PoA as watertight as possible because you are doing your homework. You are mindful of the various decisions that need to be made as part of the process, e.g. who should be your attorneys, what authority should you give them, what powers do you wish to give them. It is better for you to have thought about these questions in a quiet, non-rushed way, as part of your preparation.

Talk to a friend

Before going ahead, it may help to talk to a friend or family member whose judgement you trust, but who will be unconnected to the PoA. Ask them their thoughts on it all: on whom you are thinking of appointing, what powers you are thinking of granting etc. – essentially on all of the options that you have. Give them permission to tell you if they think you are making an ill-advised decision on any of the matters.

Consider the merit of legal advice

If you are keen to ensure you do not leave any loopholes in your PoA you may prefer to have a solicitor draft the document. There are a lot of suggestions below on which legal advice would be beneficial.

If your proposed attorney is trying to talk you out of taking legal advice or trying to persuade you to do it online yourself, especially if this is with their assistance this may be a warning flag. An attorney who has a personal agenda may suggest that you avoid involving a solicitor and will advocate the DIY option. If you do have some anxiety about a particular attorney and you think that, in the circumstances, it would be better to talk to a solicitor about this, do not let the attorney persuade you against your better judgement.

If you do a DIY, do it yourself

If your preference is for a DIY or online PoA, then ideally you should complete it personally. This way you know that you have put in it what you want and others have not influenced your judgement. If you aren't confident with form-filling or online technology, or feel particularly nervous about creating such a critical document and you want support with this, ask someone unconnected to the PoA to sit alongside you; but make it clear to them that their role is to check your IT competency, that you are putting the right things in the right place, and that it is not for them to comment on, or judge, any of the decisions you are making.

If you do not feel confident enough, even with this support, to complete the form yourself and you wish to ask someone to do this for you then my advice would be:

- Make sure you ask someone who is independent, i.e. someone other than one of the proposed attorneys, or anyone connected to them.

- Sit alongside the person as they are completing the application, so you give direction at each point and can see what they are inputting.

- If they are doing this online, ask the person to print a completed version of the document for you so you can read it before it is submitted.

- Take your time reading it.

- Ask about anything which doesn't make sense; don't just accept that it must be right because they know how to do these things online and you don't.

- Challenge anything which seems at odds with your preferences

- DO NOT agree to progress to the next step in the process until you are 100 per cent happy.

Choose your attorneys carefully

Remember: you can pick whomever you want, it is your free choice. You may wish to read Chapter 6 onwards, which covers what is involved in being an attorney; it is not an easy task, so consider who is best able to fulfil the role, pick the person who will do the best job and who will put your interests first.

As was covered above, it is helpful for practical reasons to appoint more than one attorney; but it also has the advantage of one keeping the other on track. It has been my experience that PoAs which are exploited are more commonly those where there is only one attorney. Remember, if you do choose more than one attorney, to make sure that you inform both of them about the contents of your PoA, and your Statement of Wishes and Feelings (if you have made one). There is more about Statements of Wishes and Feelings on p. 99.

Think about the attorney's authority

Consider the authority you may wish to give your attorneys, appointing them jointly, jointly and individually or with a mixture.

If you are worried about one of the attorneys taking advantage of their position, you may prefer to appoint your attorneys to act jointly, i.e. they both have to decide on and action matters. Remember, though, that this appoints them as a single unit. You may wish to reread the section on the authority of your attorneys in Chapter 3, thinking carefully about what is right in your situation.

Keep to your decisions

Having made your decisions on the various options you have, do not let others dissuade you, especially if this is your proposed attorney influencing a change of direction. If the comments of others do spark doubts then go back a few steps, redo your research, talk to independent others etc.; do not change your mind on the spur of the moment about something on which you believed you had made a settled decision.

> *A typical example may be about using a professional service for drafting the PoA versus doing it yourself. Your preference may be to involve a professional; you have thought about it, shopped around, and this is the conclusion you have arrived at. Your proposed attorney may think the cost of a solicitor is unnecessary and is encouraging you do it yourself; they offer to help you with this. They may put forward various arguments which sound persuasive. If you do find yourself changing your mind and thinking that maybe you should just do it yourself, then STOP and revisit your decision-making process first.*

This is not to suggest that anyone who offers you an alternative view has got an ulterior motive; they may genuinely see something which they don't think you have considered. Do by all means listen to all views, but arrive at your own decision and keep with it once you are sure that it is the right thing for you.

Think carefully about the powers you grant

In England and Wales, a lot of people use an online template to 'build' their own PoA. Make sure you do so from an informed position. Don't just blindly follow the template inserting what seems to be the most appropriate thing at any given point; it may be the most appropriate for most people, but not necessarily for you.

Use the list of possible powers at the back of this book to think ahead about which ones you do, and maybe do not, wish to offer your attorney and complete the template accordingly.

If you are using a solicitor, he is likely to have a fairly standard template PoA. Again, think of the powers that you are comfortable with and which are necessary for your situation. Do not feel you have to agree to a set template.

If you're not sure what a particular power means, feel free to ask your solicitor. If you don't want your attorney to have that power, then tell your solicitor; it can easily be removed. Your solicitor will tell you the impact of deleting any of the powers. Likewise, if there are specific powers that you want to include they can easily be added; just mention the situation to your solicitor and she can agree the best wording with you. You know your affairs and your family set-up better than anyone else, so make sure *your* PoA is just that, tailored to *your* circumstances.

Ensure that your attorney has to get professional opinion of incapacity

Welfare powers cannot start unless or until you become incapable of making your own welfare decisions.

If you have concerns about an attorney taking control too early, you are advised to consider requiring your attorney to get professional opinion about your incapacity before they are permitted to act, and make sure your attorney is aware of this requirement.

A professional opinion of incapacity is not required for financial powers (as these can start before incapacity), but there is nothing to stop you extending this requirement to financial powers too if you so wish.

Include a reference in your PoA to your attorney supporting you to make your own decisions

As discussed in Chapter 2, an attorney should always support you in making your own decisions, and not automatically make them without your input. It can be useful to have a note reminding them of this duty in the PoA itself, particularly if you are anxious about your attorney making their own decisions for you.

Speak to your solicitor, if you are using one, about the best wording to give this clear instruction to your attorney.

What level of confidentiality do you want?

There is a tendency for attorneys who are acting inappropriately to use 'confidentiality' as an excuse to be secretive or to cover their tracks. They may be challenged about something they have done but refuse to offer up any information, claiming it is confidential. If you are concerned that this could happen it can be helpful to be specific within the PoA, or in a Statement of Wishes and Feelings (see p. 99), about who can be told what and who can be shown what. Not being specific leaves it up to your attorney.

Defer the PoA start date?

A financial PoA can start as soon as it is registered; some people are anxious that their attorney will take advantage of this so, as has been discussed, you can defer the start date. Reread the section on deferring registration in Chapter 2, to see if this is something which you feel may offer you reassurance in your circumstances.

Supervision?

It can be helpful to have your attorney's actions and decisions overseen. Reread the section on supervision in Chapter 3, which offers more information about this. If your attorney knows that they cannot keep secrets and may be required to evidence their paperwork to others, the chances of them acting inappropriately can be minimised.

Consider doing a Statement of Wishes and Feelings

There is more information about this in the next chapter.

An attorney who wants to act inappropriately will often use the excuse: 'It's what X would have wanted.' A Statement of Wishes and Feelings will include your views on various matters and make it clear exactly what X (you) would truly have wanted.

Offering your Statement of Wishes and Feelings to others, for example broader family and good friends, as well as a range of professionals, will help the accountability of your attorney for their decisions.

Make sure your attorney is aware of the principles

As mentioned in Chapter 2, many attorneys are not aware of the principles which they are required, by law, to follow. Acting in accordance with these makes for an effective PoA. You may wish to make express reference in your PoA document to the principles and to the need for your attorney to act in accordance with them.

Make sure your attorney is aware of the Code of Practice

Attorneys are obliged to respect the Code of Practice, which was mentioned in Chapter 2; again, many do not know this, or even be aware of the code. Therefore you may also wish to make express reference in your PoA to your attorney respecting the Code of Practice.

The Code of Practice requires an attorney to keep records, but most attorneys do not do so. Having to make an entry against withdrawals from your bank account focuses the minds of people who may otherwise be tempted to be loose with your money. You may therefore wish to write into your PoA a specific requirement that the attorney must maintain a clear record of their actings – this would include their actions, decisions, deliberations and discussions for example. There is more about record keeping in Chapter 10.

Insurance?

There is increasingly available a type of insurance (technically called a security bond or bond of caution) which can reimburse money to your estate if things go wrong. The vast majority of attorneys bend over backwards to do a sterling job, but they may, innocently, overlook something which leads to a loss of money that you would have been due. There are a small number of attorneys who become tempted by the money available to them and use it for their own purposes.

A security bond covers either of these situations, reimbursing to your estate the value of the 'lost' money, so it can be advantageous to have. The cost of such a bond is generally quite moderate and tends to be a one-off lifetime payment, so it can be of value for the peace of mind it offers; but, as I would advise with the purchase of any insurance product, you should shop around, compare costs, and check the small print to be sure exactly what the product you are considering does – and, maybe more pertinently, does not – cover.

Tell others

Your attorney is obliged to seek the views of others before making decisions on your behalf. Attorneys often don't realise this, and so don't consult others whose knowledge of you may offer a different stance on a particular issue.

Attorneys who have an ulterior motive have a tendency to deliberately exclude contact with others. It minimises risk (of your attorney doing things wrong, or contrary to your wishes) if all those closest to you, including good friends as well as family, know that you have granted a PoA in favour of a particular person and what your expectations are.

The public register

The public register is, as the name suggests, a public record of all people who are appointed on behalf of an individual with incapacity: in other words, a public list of all attorneys. Your attorney should be made aware that it is a matter of public record that they are appointed. This is sufficient in some cases to prevent someone from acting inappropriately. There is more information about the public register towards the close of Chapter 6.

What about your will?

You may be doing a will at the same time as your PoA. It is not uncommon to have the same person as both attorney and as executor of your will. However, if you have concerns about how an attorney may conduct themselves then you would be well advised to think about appointing a different person as executor of your will.

If an attorney has been acting inappropriately, this often only comes to light when your affairs are being sorted after you have passed away. It leaves a lot of ill feeling if the person then sorting out your affairs, your executor, is the same person that has been acting wrongly as attorney. Obviously, this is an undesirable outcome, and it is sometimes hard to tell in advance if this will be the case; but one way of ensuring against it is to appoint two separate people for these roles.

I have deliberately given a range of suggestions for making your PoA as robust as is possible, because a lot of people express anxiety about the way their attorneys may manage the PoA; but it is important to close this section with words of balance and reassurance.

Yes, we do read about attorneys who have abused their position; these stories make headlines. Hearing about an attorney who has done a really good job is, sadly, not headline-worthy. Consequently, it skews us into thinking attorneys take advantage.

If you go through the last, say, ten reported stories on abuse of vulnerable people, you will see the majority of it is not committed by attorneys. This is because PoAs can offer a very helpful form of protection, as these next examples show.

> 'A person knocked on my door and suggested I needed my drive resurfacing. I do, it's been the same concrete for fifty years and it's cracking and looks unsightly; but my son has insisted that I am not to agree to anyone who calls at my door like this. I told them "No", but they were quite insistent; they eventually went away but came back the next day and were saying how the water could get in from my drive and get under my house foundations and endanger my house, so how critical it was that I get the drive repaired very soon. I was anxious, I was worried by what they were saying, I felt pressured. I live alone, my husband has recently died, I'm eighty-eight years old and don't walk well. I told them my son would talk to them about this, he had my authority to deal with such matters. I said if they left me a card, I would get my son to call them. They made various excuses and left, without giving me a card, and I've never seen them again.' (Bertha)

Elsie was eighty-three, recently widowed and getting increasingly forgetful. She had granted PoA to her son some years ago. One day Elsie met a 'lovely young woman' at a bus stop. This lady was at the stop most times Elsie was there, and they became very friendly. One day the lady started talking to Elsie about how important it was to have a PoA; she offered to be Elsie's attorney if she wished. This discussion gave Elsie a jolt of memory and she said she already had one of these, she thought: she had a son to whom she had given PoA and she would check with him. Elsie never saw her friend again at the bus stop. She was upset as she had enjoyed her company; she didn't know why she wasn't seeing her.

My final comment to offer balance is that the vast, vast majority of attorneys do a fantastic job, willingly and with real commitment. They use the PoA as the protective and supportive authorisation that it should be. Do not let the actions of a small minority cloud the success of the majority.

I hope that, with this knowledge and the suggestions above, you will feel reassured in appointing an attorney and in obtaining a PoA that is right for you and your circumstances.

Chapters 2, 3 and 4 have now given you all the information you need to create your PoA. We move on in the next chapter, therefore, to thinking about registering it and what to do then.

Chapter 5

Registering your Power of Attorney and what to do next

Once you have created your PoA, however you have decided to do this, it then needs to be registered with the Office of the Public Guardian (OPG). In this chapter we will look at this final step and consider what things you need to check and double-check before you submit your PoA for registration. Then we shall look at the things you need to think about after your PoA is registered, considering, for example, how you make endorsed copies of your PoA and why this is important, as well as drawing up a Statement of Wishes and Feelings, the value of which has been mentioned earlier.

Planning for registration

For a PoA to come into effect, it needs to be registered with the OPG; to allow the OPG to register the PoA there has to be a certifcation of your capacity. The next section covers this.

Certification

A certificate of capacity is a declaration, by the person completing the certificate (we will talk more about who can give this declaration in the next section), that at the time of creating the PoA you were capable of doing so; that you understand what you are doing; that you understand the significance of a PoA in granting powers to another person; that you are not under any pressure to grant the PoA; that nobody forced you to make the PoA; that no fraud was involved in making the PoA; and that there is no other reason for concern.

The different countries of the UK have differing requirements as to who can complete the capacity certificate and the form that this takes.

Capacity certificate (Scotland)

In Scotland, a certificate which attests to your capacity to grant the PoA has to accompany the PoA. This certificate can only be completed by a Scottish registered and practising lawyer or a registered and licensed medical practitioner (a doctor, such as your GP or the hospital doctor looking after you).

If you are using a Scottish solicitor to draft your PoA they are qualified to sign the necessary certificate. Completing this certificate is an integral part of the PoA process for solicitors, so they will complete this and send it in with the PoA for registration without you needing to give it a thought.

If you are compiling the PoA for yourself, you will probably approach your GP for the capacity certificate. You will need to take a blank certificate to your GP for them to complete. If you are using a DIY kit, check that it has a capacity certificate; if not, you can download one from the Forms and Publications page of the Public Guardian's (Scotland) website. If you have used the Scottish government examples they offer you a link to the necessary capacity certificate, which you will need to print off and take to your GP.

You should check ahead that your GP is willing to complete this certificate, as not all do; and if so, what you do about an appointment. For example, some GPs want you to book two, or even three, appointment slots in a row so they have twenty or thirty minutes to talk to you and assess your capacity. They may only offer this on certain days, or at certain times of the day. They may also wish to have a look at the PoA in advance, so they can familiarise themselves with its content; as they are to assess whether you have capacity to understand the nature and extent of what you are granting in your PoA, they will need to see this in order to make their judgement.

Finally, I mentioned earlier that your GP may make a charge for the completion of this certificate, which can be around £100; so you should check this with them too.

Certificate provider (England and Wales)

In England and Wales, the equivalent certificate can be completed by an impartial third party: it does not have to be a doctor or lawyer, but it could be. There is a section in the PoA form for the person who is completing this declaration to insert their signature; it is not a separate certificate as it is in Scotland.

The certificate provider must be at least eighteen years old and must have known you for at least two years – well enough for you both to have an honest conversation about making your PoA and the things they have to confirm when they are signing.

There are certain people who are not permitted to sign the certificate; you should check the OPG guidance, which accompanies the online form, to make sure the person you are thinking of asking is not excluded. If you're not sure, you can check with the OPG by looking at their website or contacting their helpline, which is included at the back of this book.

Examples of people who cannot sign the certificate include:

- one of your proposed attorneys or replacement attorneys
- a member of your or your attorneys' family

- an unmarried partner, boyfriend or girlfriend of yours or of any of your attorneys
- a business partner of you or one of your attorneys
- an employee of you or one of your attorneys
- an owner, manager, director or employee of a care home where you live or a member of their family.

If possible, the certificate provider should discuss the PoA with you in private before they sign the certificate. The certificate provider must sign after you, but they can sign on the same day as you.

The details of the certificate provider are not yet available for Northern Ireland. They are likely to be closer to those for England and Wales than for Scotland; check the government website, www.nidirect.gov.uk, which will give the position as at the time you are reading this book.

Attorney's willingness to act

Along with your PoA document itself, and certificate of capacity in Scotland, you will also need to send a declaration from the attorney that they are willing to act.

In Scotland, as with the capacity certificate, the attorney's declaration is a separate form, contained within what is called the registration form. If you are using a DIY kit check if it includes a registration form; it may well not. If not, you can download one from the forms and publications page of the Public Guardian's (Scotland) website. If you have used the Scottish government examples, they give you a link to the necessary registration form. You will need to send this to your attorney for them to complete the relevant section. You should complete the rest with your details, which are then input by the OPG to their system. Along with this registration form, it is good practice to send the PoA document itself to the attorney, so they are aware of what you are asking them to do for you.

In England and Wales there is a section within the overall PoA form for the attorney to sign to indicate their willingness to act. If they do not have digital access, you will need to print off this form and send it to your attorney for them to read and sign.

Checking the PoA document

This instruction may sound obvious, but it is crucial. Once you have a PoA document, whether you have filled it in yourself or even if you have had a solicitor draft it for you, please ensure you read it carefully before you sign it off and send it for registration, or allow your solicitor to do so. Any errors in the document may prevent it from being registered, at least until these are corrected; but, more importantly, it may mean that when the document comes to be used it is not viable and your attorney may not be permitted to rely on it.

Things to check are:

- Is your name your full and proper name, as would be found on official documents?

- Is your name spelt correctly? E.g. my name is McDonald, but people will often mis-spell it as MacDonald, which I am generally happy to let go, but not if this was on my PoA.

- Is your proper name used correctly throughout?

- Is the styling of your name the same throughout? E.g. if the first reference is to, say, Adam Benjamin Smith but the next reference says Adam Ben Smith, or even just Adam Smith, you need to correct, or challenge, this disparity.

- If any previous names for you are included, e.g. a maiden name or a previous married name, are these correct?

- Is your address full and correct?

- If you have other property which you are giving powers over, e.g. a holiday home that your attorney has authority to sell, then ensure the address of this home is also included and is correct.

- Does the document appoint whom you want?

- Is the name and address of your attorney correct; does it use their name as would be seen on official documents?

- Does it appoint them in the way you intended (jointly, individually or a mix)?

- If you have included a replacement attorney, is their name and address correct?

- Does it allow the replacement to take up post in the way you intend?

- Does it include all of the powers you wanted? If it seems to include more, ask for these to be removed if you wish. Likewise, if it doesn't include something you expected to see, then ask for this to be added.

- Have a dispassionate read of the powers; can you follow what they mean? Do they give the authority you intended?

- If you have used a DIY kit or online form, have you followed the instructions; for example, if it required a line to be put through a box if that box was to be left blank, have you done this?

Feel free to challenge anything which leaves you with any uncertainty, even if it has been drafted by a solicitor. It is your PoA, to support your future, and you have to be satisfied with and reassured by it.

'My solicitor told me that he had sent my PoA for registration, then next he was saying it had been returned to him, that it couldn't be registered until we had corrected an issue with the names. It seems there was a mix-up with the spelling of my surname. The solicitor said he was surprised I hadn't spotted it; to be honest, I didn't really read the document when he gave it to me; it seemed all legal, I didn't really know what I was reading so I just glanced through it. I now wonder if anything else was wrong.' (Alexander, sixty-three, granter of PoA)

Registration with the Office of the Public Guardian

Before the PoA can be used it must be registered with the relevant OPG. There are separate offices for England and Wales and for Scotland. You can choose to register the PoA as soon as you have completed it. The advantage to registering it early is that, if there are any errors which prevent it being registered, you can correct these while you are still able to do so. This opportunity is lost with deferred registration. You can register at any later date, or leave it for your attorney to register, if and when you lose capacity and they need to take up the role. If you are leaving the registration until later, get all the above signing done so it is 'good to go'– i.e., all that is left to do is send it for registration; the signing does not go out of date.

In Scotland, along with the PoA itself you will need to send the capacity certificate and the registration form (which contains the attorney's declaration of their willingness to act). In England and Wales these are all in the same form; just ensure before you submit it that all sections have been completed.

There is a charge for registration; you can check on the respective website what the current cost is. There is a partial or even complete exemption from the cost if you meet certain criteria, for example if you are on certain benefits. The website will tell you if you are eligible for a reduced fee or an exemption and how to claim this.

This will be the position for Northern Ireland once the MCA is fully in force and there is an OPG established.

You can send your documents to the OPG in paper form or electronically. If you have completed a DIY paper version but want to register it digitally, you will need to scan it; and, in Scotland, scan too the capacity certificate and registration form. Information on the respective OPG website guides you through how to submit your forms electronically. The decision between manual or electronic submission is one of personal preference.

The processing time by the OPG, i.e. the time that it takes to get your PoA registered, will vary depending on the volume it's handling at any given time. Typically, you should plan on about twelve weeks. If you need more certainty than this, you can check with the OPG just what their current processing time is. If you need your PoA more urgently, you can ask the OPG if there is anything they can do to expedite registration. Their websites and customer helplines both have a reputation for being informative, so please feel free to ask.

After registration

There is a temptation, once your PoA is registered, to file it and forget about it, but there are a few things to bear in mind before you do this.

Make endorsed copies of your PoA

You've now done your PoA, but before you sit back and relax, hoping, like insurance, that you will never need it, it is wise to make some endorsed copies.

An endorsed copy means you confirm that a copy of your original PoA document is a true copy, or representation, of the original. An endorsed copy is not just a photocopy or a scanned image of the original; it needs to have formal wording on it, which I provide at the back of this book, officially endorsing it as a true copy of the original. Your solicitor, if you have used one, may be willing to offer you endorsed copies; you should ask about this and whether there is an additional charge. You can, however, endorse copies yourself, even if you have used a solicitor to draw up the document; see p. 303.

You may be wondering why I am mentioning this and why is it important. When your attorney needs to use the PoA they will be asked to send either the original, or an endorsed copy, to all of the organisations that you have contact with – you will be surprised just how many this is when you count them up. The organisations will want an officially endorsed copy; they will not accept photocopies or scanned images.

It is often necessary for an attorney to contact these organisations pretty much at the same time; without any endorsed copies they have to send the original to one organisation and wait for it to be returned (sometimes upwards of a month), before sending it to the next, and so on, which really hinders the effective and timely operation of the PoA. It is better to have a number of endorsed copies, which means the attorney can send one to each organisation at the same time. Sending an endorsed copy is also safer than sending the original, as it is not unheard of for the original to be mislaid by an organisation, even though they are generally respectful of an original PoA.

Keep your PoA under review

Once your PoA is done, remember to check it periodically. Things may have changed that would make it preferable to update it.

> 'I've had a dreadful time with my husband's attorney. Paul and I married five years ago; he had a daughter from a previous relationship who never accepted me in her dad's life. Paul and I never talked about a PoA. I've since learnt he'd already done one. I don't think he was keeping it secret, I genuinely think he just didn't think to mention it. Paul had a massive stroke about a year ago and his daughter has been very fast to wave the PoA at me. She has his financial and welfare PoA and is using it to spite me, or so it feels – she is refusing to allow me to visit Paul, my own husband. I have no idea what is happening; the staff looking after him are forbidden, by her, from talking to me. She is making me move out of Paul's house and has stopped my access to his money, which was supporting the two of us. I don't know if Paul thought about his PoA since we married and decided to leave things in her hands, or if it was an oversight and he forgot to amend his PoA since we married. I suspect more likely the latter, as he would have known his daughter would probably have adopted the attitude she has and I'm quite sure he wouldn't have wanted me to be left in the position I'm in.' (Anon; Paul is an assumed name)

This very sorry situation may sound extreme but, sadly, it is by no means unusual; it really demonstrates why it is important that you review your PoA with any major change in your situation and update it if required. Things that may prompt you to review your PoA are a death of one of your proposed attorneys; the loss of capacity of one of your proposed attorneys; a marriage or divorce; a major illness of you or one of your attorneys, which may mean their ability to manage things for you the way you had originally intended is no longer possible; or a change of address.

What if I want to make a change to my PoA?

You can make certain changes, or amendments, to your PoA at any time. Simple administrative changes, for example a change of name or address, can be made without any formality by writing to, or using the form provided by, the OPG. You will need to submit proof of the changes.

You can also make more substantive changes, for example to change your powers, be this to delete some or to add some, or to change an attorney, be this to remove someone or to add someone; but for these changes there is more formality. How you do this varies between England and Wales and Scotland; the respective OPG website's 'frequently asked questions' page tells you what is required. As has been mentioned, both OPGs offer a helpline service; feel free to telephone the helpline to ask what to do in your situation if you are not sure.

You may have to pay to make an amendment; you can check this on the respective OPG website.

What if I change my mind altogether about having a PoA?

Occasionally, people do have a change of mind about their PoA. You can cancel (revoke) your entire PoA at any time, even if it has been registered with the OPG, as long as you continue to have the mental capacity to do so.

The formalities for doing this are more extensive in Scotland.

The process is similar to acquiring the capacity certificate required from a lawyer or doctor when you were making the PoA. You need a lawyer or doctor to certify that you understand what it means to cancel your PoA and that you are under no pressure to have to do so. There may be a charge for this. You then submit it to the OPG along with a written note of your request to cancel/revoke your PoA.

In England and Wales, you need to offer a written notification. The website has guidance on the wording. Your signature on this needs to be witnessed by an independent person before you submit the notice to the OPG.

You are advised to tell your attorney that you are cancelling your PoA, and so removing them from this role. It can be difficult to have this conversation. Even if you cannot, or do not, speak to your attorney they will be notified by the OPG of the cancellation. If you are anxious, and especially if you are concerned that you may encounter a negative reaction from your attorney which may impact on you, you should speak to the OPG about sources of support.

If you do decide to cancel your PoA it is important to think about making another one, possibly at the same time as revoking the original; but if not, then soon thereafter, to ensure you have the protection that a PoA offers.

'When Mum had a huge stroke we had to apply for guardianship as there was no PoA. We found out that Mum had had a PoA which she had cancelled (revoked) not long before her stroke. Her solicitor had tried to persuade her at that time to make another one but she was adamant this wasn't necessary. We don't know why she thought this. How wrong she was. If she'd known the hoops we had to jump through getting the guardianship and reporting each year to the OPG, as well as the cost, I'm sure she would have remade the PoA.' (Kate, sixty-three, guardian)

Telling others

The laws in the respective territories which govern PoAs require others to be consulted on your likely views on a given matter. It is helpful, therefore, to let those closest to you, including good friends as well as family, know that you have granted a PoA, whom you have appointed as your attorneys and what your expectations are. There is no official requirement to do this and no official way of doing so; you may just want to mention it to selected others, or you may choose to send them a copy of the PoA (here a photocopy is perfectly fine) – it is your choice. It can offer reassurance to know that a wider group of people know about your PoA than just your attorneys.

> *'Mavis and I met when we were fifteen; we're ninety this year, so we've been friends for seventy-five years. We've been with each other through marriages, divorces, births and deaths. I've talked to Mavis about things that I've not talked to my children about – well you do with your best friend, don't you. My children are to be my attorneys, but I hope they check some things with Mavis.' (Sarah, eighty-nine, granter of a PoA)*

Can my attorney use my PoA in another country?

Just a quick note on this, which I've mentioned earlier. If you know at this stage that there is a possibility that the PoA may need to be used in another country, even if this is the use of a lasting PoA in Scotland, you are advised to seek legal advice: a PoA made in one country will not necessarily be valid in another.

A Statement of Wishes and Feelings

I have mentioned a Statement of Wishes and Feelings a number of times, and how valuable this can be for your attorney. This section looks at it in more detail.

If you are not able to make your own decision on a matter, your attorney is obliged to respect your preferences on things – to act as you yourself would have done. A Statement of Wishes and Feelings can assist with this; it sets out your views on key matters. We're not talking here about what are called 'end-of-life' decisions, e.g. whether you would want resuscitation or have your life support switched off; a Statement of Wishes and Feelings offers your views on living your life the way you desire. It can be your wishes on little things, as well as more substantial matters. It can contain anything on which you'd like to give your attorney some direction.

Here are some thoughts on what you may wish to tell them:

- Any care preferences (e.g. preference for a shower or bath, need to sleep with a light on, need to be in bed by 10 p.m., preference for main meal at lunchtime).
- Religious or spiritual beliefs that you would wish respected.
- Dietary requirements you would wish respected; or just your favourite foods, or foods you don't like.
- If you have a preference for tea or coffee, or don't drink either. Milk, sugar?
- A favourite tipple if you have one, or if you prefer not to drink alcohol.
- Any preferences for clothing (e.g. some women prefer not to wear trousers; some men prefer always to be formally dressed; some people prefer to wear cotton only).

- Any preference on where your clothes are purchased from.
- Any soaps/soap powders you prefer, or cannot use.
- Any shampoos/conditioners you prefer, or cannot use.
- Perfumes/aftershaves you particularly like or not.
- Music you like/do not like.
- Television programmes you like.
- Films you like.
- If you like peace and quiet or prefer to be in the midst of the group.
- What hobbies you have.
- Places you like to visit, or to go on holiday to (you may wish to mention if you burn easily, or can't swim).
- Particular dislikes and activities; places or people you would prefer to avoid.
- If you wear make-up, any preferences you wish to offer about this.
- If you have pets, any comments you wish to make about them. What are their likes/dislikes, who would you wish to look after them if you are ill, which kennels do you prefer, which vet do you prefer etc.?
- Or maybe you have a fear of animals that you wish to mention.

There is no limit to what you can give your attorneys a steer on: anything which is important to you and which you would wish others to know about. There is a sample Statement of Wishes and Feelings at the back of this book (p. 304) if you wish to use this.

> *'I didn't know how strongly my mum disliked our local hospice; it was helpful that her Statement of Wishes and Feelings was clear that we should not, ever, place her in there. When Mum became terminal and hospice care became necessary, I was able to arrange this in another hospice; without the Statement of Wishes and Feelings Mum would have been admitted to the hospice that she hated.'*
> *(James, fifty-six, attorney)*

A Statement of Wishes and Feelings has no legal status, but it is a helpful thing to do and can assist if there is difference of opinion between attorneys, or the attorneys and others, at a later date.

A Statement of Wishes and Feelings is particularly helpful if you have complicated factors in your life, for example a difficult family situation. An example would be an estranged child who, when they learn of their parent's current situation, wishes to reconcile matters; giving your attorneys guidance on whether this is something you would wish or not is extremely helpful.

There is no formality to a Statement of Wishes and Feelings; it does not need to be in a particular style and you can hand-write it if you wish. It's not required to be dated, signed or witnessed, but signing it can help prove that it represents your views, and dating it shows that these were your views at that time; so I would advocate dating and signing it. Having an independent person witness you signing it can also assist. The witness is only confirming that it was you they saw signing it; it does not need to be a particular person, but they should be independent, i.e. not the person who is going to be your attorney.

Some people attach a Statement of Wishes and Feelings to their PoA, but it can be a stand-alone document which you can then add to as different things occur to you. If you are keeping it in your possession, it is good practice to review it periodically and, even if you aren't making any changes, update the date and your signature, so at any later stage people can see that you were consistent in the views that you held.

When you think it is complete be sure to send it to your attorneys, or tell them where they can find it and give a copy to anyone else who may have an interest, e.g. other family members or friends, your solicitor, your financial advisor, your doctor. You may wish to record in your PoA that a Statement of Wishes and Feelings exists and where a copy of this can be found.

> 'My own good friend has just made a Statement of her Wishes and Feelings and told me it's in her top drawer, in an envelope with my name on it should I need it.'

Useful/factual information

Include too in your Statement of Wishes and Feelings guidance for your attorney on your general affairs. Don't make assumptions about what your attorney might already know, and try to be as clear and comprehensive as possible about such things as who your doctor is, where you bank and what insurances you have; there is a list on p. 305 which will prompt ideas on items which you may wish to include.

Just a word about confidential information within your Statement of Wishes and Feelings: please don't include account numbers, passwords, personal identifier numbers (PINs) or the like; don't even include your mother's maiden name, the names of your children or of any pets, or your date of birth, as these are all useful information in the wrong hands.

Your PoA should include authority for your attorney to have access to such personally sensitive and confidential data. So you tell them in your factual information that, for example, you Bank with X; they can then go along to Bank X with the PoA, which permits them access to the information they need.

Hopefully, you can see real value in offering a Statement of Wishes and Feelings; it gives a lot of comfort to attorneys to know they are respecting what you would have wanted on a given issue, not just what they think you would have wanted.

Advance Decisions/Directives

Just before we leave this section, I should add a note about Advance Decisions or Directives. There is a difference between a written statement expressing preferences (Statement of Wishes and Feelings) and a statement which constitutes Advance Decisions on your future care. These decisions might include that of refusing treatment, or Advance Directives on what treatment you may wish on certain occasions, or if you wish to be resuscitated. As this book is not about advance care planning I am offering only headline information here; if you want more information about how to make Advance Directives or Decisions, a good starting point is an internet search using that term; make sure you are looking at information relevant to the country you are in, as the format and requirements are different in England and Scotland, for example.

The websites advise who should have a copy. I suggest keeping your own copy with your PoA and Statement of Wishes and Feelings, if you have made one, which should be in the same place as a copy of your will, if you have made one, so all the relevant documents are together.

My closing piece of advice in this chapter on managing your PoA longer-term is to keep an open dialogue with your attorneys. You've made all the decisions you need to make and your PoA is done, but, as obvious as it sounds, remember to keep an ongoing conversation with your attorneys; talk to them about your views and opinions on things, how you feel; discuss things you may not have spoken to them about before and update them on changes. Essentially, talk to them about anything you think they will need to know to make the decisions on your behalf in a way that you would have made for yourself. Consider, too, if you need to have similar open conversations with your wider family, so that they are also aware of your views on things. This will help them to support your attorneys when they may otherwise have opposed or challenged a decision made by the attorneys.

This concludes the chapters dedicated to those of you who are thinking about making a PoA. By now you should have a robust PoA, tailored to your needs, offering the powers you want to whom you want, and suitable for your situation. Now we will turn to how your attorney manages this.

Chapter 6

Deciding whether you want to be an attorney

In previous chapters, we have looked at what is involved in creating a PoA; now we turn our attention to the experience of being an attorney.

I regularly hear families saying, 'We need to get PoA for X'; this may just be a choice of words, but in case there is genuine misunderstanding I should clarify that a PoA is not something you 'get', but rather something you are given. If you feel it is necessary for your loved one to think about the grant of a PoA and they haven't moved to do so thus far, the earlier chapters in this book, which talk directly to potential donors/granters of a PoA, may assist. It is helpful for you to read these chapters too, as they may assist you in formulating what can be a difficult conversation about the grant of a PoA.

For the rest of this chapter, let us assume that you have been approached by someone asking you to be their attorney; do not feel guilty if your first instinct is 'I'm not sure.' This first reaction is not uncommon; it is perfectly understandable and, I think, is a good sign. Being an attorney is a formal legal role and is not something you should just assume, or agree to automatically; it is good to give it real consideration. A PoA works best if the attorney has accepted the role willingly and with their eyes open to what it involves. This chapter will look at what being an attorney involves and address those early queries that people have, which should help you decide whether this is a role for you or not.

What does being an attorney involve?

As we have seen, there are two different types of PoA: one which grants powers over property and finances, called a lasting PoA in England, Wales and Northern Ireland and a continuing PoA in Scotland; and the other which grants powers over health and welfare, called a lasting PoA health and welfare in England and Wales, and, in Scotland, simply a welfare PoA. You may have been approached to be an attorney over both types, or just one. When reading the information which follows, bear in mind what you are being asked to do, i.e. whether you are being asked to manage property and finances, health and welfare matters, or both.

Being an attorney is the same wherever in the UK you are located; this information therefore applies across the UK.

You'll see already that I've used the terms 'PoA' and 'attorney'. To avoid any confusion, I'll refer to you as the attorney, so when you see the term PoA I'm referring to the legal document. As I pointed out in the Introduction, sometimes I use the word attorney in the singular and sometimes in the plural, as works better grammatically; but all of the information applies equally to any and all attorneys.

An attorney's obligations

Being an attorney, or having the power of an attorney, is a formal and legal position. It comes with certain requirements and obligations; it can carry liabilities if you do something wrong or fail to do something you should have done. Much of the rest of this book covers the obligations of an attorney, but to give you a snapshot an attorney's obligations include the following:

- Putting the donor/granter at the centre of your thinking. *This, you may think, should go without saying: everything you do should be focused on the needs of the person.*

- You are obliged to act with honesty and integrity.

- You have a duty of care to the donor/granter of the PoA; this means you must apply a standard of care and skill. *If, for example, you feel that you are out of your depth on a given matter, then make sure you seek assistance or relevant advice, even if you have to pay for this.*

- You should support the person in making their own decisions whenever possible. *There is more about this in Chapter 7.*

- If this is not possible, you should make the decision that they would most likely have made for themselves. *This too is covered in more detail in Chapter 7.*

- You should only make decisions that the PoA gives you authority to make. *The powers in the PoA will set out what authority you have, or don't have. You do not have to use all powers, only those needed, as and when these are required.*

- You should act in accordance with the principles of the relevant Act. *The principles are detailed in Chapter 9. Please ensure you are familiar with these and how to act in accordance with them, as to overlook them could place you in breach of the law.*

- You should be aware of and have regard to the Code of Practice. *Chapter 2 mentioned the Code of Practice: this is, as the name suggests, a code of best practice which you may be challenged for not following. You should make yourself familiar with it and be guided by it.*

- You should maintain records of your actions. *I talk more about record-keeping in Chapter 10, giving ideas about what you should keep notes on.*

- You should comply with any orders of the Public Guardian and of the court. *The respective Public Guardians, as well as the courts, plus, in Scotland, the local authority of the area in which the person lives, are the supervising authorities and each has a legal status; if they issue an order in respect of anything you are doing as attorney you must pay heed to this.*

Frequently asked questions

Will I be able to do it?

Obviously, you need to know what the role involves; I have covered the obligations of an attorney above, in brief, which may assist you. Chapter 10 explains in detail what acting as an attorney involves, so do refer to that chapter too.

If you have anxiety or uncertainty about whether you will be able to fulfil the role, it can be helpful to talk to someone else. A friend or family member who has been an attorney can tell you about their experiences (bear in mind that not everyone's experiences are the same). You may prefer to talk to an organisation like Citizen's Advice, or even take your own legal advice.

If you are nervous about the prospect, but are willing in principle, talk to the person asking you to be their attorney. Discuss your fears and talk through the possibilities. There may even be a compromise which may allow you to agree to take the role.

It is important that, before accepting the role, you feel you have the confidence to fulfil it.

'I wanted my daughter to be my attorney, but she is dyslexic and was very anxious about her ability, so much so that she was going to say no, even though this upset her because she wanted to support me. Thankfully she told me this, so we spoke about what else we could do. We talked about me offering PoA to our family solicitor as well as her, so she would have his expert support. She was still anxious about 'holding her own' in conversations with him. We decided in the end that our solicitor would be my financial attorney, and my daughter was happy to take on the role of my health and welfare attorney; it had been managing the financial bits that had been most worrying her. So it all worked out in the end: my daughter could look after me as I (and she) wanted, but I could ensure she was supported and was happy.' (Emmie, sixty-five, donor of a PoA)

Will I know if I'm being nominated as an attorney?

Potential attorneys are concerned that they will be appointed and won't know until after the event, so this question comes up quite often. The short answer is yes: you will know ahead, I would hope, that the person nominating you will have had a conversation with you in advance of your being made attorney. However, even if they haven't, you do formally have to agree to be appointed and make certain declarations as part of the process, so you will find out at this stage if not before. So you can rest assured that you can't legally be made an attorney without your knowledge.

Will I be the only attorney?

Knowing whether you are to be the only attorney or whether there will be others appointed may help you decide whether you wish to accept the appointment. The number of people to be appointed will depend on what the donor/granter of the PoA wants. They may nominate you plus someone else, or multiple other people, or you may be the only (sole) attorney.

If there are multiple attorneys, you should check whether the PoA permits each of you to act independently of the other(s), or whether you have to act jointly. Being able to act independently offers you more flexibility, but also means you are liable for the actions of another when you may not have had anything to do with those actions. Chapters 3 and 10 give more information about how multiple attorneys may be appointed in relation to each other, and what this means.

If you have any concerns about the way in which you are being appointed, or who may be a fellow attorney with you, discuss this with the person making the PoA, and preferably also with the person you'll be working alongside.

Even if you are to be the sole attorney, the law requires you nonetheless to take account of the views of relevant others – for example, family members, carers, doctors, solicitors or close friends. To fulfil the role of attorney successfully requires a cordial relationship with other people close to the person. You may wish to think carefully about accepting the role if you sense that others may dispute how things are administered.

What powers will I have?

The powers you have will depend on what the PoA gives you. Ask the person for sight of the draft document and have an open and honest conversation with them so you know their expectations. You may have financial powers and/or health and welfare powers. Chapter 2 offers detailed information on the powers that can be granted. Knowing what powers you have may help you decide whether you wish to accept the position.

When can I use the powers?

If you have financial powers, these can start as soon as the PoA is registered with the Office of the Public Guardian (OPG), but you should be acting on the say-so of the donor/granter if they remain capable, not taking over from them. Let us use an example to illustrate the difference:

> *'I was quite capable, but it was a comfort to have my son able to be with me or speak for me. For example, I wanted to talk to a media company about the package of services they provide to my home, which I wasn't sure was right for me; but they talk such modern language I don't know what they mean half the time. They make everything sound like it's something I need, and really I don't know. My son phoned them, got to the right department, then I spoke to them to answer all the security questions then put my son back on with my full authority to agree with them whatever he felt was right for me.' (Sadie, seventy-seven, donor of a PoA)*

Technically, in this example and many similar situations, the son is not acting under the PoA, but under what is called 'mandated authority', i.e. with the express permission of the person. While the person remains capable, you should only act on their behalf with their explicit consent and instruction.

While financial powers can start as soon as they are registered, welfare powers cannot start unless or until the person is incapable – and even then, this incapacity must be assessed in relation to each decision that needs to be made. Chapter 8 explains how you decide whether the person is incapable or not.

In advance of the welfare PoA coming into effect, you should also check whether there are any stipulations contained in the document which must be met before the powers can start. Most typically, this would be that you are required to get medical opinion to confirm that the person is incapable. This may be the case in Scotland particularly.

How much time does it take to be an attorney?

This is an understandable concern: you will want to give the role commitment, but may be anxious about how much time this will take. You may already have a lot of other commitments, for example, family and work, as well possibly caring for the person now asking you to be their attorney.

The time that needs to be given to being an attorney will depend on the individual circumstances. At the very least, attorneys are advised to see the person twice per year, but in an active phase there can be some attorney duties most weeks. It can be hard to juggle competing demands. Recognising this level of commitment can put some people off, but in reality the time you have to give may stem from being a carer, or from the support you are giving to the person anyway; it may not be linked to being their attorney per se. Having the authority of attorney can actually ease time commitments, since it opens doors that you may otherwise have had to spend even longer trying to access – like trying to speak to care, banking and utility organisations, potentially with little success without being an attorney.

Will I get any support?

Knowing that there is support may make it easier for you to accept the role. If you need support, because you have a specific question that isn't covered by this book, or you want a more authoritative opinion than that of a friend, there are a range of organisations that can offer you guidance. Among these are:

- The local authority social work department

- The Office of the Public Guardian
- Citizens Advice Bureaux
- Voluntary organisations
- Independent banking/financial/mortgage advisors
- Legal advisors
- Government websites
- Online searches.

This list is not exhaustive; ask around. If other family, friends or neighbours have been attorneys, where did they go for advice; ask them for any hints and tips they may have. Informed insight from people who are, or have been, in your position can be invaluable and a great source of support; but double-check that any suggestions they make are right for your situation – just because it worked for them doesn't necessarily mean it is the right thing for you.

You may find 'chat' sites online to which you can pose your query, or maybe there is a group in your area where people in a similar situation to yours come together in a relaxed surrounding for mutual support and an exchange of views. You may well be surprised how much is happening in your area that you didn't know about until you start asking around.

If you have to pay for advice to keep you on the right track in your role as attorney, check if the PoA allows you to be reimbursed for expenses you have incurred.

Do I have to do everything myself, or can someone else act on my behalf as attorney?

Your decision on accepting the role may be influenced by whether someone can take over from you every so often, for example to give you a bit of a break. This will depend on how you are appointed – which is covered in Chapter 3.

If you are appointed jointly with another, or other, attorneys, then you all have to action every matter together; but at least you have each other for mutual support. If you are appointed jointly and individually with another, or others, you can each action something individually, but again you should be discussing and agreeing the path you wish to pursue, and so giving and getting mutual support.

The position is more difficult if you are being appointed as a sole attorney, as you are not permitted to delegate responsibility; there is more about this in Chapter 10. That said, you are required to consider the views of others in your decision-making, so consult those who know the person well to help you formulate your direction, and maybe in so doing validate your decision; but the end decision has to be yours – you cannot pass this responsibility to someone else.

In Chapter 3 we discussed replacement attorneys. A replacement is a person who takes over from you permanently. If you are being appointed as the sole attorney and you think you will need a break from the role from time to time, you will need to speak to the person creating the PoA about appointing at least one other person, and appointing you jointly and individually, so that the other person can hold the reins while you have some downtime.

Can I, or will I, be paid?

Knowing whether you will be paid for acting as an attorney may influence your decision on whether you accept the role.

Whether you can be paid will depend on whether the PoA permits this. If there is no payment power, then no, you cannot be paid. If it does allow you to pay yourself, this is only for the occasions when you are acting as attorney and would usually only cover losses and outlays; i.e. it is not an active payment and is not like having a job for which you are paid a wage.

> *Your mum has lost capacity and is in care. You visit your mum each day; this involves a round trip totalling fifty miles. You cannot reimburse yourself for the cost of the petrol as you are visiting in your capacity as her daughter, not in your capacity as her attorney. However, today you are required to travel the same fifty miles to meet with the doctor to agree treatment for your mum, as her welfare attorney. If the PoA permits, you can reimburse yourself for the cost of this visit – but this would only extend to actual losses; for example, you can reimburse yourself for fuel costs as this is a cost you have borne, but you cannot pay yourself for lost hours of work if you did not have to work that day, or had paid leave from work.*

Will I be able to change my mind?

It may assist you in deciding to accept the role to know that you can resign at any time, even if you have already taken up the post. If you wish to resign as attorney, there are a few formalities to comply with, which differ slightly depending on your appointment.

You are appointed as a sole attorney and wish to resign some or all of your powers

You should notify, in writing:

- the donor/granter of the PoA
- the person's primary carer, if this is not you
- the Public Guardian
- the local authority.

You should be aware that, if the person has now lost capacity and is therefore not in a position to appoint someone to replace you, your resigning leaves the person without anyone in an official capacity to support them or authorise matters on their behalf.

This would likely, therefore, have to proceed to a deputy-ship/guardianship, which is a more onerous and costly process by which someone is appointed by the court to act in an official capacity for the person. Additionally, as a court appointment it can take some time to process; the person may be left with no one officially appointed to support and act for them for a period. To prevent this void, if you can, you should remain as attorney while someone else applies for deputyship/guardianship; upon their appointment to this post your PoA would come to an end.

You are appointed alongside someone else, or there is a replacement/substitute person named. You wish to resign some or all of your powers.

You should notify, in writing, the same people listed in the previous section, and in addition the person appointed with you, or the replacement/substitute. A written confirmation from them that they are willing to act either alone, or as your replacement, should accompany your written resignation.

You should be aware that, even if you are appointed with someone else, the impact your resigning has on the PoA will depend on the construction of the PoA. You should have a look at Chapters 3 and 10, which tell you more about how attorneys are appointed in relation to each other, and thus what would happen if one resigned.

What if I don't want to accept the role?

Hopefully, reviewing these questions has helped you decide whether you are willing to be appointed; but what if you don't want to do it?

When you are approached by someone asking you to be their attorney, whether that is in advance of signing a document or because you have received the documentation nominating you as attorney, you may feel some pressure to agree.

You may feel a natural obligation to accept the role, but agreeing to be an attorney is not something you have to do. There are many reasons why people decide that being an attorney is not for them, and there is no shame in saying no. The PoA works way better if the attorney is willing, rather than having felt pressured into the role. Don't accept because you think you should; have an honest conversation with the person who has asked you to be their attorney about your concerns. This gives them the opportunity to nominate an alternative attorney.

The role of the Office of Public Guardian

Before closing this chapter I should touch on the role of the OPG, which has been mentioned a few times. The Public Guardian is the head of the OPG, which is a statutory position, i.e. one created by law. There is a Public Guardian for England and Wales and a separate office holder for Scotland; longer-term there will be a Public Guardian for Northern Ireland too. The Public Guardian has a range of responsibilities related to the care and support of incapable persons, but in respect of PoAs, for ease, let me describe the role as one of regulation.

The OPG in each country is often seen as central to the operation of PoAs. The respective OPGs both have a Twitter account, via which they provide useful information; you may wish to follow them. Their websites are also very informative and can offer a steer on how to progress with something if you are not sure. Both, too, are very willing to give telephone advice; they would rather you asked than carry on in a direction which is wrong. They are used to being asked all sorts of questions, so nothing is off-limits; they have a reputation for being very helpful. If they are not able to assist directly because of the nature of your question, they will signpost you to the best agency to contact. They are not, however, able to offer legal advice.

The PoA must be registered with the OPG before you gain legal authority as attorney. Thereafter the OPG does not have any routine function in respect of a PoA or your role as attorney, but can receive complaints about how you have exercised your function. So in making this decision about being an attorney you need to know that you are, in the main, an autonomous practitioner, but that there is an official body there if you need their assistance, or if they need to regulate your practice.

The public register

The final thing for me to mention in this chapter is the existence of the public register; you should be aware that the OPG in both England and Wales, and Scotland maintains a register, which is open to the public, which lists PoAs that are registered with them. The register also names the attorney. As the PoA has to be registered with OPG before you can start acting as an attorney, it will be a matter of public record that you are appointed as an attorney. Anyone is allowed access to this public information. The information on the register is limited to high-level facts: that a PoA exists and who the attorneys are.

In conclusion, the decision to act as an attorney, even if this is for a loved one, is one which you should spend time thinking about. Being an attorney comes with certain obligations; you should be aware of what it involves and be satisfied that you are willing to take up the appointment before saying yes. There are a whole range of reasons why people may hesitate to accept the role of attorney. Please don't feel guilty if you think you should accept but have some of these concerns; this is quite common. Try to explore and get answers to any doubts you may have before deciding. There is no shame in refusing, and many people end up saying it is not for them. The PoA works best if you have satisfied yourself that this is a role which you are willing and feel confident and able to fulfil. If you have agreed to be the attorney, the next chapters put your role in context, providing you with the framework within which you should act.

Chapter 7

Supporting decision-making and respecting rights, will and preferences

Supporting a person with their decision-making

One of the key tasks of an attorney is supporting the person with their decision-making. Indeed, you could argue that doing this comes before you begin operating as attorney: as you will see, you should not be stepping in as attorney unless or until the person can no longer make their own decisions and after you have offered them every support with this. Consequently, this chapter precedes the chapters which offer you detail about operating under the PoA.

Before I go further, I should point out that you will see numerous references, throughout this book, to supporting *decision*-making: this is shorthand, as the term 'decision' also extends to supporting a person in taking action on a decision they have made. Supporting a person to make a decision would be a fruitless exercise if they then could not take the necessary action. So wherever you see 'supporting decision-making', it also covers supporting the person in taking action.

An attorney's role is not to take over someone's life, but to empower them as far as is possible to make decisions for themselves; this extends from what they might want for lunch to more significant decisions such as whether they want to sell their house.

This requirement, to support a person with their decision-making, applies equally across the UK to anyone fulfilling any function with, or for, a person with impaired, or lost, capacity. That means nurses, carers, bankers and, of course, attorneys.

The requirement comes from the United Nations Convention on the Rights of Persons with Disabilities (UNCRPD), which the UK has ratified (agreed to respect). The Convention sets out a framework for the rights which a person with disability can expect. This covers people with physical disabilities, but also those with intellectual disabilities, or cognitive impairment, so it includes people with incapacity. There are two rights within the Convention which are of particular importance for attorneys and which we will explore in this chapter: these are the right that a person will be supported in making their own decisions, and that their rights, will and preferences on a given matter will be respected. We shall cover this second aspect later in the chapter. For now, the focus is on supporting decision-making.

Technically, what the UNCRPD requires is support for a person in the exercise of their legal capacity; I include this phrasing as you may hear professionals referring to it and wonder whether this is something different to supported decision-making. One could have an academic debate about the semantics – the differences between supporting decision-making, or support for decision-making and supporting the exercise of legal capacity. For the purposes of this book we need to think in practical terms; so it easier to see this simply as a requirement to support a person to make their own decisions and to act on these decisions. But how do we do this?

What is your responsibility if you are supporting a person with incapacity?

A person with incapacity has exactly the same legal rights and entitlements as a person of full capacity.

The law requires you to maximise the ability of the individual to make decisions, or to participate in decision-making, as far as they are able to do so. Your responsibility is therefore, as far as is possible, to support the individual in making their own decisions; this may require you to think creatively about how to achieve this, as previous methods of decision-making may no longer be possible. It will usually take more time than you feel you have, but do not fall into the trap of just making the decision yourself for ease or speed. This is called substituted decision-making and is not considered acceptable.

Alex and Lynn were with David in a café. David has a learning disability and impaired decision-making. Alex and Lynn spent about fifteen minutes supporting David to choose his lunch; he opted for tuna panini. Alex and Lynn were both having a toasted teacake. Alex went to order and came back saying she just ordered three teacakes – it was easier. Lynn was annoyed. She said that if she, Lynn, had wanted tuna panini and David had wanted a teacake, would Alex then have ordered three teacakes? No, she would have respected Lynn's right to choose; so why was she disrespecting David's right to choose?

This example illustrates substituted decision-making. Despite doing a textbook exercise in supporting David's decision-making, Alex, at the last minute, simply substituted her own choice for his. Lynn was justified in challenging Alex; she recognised that David had as much right to have his choice respected as she herself did.

Substituted decision-making is when you make the decision based on your own values. For example, if you are vegetarian but the other person is a meat eater, and when shopping for them you only choose vegetarian meals as you cannot bring yourself to purchase meat products, you have 'substituted' your own values, and therefore decisions, for those the other person would have made.

You will get to recognise a substituted decision when you become familiar with this concept, as the next personal example shows:

> *'I went into the store to buy lunch for my husband; he had asked for a sandwich, telling me to just pick, as I knew what he liked. There were only about three packets of sandwiches left, none of which he would have liked, so I got him a warmed pie, which I knew he liked. When I told him about the exchange, he replied straight back at me: "I asked for a sandwich you chose a pie, substituted decision-making, shame on you Sandra McDonald."'*

So, we know that we are required to support a person's decision-making; why is this?

What are the benefits of supported decision-making (SDM)?

As well as helping someone make a decision for themselves, SDM can have wider positive effects on both your life and that of the person in question. The benefits of SDM, when carried out appropriately, have been shown to include increased confidence for the individual being supported, increased autonomy and a resulting participation in a greater range of activities. There is less need for deputyship or guardianship; indeed, a few such orders have been recalled as a result of improved SDM, because with the increased level of support the person is able to make their own decisions. The person offering support often reports satisfaction in seeing the increased autonomy of the person they are helping. One might suppose that these benefits are only visible with longer-term and more consistent use of SDM; but they can occur, for both giver and receiver, as it were, even when support is given for a single decision.

Decision-making ability

Assessment of decision-making ability should not be confused with assessment of capacity. They are distinct: someone may, by definition, be incapable, but may nonetheless be able to make a decision on a given matter, albeit with support. We will see in the next chapter that capacity is not an all-or-nothing matter; so it is with decision-making ability: it is not the case that one passes a point after which one is not able to make any decisions. Neither is decision-making ability linear: it is not the case that a person is able to make a low-level decision but not a higher-level one. Decision-making ability must be assessed for each decision.

Factors that affect decision-making

When considering how you can support someone in their decision-making, it's important to examine the various things that may be impeding their ability in the first place. There are many factors which affect anyone's ability to make a decision. Here we look at some of the more common ones, in no particular order.

Experience and confidence

If you have had a positive experience in making a particular decision, this may give you confidence to make a decision of a similar nature; conversely, if you've had a bad experience you may lack the confidence, or be hesitant, to make a similar decision at a later date.

Understanding

If you don't have all the information, don't recognise the importance of the situation, don't appreciate the risks, benefits or rewards, you won't be able to make a properly considered decision, or a decision at all.

Emotion

If you are having a difficult time emotionally, you may find it hard to make a decision, or make a well-judged decision. If you are stressed or anxious about a matter, your decision-making ability will be affected.

Other people

You may feel inclined to make a decision to please, or maybe annoy, someone else. You may feel pressured by someone. Someone whose views you value may put you off a decision you may otherwise have made, or may spur you on.

Time of day

We may be naturally better at making decisions at a particular time of day; or we may be affected by external factors. For example, for a parent under pressure in the morning to get the kids up, dressed, with lunches sorted and off to school, it may be better to wait until later in the day to consider a key matter.

Pain

We will be less equipped to make good judgements if we are in pain. Medical treatments may impact on our ability.

Lack of support

You may feel you wish to chat the decision through with someone but have no one, or no one suitable, available.

Location

An unfamiliar location may adversely affect one's ability to make decisions; lawyers, when taking instruction on a PoA, may attend the person's home to optimise their ability to have the necessary discussion.

Environment

A calm, quiet environment may assist decision-making; many people say they make their best decisions in the bath, or in bed. For others, background noise helps them think.

Tiredness

Your decision-making ability will be affected by tiredness, e.g. from lack of sleep, or at the end of a hard week's work, or after a long drive.

Lack of concentration

You will find decision-making harder if your thought process is being interrupted or if you are being distracted or lack concentration for other reasons.

Money

A lack, or even an excess, of money may influence a decision. Certainly, anxiety about money, debt or the cost of things will have an impact.

This list is by no means exhaustive. It would be easy to go on, but there is sufficient here to demonstrate just how many factors influence decision-making. When supporting someone in making a decision you should take these factors into consideration and ask yourself if you can alleviate them in any way.

Things get even more complex when one takes into account issues specific to a person's medical condition or character which impact on their ability to make a decision, such as:

- attention deficit
- panic disorders
- irritability
- rigid thinking
- paranoia
- controlling impulses
- hearing loss
- suspiciousness
- apathy
- lack of motivation.

How do you support someone with their decision-making?

The kind of support people might need to help them make a decision varies. It depends on, among other things, personal circumstances, the kind of decision that has to be made and the time available to do so. Here are some of the common things which you can do to help.

Eliminate all of the obstacles

To support someone in their decision-making successfully requires you first to get an optimal position on all of the factors, some of which are outlined above, which impact on the person's ability to make a decision. So, for example, make sure they are pain-free, not overly tired and in a familiar environment.

You may have to use a different form of communication (for example, non-verbal communication). You may have to provide information in a more accessible form (for example, photographs, drawings or tapes), or you may need to have a structured programme to improve the person's capacity to make particular decisions.

Be clear about the decision to be made

If we are asked multiple questions in the same sentence it gets confusing, and even more so if the answer to one of the questions is yes and the other is no; the person awaiting your response is then also confused as to which response you are giving to which question. In a similar way, it is hard to get to a definitive decision on something if one is not clear, from the outset, about the matter on which a decision is required. Thus, make sure you clarify to the person you are supporting, in easy-to-understand terms, what the matter is you are asking them to consider and decide on.

Take time

In making a decision, many of us need time to consider the issue, then further time to ruminate on our decision, before confirming whether it is the way we wish to proceed. And likewise, we can feel constrained in our ability to make a decision if we feel under pressure.

Ensure you take sufficient time when supporting a person with their decision-making. The time necessary will vary from person to person and depend on the issue – be guided by the individual.

Be sure not to apply pressure

A number of things we have touched on can put undue pressure on the person, which will inhibit positive decision-making ability. For example, if you rush the person, or stand over them, or influence them by way of your behaviour or body language, from which the person infers that they are making a poor choice, or one that you disapprove of – they may be keen to try to please you. Watch your own interactions, therefore, to ensure that you are not, even unintentionally, negatively affecting the person's freedom to choose.

Appropriate questioning

Check that you are not influencing the outcome by the way you ask the question. A closed question, for example 'Do you want a sandwich for lunch?', closes the person's choice, whereas 'What would you like for lunch?' leaves them free to tell you their preference.

Having considered the concept of supporting a person with their decision-making, let us now look at the how – the approach you need to adopt to be successful, or as successful as may be possible in the circumstances.

Your approach

Check first that the decision maker wishes you to support them in the process. The decision maker has the right to decide whether they want decision-making support in any specific instance.

Check, too, if they wish you to be that supporter. The decision maker has a right to choose whom they want to support them to make decisions. Even if you are their appointed attorney, the nature of the decision may be one that they would prefer someone else to support them with.

Assuming you are progressing with supporting the individual's decision-making, then your approach should be:

- stay calm, have patience
- build trust
- use touch
- maintain eye contact, be on the same level as the individual
- have open body gestures, smile
- be matter-of-fact and relaxed
- remain objective – ensure you are not inadvertently influencing the person's decisions by your words or gestures
- do not use excessive persuasion or undue pressure
- speak at a steady rate and normal volume
- make sure your comments and questions are clear and unambiguous
- use language the person understands
- use short sentences
- if the person is struggling for words, do not be tempted to offer them a range of options hoping one of these may be the one they are searching for

- listen actively, be observant: a change in the person's body position or facial expression may indicate something different to the words they are conveying
- if you don't understand something, apologise and ask the person to repeat it
- check your understanding of what they have said by repeating back what you believe yourself to have heard and understood
- be alert to the person's emotions; acknowledge these.

The process:

- offer only as much support as is needed
- provide appropriate advice and information
- explain things in simple terms
- break the matter into bite-sized chunks; offer the person choices and options
- focus on one decision at a time; don't expect more than a couple of decisions to be made within the same time frame
- use, and encourage the person to use, simple gestures if this helps, e.g. thumbs up, down, pointing, head or eye movements, mimes
- use drawings, pictures, recordings etc. if this will be better for the individual than words, or will complement the words
- in any event, keep paper and a pen handy, be this for you or the individual
- writing down key words can assist with the focus of the conversation
- writing down choices can also assist
- Will past examples help? Has the person had to make a

decision of a similar nature previously which you can discuss with them? However, remember that circumstances can change; and just because they made a decision one way in the past does not mean that they will make that same decision on another occasion.

- Can someone else help? No one person has the monopoly on supporting another's decision-making, even if this person is appointed as their attorney or guardian. There may be others who can assist, for example a long-term friend or a daughter rather than a son.

- Can professional input help? It may be more appropriate for an independent person to support the incapable person's decision-making. Speech and language therapists, who have expertise in complex communication, may be able to assist, as too may independent advocates; the last section of this chapter gives you information about independent advocates.

- Can it wait? As has been touched on above, a person may be better able to make a decision on some occasions than others; if they are struggling today can the decision wait until later, or another day?

Once a decision has been arrived at, the supporter should:

- respect the person's decision
- facilitate action, if required.

Supported decision-making should be attempted first on every occasion. Do not assume that, because the person cannot make certain decisions, they will not be able to make the decision today, and then move straight on to making the decision for them.

You should also assess whether the person might regain

capacity, or sufficient capacity to be supported with their own decision-making, and, if so, if the matter can wait until then.

Regaining of capacity may not be likely, and thus there may be occasions when it is just not possible for the individual to make a decision personally, even with every support; in which case, you should move to best-interpretation decision-making.

Best-interpretation decision-making

Sometimes, no matter how much you optimise the decision-making environment and offer every support, the person will not be able, on that occasion at least, to make a decision personally. This is sometimes referred to as having lost the capacity to make that decision. We will look at how one determines capacity in the next chapter; for now, let us simply accept that if a person is not able, even with support, to make a decision for themselves, then we may then have to make the decision on the person's behalf. If we are in this situation, the decision we make should be that which is the best interpretation of the decision the person themselves would have made – which may be different from the decision we think is advisable and may be different from the decision we would have made for ourselves had we been in the same situation. Decisions made in these situations are often among the hardest ones you have to make.

> *Brian has terminal dementia. He made it clear to his family that he saw dementia as a 'slow demise' which would only end one way; he would welcome his reprieve from this. After Brian lost the ability to make decisions for himself, he developed a cancer which the doctors told his family would kill him without treatment, but the treatment would be relatively simple and would likely be effective.*   →

Brian is not able to make this decision. His family have a health and welfare PoA; they have to make a decision based on what they think Brian would opt to do: would he accept an effective easy treatment, but live longer with dementia; or decline treatment and allow the cancer to take him sooner, hoping, though, that the cancer can be controlled and that his end can be comfortable and pain-free? But what if the cancer cannot be controlled and his end is not as smooth as one would hope?

It is maybe worth reiterating here that such decisions are not entirely the preserve of the attorneys, as health and social-care professionals are permitted, by law, to authorise treatments. Consequently, if Brian's relatives had not had his health and welfare PoA the doctor treating him could have authorised the procedure.

Making a best-interpretation decision

If you are facing making a best-interpretation decision, the following prompts may help:

- First, ensure you avoid discrimination, or any personal bias.
- Ensure you are not making assumptions about someone's best interests simply on the basis of the person's age, appearance, condition or behaviour.
- Consider what the person's current wishes are; do you know?
- Can you glean anything from current behaviours? Is their mood, their tone or pitch of voice, their attitude, even their physiological response telling you anything about a preference?

- What would their past wishes have been? Can you draw anything from their approach to similar decisions?

- Is there a Statement of Wishes and Feelings? Increasingly, people are making such a statement, which may assist with best-interpretation decision-making (see Chapter 5).

- Have you respected the person's rights, will and preferences (see the next section). Can anyone else offer a view? You can involve others, e.g. an independent advocate, or a close friend of the person, who may be able to offer a fresh perspective on what the person would have wanted, or may be able to elicit information, or even a decision, from the person that you yourself were unable to obtain.

- Is the decision one which meets the respective Acts' principles? (We will look at these in detail in the next chapter.)

Ensure you record the process, especially if the person's wishes cannot be established, or the views of someone else involved are not going to be followed. I offer more information about record-keeping in Chapter 10.

Now that we've established the basis for making a best-interpretation decision, I shall introduce you to Audrey, who features in the next few examples, which illustrate further the ways in which you can help yourself make a best-interpretation decision.

> *Audrey lives in her own home; she is desperate to live there as long as possible, but of course she wishes to be safe. Audrey senses there are prowlers around her house, and she says people are coming to her door asking for money. She is getting anxious.*   →

> *Graham, her son and attorney, thinks that external CCTV and a*
> *video doorbell would assist; it would allow him to monitor the situ-*
> *ation and intervene if required. Graham has tried explaining the*
> *idea to Audrey, in a number of ways, but she cannot grasp what he is*
> *suggesting and why this would help, but she keeps saying she wants*
> *to be safe and in her own home. Graham concludes that Audrey does*
> *not have capacity to decide on the use of the technology – but he does*
> *know she wants to stay in her house and be safe. He needs to make*
> *a decision about the technology based on the best interpretation of*
> *what Audrey would have chosen had she been able to do so.*

If you are an attorney, it is important to keep open communication with the person you are supporting so that you are aware of their views on a range of topics. This is easy when a situation may be reasonably foreseeable, but the situation which arises may not have been foreseeable, in which case you cannot know what the person would have done or would likely have done.

You may then have to draw parallels with equivalent situations or from a broader situation. For example, we know that Audrey wants to stay in her own home as long as possible, but that she wants to feel safe; so perhaps one can say that, had she understood how technology can assist with this, she would have agreed to it. This is an example of a decision which best interprets what Audrey may likely have opted for.

Best-interpretation decision-making is decision-specific, so a proper and objective assessment of what the person's wishes may have been, what may be in their best interest and is for their benefit must be carried out on every occasion. What is in a person's best interests may well change over time. This means that even where similar actions need to be taken repeatedly, the position should be regularly reviewed and not just assumed.

Sometimes, to go with the decision you think the person themselves would have made places you in conflict with what you yourself would have wanted for them; but you are advocating for the now-incapable person, standing in their shoes, acting as their voice, making the decision they themselves would have made, no matter how much it may differ from the decision you may wish to make for them, or you would make if it were you.

Let us now look at the second requirement that comes from the United Nations Convention on the Rights of Persons with Disabilities (UNCRPD).

Respecting rights, will and preferences

We have looked at the first of the UNCRPD requirements, that of supporting decision-making, or as it is actually referred to, support for the exercise of legal capacity; the second requirement is that we should respect a person's rights, will and preferences. We will now look at what this means, both as a concept and in practice.

Rights

There are a range of legal rights to which any one of us is equally entitled without discrimination, no matter our nationality, place of residence, sex, ethnic origin, colour, religion, language, or any other status. Examples would be rights to life, liberty, freedom of opinion and expression, the right to education, to equality, to a fair trial, to privacy, to family life, to freedom of belief and religion.

These rights are guaranteed by law, in the forms of various Acts, treaties, conventions and principles. Human rights law is a vast and extremely complex subject; it is not the intention of this book to give you even an abridged tutorial on this.

So what do you need to know? That a person with incapacity loses none of their human rights and that the UNCRPD requires us to respect these rights when working with, or for, that individual. Your rights are inalienable, no matter your mental capacity.

Will and preferences

Often you will hear 'will and preferences' linked together, as if they are a single entity. It is important to remember that they are distinct. Will, in this context, refers to a person's motivation, determination, intention or drive. It does not refer to any other form of 'will', for example a legal bequest on death, or a living will. Preference is, as we would understand the word, a choice, or partiality.

It can be difficult to separate what is a will and what is a preference. For example: I would like to lose weight, but I like regular takeaways; at the moment these are both preferences. My 'preference' may be for takeaways, but if I have 'a will' to lose weight then I have to reduce the number of takeaways. You will see from this that 'will' tends to be evidenced by some action or behaviour.

Both a will and a preference can be expressed in many and varied ways: in words, of course, but also in tone and pitch of voice, in behaviour, mood, posture, facial expression, eye movement or self-harm. Some of these may be intentional, some the person may not even be aware of. In this sense, you need also to be alert to uncontrived physiological responses such as increased breathing rate, headache, needing the toilet more frequently, or being sick.

In summary, people don't just use words to tell you their will or preference. In order to recognise a will or a preference being expressed you need to be alert, to watch and to listen.

Respecting rights, will and preferences in practice

Having introduced you to the requirement to respect a person's rights, will and preferences, we will consider how this works in practice.

Respecting rights in practice

As stated above, there are a range of legal rights to which any one of us is equally entitled. You must ensure you do not restrict a person's rights, but it may be difficult for you to know if the decision you are now making is a matter which is protected by right. If you are unsure, ask the person you are dealing with, for example the health or social-care professional, what rights, if any, the person you are supporting has in respect of this issue that you must consider.

There is no simple way of advising you how to go about ensuring that you respect the individual's rights; it can all be a matter of perspective.

Back to Audrey and Graham. You will recall that Graham has decided to install external CCTV and a video doorbell so he can monitor for potential prowlers and scammers and intervene as may be required to keep Audrey safe. Audrey was reassured by this; she felt that Graham was there, even when he wasn't physically present, and that he could take action if necessary. Audrey's friend had a different view on the situation. She felt, quite adamantly, that Graham was invading Audrey's right to privacy and that it was inappropriate that he should have free access to and intrude on Audrey's life in this way.

You will see from this example that whether one's rights have been, or are being, breached can be a matter of opinion. Audrey seems reassured by the monitoring which the technology allows; her friend, however, is of the opinion that the cameras are a breach of Audrey's rights. The opinion that counts is that of the individual themselves.

That said, even if the action is consented to – in this case, Audrey agreeing to use of the cameras – it still has to be proportionate to the problem. To explain, let's use Audrey again.

> *Let us assume that Audrey was not having any concerns about her safety and had had no suspicious callers to her door; but on the off chance that this may happen, Graham had suggested that she have CCTV and a video doorbell. Audrey agreed, to keep him happy, but she herself felt it was unnecessary.*

In this case, although Audrey has agreed, it may still be a breach of her right to privacy because there is no evidence that this action is required – *and* Audrey sees it as unnecessary. One could say she has assented rather than consented, i.e. that she has agreed to keep the peace rather than being genuinely accepting of the position.

Or:

> *The situation with prowlers and suspicious callers is as first described and Audrey is reassured by the presence of cameras, but Graham uses them to monitor Audrey's life: to see when she goes out, when she comes in, and starts asking her where she went, who she saw, why she saw them etc.*

In this case, Audrey readily consented to the installation of cameras for the purpose of safety, but the way in which they are being used is disproportionate to the prowler problem and so, in this respect, the use of the cameras is an invasion of her privacy.

In both these latter cases, Audrey's rights have been abused.

In summary, therefore, on the matter of respecting a person's rights:

- Be aware that the person you are supporting, even if they have a loss of capacity, does not lose any of their human rights. You are obliged to respect their rights. It is unlawful to breach an individual's human rights without due authority.

- For an attorney, this due authority can only come from one of two sources, either:

i) The person agrees to whatever it is; another way of putting it would be to say that they consent to it – but be sure the person is truly consenting and not just agreeing for the sake of keeping the peace; this may be called assenting rather than consenting. We saw this with Audrey in one of the examples.

ii) Because you have been given the power to agree a decision of this nature on the person's behalf within the PoA. Remember, though, that if you are making a decision, it can only be if the person can no longer do so themselves; and you then must respect the decision they would have made.

- Whether the person's rights have been breached will depend on their opinion.

- Even with due authority, any intervention has to be proportionate. Excessive use of powers, even where there is a basis of authority, is still a breach of human rights.

Respecting will and preferences in practice

As well as the person's rights, you must also take into account their will and preferences on a given matter.

The requirement is for us to 'respect' a person's will and preferences (as well as their rights). To 'respect' does not mean there has to be unqualified deference to the person's will and preferences, i.e. that we have to go unquestioningly with whatever the person's will and preferences are; but more consideration must be given to the person's views than just a fleeting nod. We have to give genuine consideration to their position; we cannot just pay their views lip service.

> *Sue and her sister fell out with each other in their early twenties. Sue is now seventy-two and has dementia. Carol, Sue's daughter, has no idea what her mum and aunt fell out over, her mum would never say; she just said 'it was over a stupid matter', but both are so obstinate that neither was prepared to be the first to say sorry. Sue always said she would see her sister again if she would apologise, but not if she wouldn't – even now, after all this time.*
>
> *Sue's sister has now approached Carol to ask if she may come to see Sue. Carol has asked her aunt if she will apologise for whatever the falling-out was about; her aunt says no, it is for her sister to do that. Carol decides that, in the absence of an apology, she thinks her mother's preference would be to decline to see her sister – even now. So she refuses to allow her aunt to visit.*

There are two elements to consider when thinking about a person's preferences: those that they may have expressed for many a year when capable, and those that they are expressing now, which may be different. To explain this, let's take Sue and Carol a bit further.

> *Instead of making the decision to refuse her aunt's request to visit, thinking this was what her mum's preference would be, Carol, as she should, tells her mum of the request and supports Sue to make her own decision. Sue says: yes she would like to see her sister, she has always wanted to see her. Carol reminds her of the discussion about an apology being due; Sue laughs and says there is no apology due, she doesn't know what Carol is talking about and accuses Carol of keeping her sister from visiting her.*

You will see from this how Sue's clear past preference is different from her preference now; which of these is Carol to respect? There is no right answer to this; it will very much depend on the situation. This is when the views of another person can be valuable, for example if Sue has a good friend who may know more about the falling-out, or Sue's views, than Carol does as her daughter.

Sometimes, will and preferences can conflict. Let's take Sue and Carol on to another stage.

> *Carol decides to respect her mum's current preference and to allow her aunt to visit. Her mum seems excited to see her sister again. When her sister arrives, however, Sue starts shouting and kicking out; she becomes both upset and angry. She throws the cup of tea that Carol has made her at her sister. Carol asks her aunt to leave. Her mum asks Carol why she took it upon herself to let 'the she-devil' into the house. How dare she.*

This example illustrates how fluid one's preferences can be, but also how a will and a preference can conflict with one another. Sue's current preference had been to see her sister, but her expression of will suggested, quite forcibly, that she did not wish to see her. We will now look at how you manage situations when there is such conflict of rights, will and preferences: which one do you respect when you can't respect all three?

When rights, will and preferences conflict

As the example above illustrates, there will be times when rights, will and preferences conflict with each other, when to respect one will mean disrespecting the other. Or, there will be times when the rights, will or preferences of one person may conflict with those of another.

> Ann lives in a shared house; she is currently in hospital having treatment for serious burns – caused when she did not put out her cigarette properly. Ann also caused a fire in the kitchen by leaving a cloth next to a lit gas ring which she had not turned off. Discussion is ongoing about Ann's care once she is ready to leave hospital. Ann's preference is to return to her shared house; she loves her home and sharing with Brenda, her housemate. But Ann is considered to be at significant risk of, inadvertently, endangering herself as well as Brenda.

In this example, the preferences of Ann, to move back to her home and to share with Brenda, conflict with the rights of Brenda to live in a safe environment.

There is no easy answer when rights, will and preferences conflict like this, and no single piece of advice that can be given; yet as an attorney you must ensure that the conflict is managed.

Managing such conflicts

The first thing to consider is whether a compromise is possible. Is there a different way of achieving the same end result in a way which is acceptable? For example, in Sue's case her sister came into her home; would meeting in a neutral venue have been an option?

Sometimes, though, it is just not possible to eliminate conflicts; then it is a case of making sure you have a correct and comprehensive understanding of the full situation, from which you have to reach what you believe to be the right decision in the circumstances.

A review of the section above on best-interpretation decision-making will assist, as will the following prompts:

Am I clear what the central issue is and what outcome we need to reach?

In conflict situations it is easy to lose sight of the key issue; ensure you are clear about exactly what outcome you are trying to achieve.

Have I fully supported the person to make their own decision?

Are you satisfied that you have fully supported the person to offer their own views? Do you need to involve anyone else, including, for example, independent advocacy, to ascertain the person's views impartially? There is more about advocacy below.

Is the individual free of undue pressure?

Is the view being expressed by the person their 'unencumbered' view, and are you sure they are not saying what they think they should say? Ensure that they are not being influenced by you, by someone else, or by the situation into thinking they have to say a certain thing.

What are the person's rights in the given situation?

Are you clear what the person's rights are? Have you given more than mere consideration to these? Are you going to be able to respect these? If not, have you got a clear rationale for disregarding their rights?

What is the person's own view on the matter? What is their preferred outcome?

Are you clear what the person's own will and preferences are? Have you given more than mere consideration to these? If you are not going to be able to respect these, do you have a clear justification?

What is the best interpretation of the person's views?

If the person has not been able to offer their opinions, do you know what the best interpretation of their views is?

Do you need to know anything more about the circumstances or the situation?

Make sure you know all you need to know; do not make the mistake of working with only a portion of the relevant information.

Are you clear of time frames?

Do not feel pressured into making a decision under the false assumption of a tight time frame. Do you have longer than is assumed? If not, can you negotiate longer – to allow for a properly considered decision? If yes, be clear how long may be required for this.

Have you reviewed the position objectively?

Challenge yourself on this; make sure your own values are not, even inadvertently, creating the conflict. Have you asked the views of others? Can someone else offer a view which may help?

Are all possible options under review?

Ensure you have thought laterally about all possible options. Do not make the mistake of going with the one which seems the most viable, or obvious, or even the only one, without first having considered whether there are others. It may be obvious to you that these other options will never be viable solutions, but an objective, systematic review would include them anyway, even if only to exclude them in the end.

Have you conducted a review of each option?

For each option consider:

- What are the views of the person?
- What are the views of others?
- How would this option benefit the person, and is this option in their best interests?
- Would there be any risk or detriment to the person from this option?
- Is this the least restrictive way of achieving the outcome needed?

Is there any compromise option?

Is there an option which the person would tolerate, even if it's not ideal? This still has to be a viable solution. It may be that it presents a short-term option while time is taken to consider the longer-term, or broader, options.

Have you sought the opinions of all relevant people?

Ensure you have not omitted a relevant player; the views of all relevant people involved need to be considered.

Are there wider things you need to consider?

It is appropriate to consider wider things in such a review; for example the costs, or the impact on, or risks to others that any of the options may present.

Is there anything else you need to consider?

This is a generic template: is there anything particular to your current case/situation that you need to consider before reaching any conclusions?

Would it be wise to consult someone else or obtain authority before making a decision?

Do you wish to, or need to, run your proposed decision past someone else, for example the local authority, the Office of the Public Guardian, a lawyer?

Have you made a clear action plan?

Am I clear about who is doing what, in what time frame, when this will be reviewed etc.? Are all relevant others also clear about this action plan?

Whom do you need to tell?

When you have reached a decision on the way you wish to progress the matter, make sure you advise everyone who is relevant.

Have you made a comprehensive record?

When you have completed this formal assessment, you are advised to make a clear record of all the things you considered – discussions, actions, your rationale for your decision etc. – as this will be of great assistance should there be any challenge to why or how you arrived at the decision you have taken.

Can I force treatment?

Let us think of a person with severe pain from an infected tooth abscess but who was too afraid to go to the dentist. In this scenario their preference, to be pain-free, is in conflict with their will to avoid the dentist. You have used the above prompts to try and find a solution, but let us assume that this has been unsuccessful and you still cannot get the person to agree to see the dentist. Their tooth has now become majorly infected; it is creating more widespread complications; they are gouging at their face to try and rid themselves of the pain, and these gouges too have become infected. There is no alternative: the person absolutely has to have some treatment. You have welfare powers to decide on necessary treatment; this treatment is clearly justified; can you compel it?

You may have welfare powers to decide on necessary treatment, but you cannot insist that a dentist effectively holds the person down to sedate them, or anaesthetises them against their will, to deliver this treatment. In such a scenario you would need to speak to the dentist about what they could lawfully agree to, or offer, and thus as to their suggestion on the best way forward. The ultimate approval may have to come from a court, or an order for treatment under the mental health legislation. The professional involved, the dentist in this case, will have had similar situations and will guide you. This may be a specific example, but I cannot think of a situation when you could rely on your health and welfare PoA to compel treatment against someone's adamant will. I talk more about using your powers in Chapter 10.

Before we leave this chapter, I am going to touch on the role of independent advocates.

Independent (mental capacity) advocates

In this chapter we have looked at the requirement for us to support a person's decision-making and to have regard to their rights, will and preferences. This final section explores the role of an independent person called an advocate who may be able to assist when there are challenges in decision-making.

An advocate is an independent person who can impartially represent the voice of the incapable person; they have training and skills in communicating with people who have loss of, or impaired, capacity. In cases where there may be dispute, for example if two attorneys have differing opinions on the way forward, it can be particularly helpful for the views of the incapable person to be independently represented.

The MCA (the law in England and Wales) refers to advocates as independent mental capacity advocates, or IMCAs, whereas the AWI (the law in Scotland) omits the 'mental capacity' bit simply calling them independent advocates. The MCA gives some people who lack capacity a right to advocacy, whereas at the time of writing the AWI advocates this (no pun intended) but does not give a right to it – this may change. The role, however, is broadly comparable. A web search for 'independent mental capacity advocates' or 'independent advocates' brings a range of documents which explains their role in more detail than can be given in this book.

If appointed, an advocate's role is to support and represent the person who lacks capacity. Because of this, they have the right to see relevant records. Any information or reports provided by an advocate must be taken into account as part of the process of deciding whether a proposed decision is in the person's best interests, or for their benefit, and accords with their wishes and preferences.

As an attorney, you should consider whether you should instruct an advocate in a given situation to act as an independent representative of the incapable person's position. Details are given at the back of the book for contacting advocacy services.

> *'My brother and I are Mum's welfare attorney. She has lost capacity. Mum's ex-husband, our dad, wants to visit her. She can no longer make this decision for herself. My brother and I have different opinions. I think Mum wouldn't want to see him. He cheated on her, she has no feelings for him any more; she's moved on, she's married again; it would be disrespectful to Mum's new husband. My brother thinks I'm overly emotional; he says Mum often asks him how Dad is and says she would enjoy a catch-up. She recognises that she loved him, even though he hurt her, and that it's been so long now and time has healed.'*

In this case, an independent opinion would not only ensure a) that the incapable person's own views are taken into account and that the matter does not turn on the views of her respective attorneys, but also b) that the attorneys themselves are supported in a matter which may create a fracture; impartial assistance may preserve their longer-term relationship, critical to them working together to support the incapable person.

The disagreement may not be between family members but family and professionals. The inclusion of a third, independent and impartial party who can represent the incapable person in this is hugely valuable in ensuring that sight is not lost of what the person themselves would have opted to do had they been able to input personally. In such situations one may expect the professionals to suggest advocacy involvement, but as an attorney you can ask for this too.

This concludes this chapter on the requirement to support a person in their decision-making and to respect their rights, will and preferences, with information on how to comply with these requirements. This chapter precedes the one on acting as an attorney because, before you can start acting on your powers as an attorney, you have first to make every effort to support the person in making their own decisions.

You may have noticed that interwoven with the requirement to support decision-making is the concept of capacity. On many occasions through this chapter I have said 'X had capacity' or 'X was now incapable'. Supporting decision-making and determining capacity go hand in hand, so in the next chapter we go on to consider what is meant by capacity, or its opposite, incapacity.

Chapter 8

Knowing when a Power of Attorney can be used: the art of determining capacity and incapacity

You cannot start acting on your powers as an attorney unless the person for whom you are acting is unable to offer you their own views. Consequently, knowing what capacity is and how to assess it is critical to knowing whether you can act as an attorney and use the PoA or not.

I have already used the terms capacity and incapacity a number of times. Capacity and incapacity are the lynchpins of the law in this field and govern whether and when one can intervene lawfully. It's critical, therefore, that you understand what is meant by capacity and its opposite, incapacity, in order to know when you can rely on a PoA.

We are going to consider capacity and incapacity in some depth. There are three distinct sections to this chapter:

1. The concepts of capacity and incapacity: this is an introductory section to the principle of capacity and incapacity.

2. The definition of capacity: in this section we will consider how the law defines capacity and what the definitions mean in practice.

3. Assessing capacity: in this section we will look at how you use the various aspects of the legal definition to objectively assess someone's capacity and decide whether or not they are capable.

I should start, however, by saying that the terms 'capable' and 'incapable' sometimes create tension. It may be that in years to come we won't use this terminology, and indeed that we may be frowned upon for ever having done so. It may help to think instead in terms of ability. A person whom we would call capable is someone who is able to determine matters for themselves, even if this requires them to be supported in doing so. A person whom we would call incapable is someone who is not able, even with every support, to determine something personally, or to act on the decision they have made. For now, since the law does talk in terms of capacity and incapacity, I will use these phrases.

The concepts of capacity and incapacity

Presumption of capacity

In common law there is a presumption of capacity, but the MCA of both England and Wales and Northern Ireland include 'presumption of capacity' as the very first principle (we will look at the principles in detail in the next chapter).

A presumption of capacity is, as the words suggest, a presumption that the person is capable. When deciding whether you should intervene for a person, for example in your role as attorney, the starting point should be one of presuming the individual has the capacity to make whatever the decision is that needs to be made. It is discriminatory to behave otherwise.

You must not assume that an individual lacks capacity solely, for example, because of their age, disability, appearance, behaviour, medical condition (including mental illness), beliefs or apparent inability to communicate.

> *'If I am talking to a group of lawyers as part of my training role, I presume they all have capacity; why would I not? If I am talking to a group of people with dementia as part of my training role it would be discriminatory of me to assume, based on that diagnosis, that they were not capable.'*

This doesn't mean that you treat everyone exactly the same: you are required to give a person all appropriate help and support to enable them to make their own decisions or to maximise their participation in any decision-making process. In the example above, I shouldn't assume that people with dementia lack capacity because they may not understand the same legal jargon as the lawyers. I must use the tools at my disposal – plain English, images, text, audio, etc. – to ensure that people are able to participate. There is more discussion about this in the previous chapter.

Capacity is not all or nothing

Capacity is not all or nothing, it is not black and white; it may be a spectrum, with capacity at one end and incapacity at the other, but it is not a spectrum along which one makes a smooth journey, passing at some point from capacity into incapacity. There is much to-ing and fro-ing along the spectrum. There is often a large grey area. It is common for an individual to be capable on some days (or at certain times of day) of making some decisions, or taking the necessary action, but not on other days. There are *many* things which affect an individual's capacity: for example if they are in pain, feel rushed, are frightened, are under-confident with the decision to be made, have insufficient knowledge to understand the decision to be made, all of which can be exacerbated by a person's illness. There is more on this on p. 170, where we consider how an attorney assesses capacity. For now, it is important to recognise that capacity can fluctuate – quite markedly sometimes – and thus that capacity to make a given decision can only be assessed at the time the decision needs to be made.

Capacity is not linear

You will often hear people say, 'He can make day-to-day decisions [for example, about what he wants for tea], but he's not able to make more complex decisions [for example, about his finances].' This may be true of some people, but not of others: capacity does not always move neatly from 'easy' to 'difficult' decisions. There are many reasons why capacity will fluctuate, and why some individuals may be able to make higher-level decisions, like whether they want to sell their house, while at the same time being unable to make a lower-grade decision, like what they want to eat.

Ann was having a conversation with her dad about him needing to go into a care home. Dad was participating fully; he was keen on the same care home that his wife and sister were both in. Although this wasn't the best care home for his condition, and there was a different one which would have suited his needs much better, he commented that he was aware of this but he wanted to be near his wife and sister. He said he knew the staff in their care home, he knew the routine and they knew him. He even mentioned that he and his wife had always looked out for his sister, who had never married, and that he wanted to make sure he could continue to do this. It was clear from this conversation that he was very able to weigh up complex →

> *information. Immediately after this conversation Ann asked her dad what he wanted for his tea, and he asked what she was having. When she told him she was thinking of poached egg, he asked her what a poached egg was, and whether he liked poached egg. Ann then spent about fifteen minutes supporting her father, with the use of drawings and explanation, in making a decision about whether or not he wanted a poached egg.*

You can see from this example that Ann had to give her dad a higher level of support to make what would generally be considered a lower-level decision, about his tea, than about a higher-level decision, his ongoing care. Do not assume, therefore, that low-grade, day-to-day or simple decisions or actions may be possible but that complex or higher-grade decisions or actions are not. You should always assess the individual's capacity to make the decision, or take the action, at the time it has to be made or done.

Capacity is decision- or task-specific

You will see from this that capacity is decision-, or task-, specific. Ann's dad had clear views about his care, perhaps born from his emotional bond to both his wife and sister and wanting to be near them. This allowed him to make a capable (or capacitous) decision on the matter.

There should be no assumption that the person cannot make a given decision just because, typically, they cannot: assessing capacity is an ongoing process that must be applied at every decision-making moment. So in the example above, Ann would ask her dad every day what he wanted for dinner.

Unwise decisions

We may not always agree with a decision that a person makes; we may think it unwise, risky or not thought through properly; but if a person is capable of making this decision, then they have a right, like any one of us, to make a decision that others might disagree with. Everybody has their own values, beliefs, preferences and attitudes. A person should not be assumed to lack capacity just because they are making a decision which most people would see as unwise, or which family members, friends, health-care or social-care staff are unhappy about. When the person is making a decision with which you disagree you must take particular care to ensure you are not letting your own values, motives or biases affect your judgement.

The next section on assessing incapacity will help you decide whether a person who is making an unwise decision, as you see it, is making this decision with the capacity to do so, or whether they lack the capacity to appreciate that their decision is unwise.

We have spent some time considering what capacity is; let us now look at this from the other side and consider what incapacity means.

Incapacity

We have established that a presumption of capacity is the essential first step in any situation. Determining whether someone is capable, or incapable, is crucial in giving you authority to intervene in their affairs or in applying a PoA. I shall go on to explain how you assess capacity; but first we need to look at what incapacity is.

In considering the concept of capacity and incapacity we are going to have to look at the legal definitions; don't worry, I'll explain them in plain English. The legal definition of incapacity under both the MCA and AWI is very similar; both have what may be referred to as a two-stage test.

Stage one is that a person must have a mental disorder or impairment of the mind or brain. The conditions that fall under this are extensive, for example, dementia, learning disability, acquired brain injury and alcohol-related brain damage; so it is likely that the person you are supporting will meet this stage-one requirement.

A diagnosis of a mental disorder does not automatically mean a person is incapable. Many people with dementia, for example, remain capable of making many decisions for a lengthy period, and sometimes throughout, and likewise with any other mental disorders or impairments of the mind or brain. Stage one involves checking that such a diagnosis is present – to allow progression to stage two, where the actual assessment of capacity, or incapacity, occurs.

Stage one is sometimes referred to as a 'gateway entry test', 'gateway' because the person must 'meet the test of' having a mental disorder or impairment of the mind or brain before the Acts can apply to them. The diagnosis thus becomes the gateway: you cannot progress to stage two if you do not pass the gateway entry test, i.e. that you have a mental disorder or impairment of the mind or brain.

Alternatively, stage one is sometimes referred to as a 'diagnostic threshold test', because you have to have a certain diagnosis (of mental disorder or impairment of the mind or brain) before you can progress to stage two; so the diagnosis becomes a threshold that you have to cross.

There is criticism, on the grounds of fairness, of there being an entry threshold which requires a certain diagnosis. The argument is that it shouldn't matter *why* a person lacks capacity. If a person lacks capacity, for whatever reason, they should be afforded the protections that the Acts offer. There is a view that both Acts should be reworked in order to focus on an individual's ability to make decisions, rather than on a legal assessment of their capacity. With these arguments gaining force it is possible that the Acts will be amended in the long term, but neither Act is likely to be changed in the foreseeable future. Northern Ireland has listened to these criticisms and therefore its new Act does not have a diagnostic entry test for the application of a PoA.

The definition of capacity

Let us assume we are supporting a person who has met the stage-one test, in that they have a mental disorder or impairment of the mind or brain; so they have, for example, dementia, a learning disability, an acquired brain injury or alcohol-related brain damage. As such we can move on to look at what we have to do under stage two to assess their capacity.

Capacity should always be assessed objectively, against the definition, so let us look at how all three Acts define mental capacity. A person is considered capable if they:

- have a general understanding of what decision they need to make and why they need to make it

- have a general understanding of the likely consequences of making, or not making, this decision

- can use and weigh up the information relevant to this decision

- can make a decision

- can retain the memory of their decision

- can communicate their decision

- can act on their decision, or act to safeguard themselves (Scotland).

Or, to flip this, a person is incapable if they do not have a general understanding, cannot weigh up information, etc.

This conflates the definitions in the three Acts, but they are sufficiently similar; for the purposes of this book it is easier to have a single list to consider.

For a person to be judged as capable in a specific situation, *all* of these factors have to be present; or, to look at it the other way round, a person would be judged incapable if any single one of these factors was absent – remembering always that capacity is decision-specific, not all or nothing.

To help us when it comes to making the judgement call on capacity or not, let us look in more detail at what the criteria mean.

Understanding

A person needs all the facts relevant to the decision, to be aware of the disadvantages as well as the advantages, must be able to weigh up the pros and cons, risks and benefits, giving each due consideration as they apply, or may apply, to their situation.

In order to assess if a person is considering things in an appropriate way (for them), it is necessary for you to know relevant things about their situation.

> In the example above about Ann's dad making the decision about his care home, the fact that his sister was a spinster for whom he felt a lifelong level of responsibility was something that one needed to know in order to put his decision-making in context.

To aid understanding, every effort must be made to provide, or present, information in a way that meets the individual's needs and circumstances. For example, if someone doesn't speak

English as a first language, or is deaf, then to help them understand the information you would offer interpreters, including sign language.

The level of understanding expected is that of 'the man in the street'. A person only needs to understand what the average person would be expected to understand in the same situation. They do not need to have knowledge at expert level. With this in mind, information should be communicated in a simple way, avoiding the use of technical jargon or highly convoluted sentences.

Making a decision

As we saw in the last chapter, there are many, many factors which affect one's ability to make a decision: for example, one may need time, a quiet environment, or support. All such obstacles to decision-making should be removed and every support given before one can conclude that a person is incapable on the grounds that they are unable to make a decision.

Retaining the memory of a decision

There are several aspects we need to consider under this heading:

- retention of memory per se
- ability to recall, even if prompted
- accuracy of retained memory or recalled response
- consistency of retained memory or recalled response.

Retention of memory

The definition requires someone who is capable to be able to retain the memory of a decision they have made; but what does 'retaining the memory mean' when we all forget things from time to time? If you forget where you put your keys, or can't remember what you had for your tea, even yesterday, does that make you incapable?

Also, for how long is a person expected to retain the memory of a decision before you can conclude that they have retained that memory – for ever, or for just a few minutes?

More complex decisions tend to take longer, and need more thinking about, so a person may be able to retain the memory for a lengthier period of time. On the other hand, someone may be able to make lower-grade decisions very quickly, in which case we'd expect their retention period to be lower.

> *Using Ann and her dad again, the conversation and his decision about his care home is something which usually spans a long period, with significant consequences, so requires him to retain the memory, or recall his memory, for longer. Whereas the decision to have a poached egg for tea can be made quickly – the egg is ready soon after, so retention of memory for this decision can be very short.*

For how long anyone can retain the memory of something will vary depending on a number of things, for example how important the decision is and even how your brain processes information.

> *'On 30 January 2010 I can recall that my husband and I went to meet with my sister as it was her fortieth birthday. We went out for a meal; I can recall generally the restaurant but would struggle beyond that. For me, all I need to remember is that we celebrated with my sister on her fortieth and we had a lovely family evening. My husband, however, would be able to tell you that it was a Saturday because his football team were playing such and such a team, his team won 2–0, goals by Smith and Brown. We went to the Dog and Duck in New Town and he had steak.'*

Just because the husband can retain a memory of this event in such detail and his wife can't does not make her incapable; it simply demonstrates that we retain and process memories differently. You have to assess the person's ability to recall situations against their own benchmark.

The physiology of memory is extremely complex; whole books have been written on the subject, so no one is expecting you to be an expert. Family and friends often find it easier to assess memory retention than professionals, as family and friends have a person's normal behaviour to benchmark against.

> 'My dad and I love mushrooms; when eating out, Dad and I most often share a mushroom starter. On this occasion, as usual, I suggested to Dad that we share a mushroom starter; his response was: "That'd be nice, do you like mushrooms?"'

A professional would not have recognised this as an inability to retain memory as Dad's response was perfectly natural, whereas his daughter thought how odd it was that he didn't remember that she liked mushrooms and that they nearly always shared a mushroom starter. With hindsight, it was one of the first indicators she had of her father's dementia. It was easy for her to spot his impaired memory – although she didn't know at that time what it signified.

Ability to recall

We have looked in some detail about what retention of memory means. Retention of memory does not require a person to be able to retain the memory of their decision for ever, or even necessarily for any lengthy period of time. But if they have not retained the memory, they should be able to recall it if prompted, for as long as it takes to make the decision. Items such as note-books, photographs, posters, videos and voice recorders can help people record and so recall information.

To remember where you put your keys you may go through a recall exercise: I had them in my hand when I went into the kitchen, I went straight to put the kettle on, I reached into the cupboard for a cup and the coffee, the fridge for the milk and the drawer for a spoon. I sat down at the table to drink my coffee; I didn't have the keys in my hand then, so I must have put them down at some point on the coffee-making journey. Ah, there they are in the drawer, how stupid am I.

Steve thought a large tree near his house needed to be felled, as it was in danger of falling on the building – but he really didn't want to arrange for this unless it was absolutely necessary. Steve had worked as an engineer and had high-level mathematical ability. His son thought the use of a mathematical diagram would assist. He took Steve outside and together they measured the distance of the tree from the house, then used a protractor and string to calculate the height of the tree. This showed there was enough distance between house and tree for it not to hit the house if it fell. This was then drawn up as a scientific diagram, showing the house, tree and the various distances and measurements. Steve kept the diagram beside his chair. The next week, when Steve talked about whether he should have the tree felled, his son reminded him of the measurements they had taken and advised Steve to check the diagram beside him. On doing this Steve could recall the exercise and was, again, reassured that there was no problem. This was a regular conversation with Steve, but on each occasion a review of his scientific diagram assisted his recall and provided reassurance.

You can use tools to aid recall.

For most of us, a scientific drawing would not have meant anything, but it did for Steve, and shows that things other than words may assist recall; but these things have to have meaning for the person concerned. Showing them a photograph of another elderly person with their grandchildren will not necessarily remind an elderly person that they themselves have grandchildren; but showing them a photograph of them with their own grandchildren may generate this recall. Consider, therefore, how you may use things which are of meaning to a person to assist with their recall of a memory.

But retention of memory is more than just an ability to recall. It relates too to both accuracy and consistency of the recalled response. We'll look at those aspects now.

Accuracy and consistency of response

Let us use an example to consider accuracy and consistency of response.

Last Friday, you were late in, not hungry, had to get this and that sorted before bed so, for speed, you just had beans on toast. When I ask what you had for your evening meal last Friday you can't remember, so I offer you prompts for recall: I remind you that you were late in, weren't hungry and had to get this and that sorted before bedtime. With these prompts you recall: 'Of course I had *cheese* on toast, for speed.' The recall exercise has reminded you that you had something quick, but you didn't recall accurately what that was.

If I ask you about this again, in, say, half an hour, you may again reply that you had cheese on toast, so here you have a consistency of response, albeit inaccurate. If, however, on this later occasion you then recall that you had *egg* on toast, you have neither an accurate nor a consistent response.

Questioning to check accuracy and consistency of recall can be tricky. The person can feel under interrogation, or that you are not trusting them, or they may even worry about your own ability to recall given that you are asking them the same question so often. It takes time to learn how to make this questioning subtle, so don't worry if you get some resistance at first.

You can see from this rather lengthy section how complex the criterion of retention of memory is. We shall consider in the next section, which is on assessing capacity, how you apply this in practice to decide whether a person is capable.

Communicating the decision

Within the definition of capacity there is the criterion which requires the person to be able to communicate their decision. This doesn't need to be verbally: it may be by drawing, by non-verbal signs or signals, or with the use of communication aids. A person is not to be considered incapable if an inability to communicate can be rectified by human or mechanical means.

Inability to act

Having capacity means that a person has ability to act. They must be able to action the decision they have made; or be able to act to safeguard themselves. For example, a person who is under the coercive control of another may be able to understand that they are in an unacceptable position, know that they need to do something to remedy this, have assessed the pros and cons of the options and have made their decision. They have no problem with retention of memory or communicating their thoughts, so, on the face of it, this person may seem capable. However, the coercive control of another person may inhibit them and so prevent them from being able to act on their decision.

> *Mary, who is in the early stages of dementia, lives with her son Paul. Paul has her PoA. She knows that Paul is taking a lot of money from her account to 'feed' his drug habit. She doesn't want Paul taking her money, but she is too afraid of Paul to say anything. He can be very temperamental and occasionally quite abusive. She doesn't want to upset him. She loves Paul and needs his care and support. Mary wants to talk to the family solicitor: she feels he would have some advice for her. However, although she understands the situation and has made an informed decision, she is too afraid to ask Paul to take her, or risk Paul finding out that the solicitor has visited the house. And so she does nothing.*

This example shows how Mary is aware of what is happening and that something needs to be done. She even knows that taking the advice of her family solicitor is a good idea – so in this respect she seems mentally capable. But because of her fears she is not able to progress this, and she is unable to take the necessary steps to safeguard herself and so prevent the abuse. The lack of ability to act, being one of the factors which is required for capacity, means that, in this case, Mary can technically be classed as incapable.

Undue pressure

Before we finish looking at the meaning of capacity/incapacity, as the law sets it out, we should consider the concepts of undue pressure and consent versus assent.

A person should make a decision of their own free will. The person should be free of undue pressure, including pressure from you. Make sure you're not leading them or influencing them, even inadvertently. Make sure they know they can make a decision which may go against what you would have wanted or preferred.

> '*I was making breakfast the other morning, and my husband asked for cheese on toast. I tutted: he is quite particular about how he likes his cheese on toast, it's a faff, we didn't have a lot of time and I wasn't putting the grill on for anything else. His response was, "OK, it doesn't matter, I'll just have toast." He was very willing to have toast and he was making no issue of it, but his preference was to have cheese on toast; he was moving away from this because of my influence (my tut); he did not wish to put me to the additional trouble he knew cheese on toast takes.*'

This example shows how even a capable person can easily be influenced by the inadvertent expression of another's opinion. Imagine how much this is magnified when the person lacks capacity and may be compliant, wishing to please and feeling reliant on the other person. You therefore have to work additionally hard to make sure you do not inadvertently influence the situation by your words, or silence, or gestures.

Consent v. assent

The final thing for us to consider in this section is the difference between consent and assent. The person's decision needs to be one they have consented to, as opposed to simply assented to. This is the difference between active agreement and passive acceptance. It can be a very hard call to make, increasingly so as people lose capacity.

By way of example: you ask Mary what she wishes to wear today, she picks the blue frock; you dress her in this, and she seems happy – she has consented to this outfit. Whereas if you dress Mary in a blue frock and she seems happy, she has assented to this; she has passively accepted your choice, as opposed to having actively participated by choosing the outfit herself. I mentioned how interwoven capacity and supported decision-making are; this is a good example.

That completes our survey of what the Acts say about the definitions of capacity and incapacity and related issues. We'll now look at the practical application of this.

Assessing capacity

This is another matter on which whole books have been written, so I will only give you an overview here. It's important to say, right at the outset, that assessing capacity is not easy, and even professionals can be anxious about it; that said, family members and friends can instinctively find it easier, probably because you know the person that much better and have many more experiences against which to benchmark how they are now compared to how they have always been. On the other hand, family members and friends can become over-protective and much more easily slip into making all the decisions for the person, so a balance has to be found.

Perhaps the most important thing to remember here is that capacity or incapacity is not all or nothing: it must be assessed in terms of the decision that needs to be made in that moment. Assuming you have the authority to do so, you can only make decisions on behalf of the person you are supporting if they are no longer able to do so themselves, so being able to assess capacity is critical.

So, how do you assess capacity in practice? The information that follows is a helpful steer, but should always be adapted to the circumstances and the decision to be made.

To assess capacity you end up, effectively, asking a series of questions which fall under three categories:

- establishing the situation
- understanding the perspective yourself
- assessing the person's perspective.

Establishing the situation

1. Am I clear what the decision is for which I am assessing capacity?

Capacity is decision-specific, so before you can begin to assess it you have to be clear that you know what the decision is for which you are assessing capacity. Assessing the wrong decision is one of the most common errors, so even if you think you are clear, take a moment to consider the specifics of the situation.

> *For example, a person may be unable to make decisions about their financial affairs, but they may know who they would wish to look after their money for them and know that they have to give official authority for this.*

In this example, an assessment of the person's capacity to manage money would likely have led to the conclusion that they were incapable, whereas an assessment of their ability to grant a PoA may have concluded them capable. This person would have been denied a critical opportunity to do a PoA if they had been considered incapable of this, because the wrong decision had been assessed.

2. Have I made it clear to the person exactly what decision they are being asked to make and why they need to make it?

You may have experience yourself of occasions when you have

found yourself thinking: 'I'm confused, what's the question here? What I am being asked to answer?' It may be because of the way someone phrased their question, or a simple misunderstanding. Your confusion about what's being expected of you affects your ability to respond meaningfully. You have the ability to ask for clarity, but a person with impaired capacity may not. Thus it is important that you ask single questions, framed clearly, so the person can understand what decision they are being asked to focus on.

If the person seems unable to offer a clear reply, replay your question in your mind to be sure you have asked it in a way which would allow them to respond; perhaps try rewording it, to see if hearing it expressed differently assists them.

It is also important that the person, as we all do, appreciates why they are being asked to make a particular decision. Let's use the example of the person needing respite care; you ask whether they would prefer care home A or B. The decision to be made may be clear – is it to be A or B? – but how can they make this decision unless they know why it is relevant?

3. Am I starting with a presumption of capacity?

If you find yourself thinking, for example, 'I know they won't be able to make that decision because they haven't been able to do that for months now,' then you are starting with a presumption of incapacity.

We know that capacity is fluid and is not all or nothing; just because someone typically cannot make a particular type of decision does not mean they will not be able to do so today. There are many stories of people who have lost capacity for many things, and for lengthy periods, suddenly having what seems to be a flash of insight. Ensure, therefore, before proceeding, that you have tested whether the person can make, or be supported to input to, the decision at the time it is to be made.

Understanding the perspective yourself

These first three questions are the bedrock of assessing capacity, but of course they lead to further questions. The following are designed to clarify the situation even further and allow you to make fully informed assessments.

You need to assess whether the person can understand the information required to make the decision and then assess whether they are weighing it up in an appropriate way. In order to do this, you must be clear of your own understanding.

4. Do I know enough about whatever it is to assess whether the person has gone through an appropriate thought process?

> *'My mum was told she needed to go on statins. She's not sure if she should say yes and she wants me to help her make this decision. I've heard of statins but have never examined the facts. I think they come with mixed press, but I don't really know, this may be wrong; I don't know the pros and cons, is it one tablet a day, do you need to watch your diet as well?'*

This example illustrates how, without knowing enough about the topic herself, the daughter could not assess whether her mum was considering things appropriately. As you would if you were making a decision for yourself, you should do your research, ask questions, seek advice and make sure that you have a good grasp of the issue. In the example above, you could talk to your mother's doctor, or accompany her to the appointment, in order to be better informed.

5. What do I need to know about the individual's personal circumstances in order to assess the appropriateness of their thought process?

> A man who had been admitted to hospital as an emergency was asking his son, when he visited, to go round to his house to secure the back door, which the Fire Service had had to break down in order to let the ambulance staff in. This sounds a very sensible, security-conscious, request.
>
> The man lives in sheltered accommodation; the ambulance was called by the warden, who let the medics in. The house he seemed to be talking about was his former home. His son has no idea where the notion of the Fire Service and breaking down doors came from.

This example illustrates how, in order to assess a person's capacity, you may need to know aspects of their background or situation.

Another example is a young man with a learning disability who was considered to have sufficient capacity to grant a PoA, asked for this in favour of his mother, which seemed sensible until it was realised that his mother died some months previously. You need to know this element of his background to judge his decision in context.

6. What would you expect the average man in the street to consider in order to enable them to arrive at a decision?

You should consider what the pros and cons are that you would expect this average person to weigh up. Then you have to decide whether you can assess the individual against this benchmark, or if you need to make any adjustments. For example, if a person is choosing between buying a red or blue dress I may expect the average person to think about such things as cost, durability of the fabric, style, how frequently they may wear it, whether it works with other things in their wardrobe, or is suitable for the occasion that it's being purchased for. Ask yourself: is the person I'm supporting capable of this level of thought processing, or do I need to make adjustments?

The benchmark against which you assess a person's ability to understand and make decisions will vary from person to person and decision to decision. For example, you would ordinarily expect a person to be more readily able to choose between a red or blue outfit than to select treatment A or B for their cancer. The considerations required to determine a clothes choice would be more familiar to most of us. However, if the person was a doctor, whose partner did the majority of their clothes shopping, then they may be better able to choose between the treatment options than the outfits.

You can see from this that you cannot apply a single benchmark by which to judge everybody and every decision; your assessment has to consider both the person and the decision that person is being asked to make.

Assessing the person's perspective

The previous questions are designed to make sure that you yourself have the deepest possible understanding of the decision which the person is being asked to make, against which you can assess their response. This next section considers the logistics of putting the issue to them, and of reviewing their response and using the criteria that we looked at under the definition of capacity to ensure we assess their perspective objectively.

7. Do they have information about all possible options?

You need to ensure that the person has been given all the information they need and in a way which they will understand, if this is at all possible.

At point 2, you established that the person was clear that they knew what the decision was on which they were to focus, and why. In the example, the issue was the selection of care home A or B. Let's stay with that. In order for them to be able to choose between care home A or B, they will need any relevant information. So, for example, they know, and are known at, care home A because they visited regularly to see their sister who was there, the surroundings are familiar and they know the staff; but care home B, although unfamiliar to them, is round the corner from their son so he can pop in each day while they are there.

Every effort must be made to provide information in a way that is most appropriate in helping the person to understand. Quick or inadequate explanations are not acceptable unless the situation is urgent.

8. How has the person come to their decision?

At point 6 you satisfied yourself that you understood the decision-making considerations; now you can assess how the person has approached this. Are they able to understand the information to enable them to come to a decision? Can they, and have they, weighed up the pros and cons appropriately? Have they thought about the long-term implications of their decision as well as the here and now?

Using the care home example, let's say the stay in care home A will cost £995 and care home B will cost £1,000. The person really wants to go for care home B because they wish to see their son every day, but thinks that it is too expensive, so they choose care home A because it doesn't cost £1,000.

Hopefully, this example illustrates that, for whatever reason, but most likely related to their condition, the person is unable to recognise that there is only £5 difference in the price; they are so focused on how much more expensive care home B is because of how much £1,000 sounds that they cannot weigh up that paying £5 more is worth it to be in the home closer to their son, whom they can then see each day.

If the person isn't able to understand the information properly or is unable to weigh it up, you need to think about whether you can offer this information in a different way. What may assist them? Have you thought about this laterally and considered anything that may help them understand the situation, or at least elements of it, so they can input even if only to a point?

Finally, on this point, remember that a person is not incapable just because they make what you may consider to be an unwise decision, or a decision that is different from the one you would have made, either for them or for yourself, if you had been in the same position. As difficult as it is, you have to assess objectively the person's capacity to understand, and so make a decision.

Retention of memory

Assessing memory is fundamental to assessing capacity, so I have given this its own subsection.

We have looked at the person's ability to understand and weigh up the information they have been given, satisfying ourselves that they had been given the necessary level of information and in a way in which they could hope to understand, if this was possible. We now have to consider retention of their memory.

The concept of retention of memory was covered above; you will recall it broke down into the four sections:

- retention of memory per se

- ability to recall
- accuracy of retained memory or recalled response
- consistency of retained memory or recalled response.

In our example, the person opted for care home A because it was cheaper, even though this meant they would not see their son.

They may not have to retain the memory of this decision for a lengthy period, as the respite care in question may be coming up shortly. Even if they cannot or do not retain the memory, are they able to recall it if prompted? So you would go through the basic options again – that there are two homes, one where the sister was, one round the corner from the son, who will be able to visit each day; one will cost £995, the other £1000. You will see if they then recall picking the cheaper one.

If you want to double-check it can be useful, if and when you are next covering the ground, to offer the information in a different order, to ensure that they are not just focusing on the last thing you said – so for instance you would give the costs first, then mention the familiarity of one but the proximity of the other so the son can visit. They may not be able to recall having made a decision on it previously, but they go through the decision-making exercise again and opt for the same decision – so you have consistency of decision-making.

What happens, though, if they go through a repeat decision-making exercise and come up with a different response, so you have inconsistency of decision-making? It is likely that you will conclude that they are incapable because of their inability to a) retain the original memory of the decision, b) recall it when prompted and c) be consistent in their decision-making process when they repeat the exercise.

Ability to communicate

We are still in the section on assessing the person's capacity, but ability to communicate is such an important aspect that it too is worthy of its own subsection.

It is vital to remember that a person is not incapable simply because they cannot communicate their decision to you. As you go through the questions above you may need to find creative ways in which to assist the person in communicating with you. Encouraging them to have a pen and paper to hand can be useful so they can write down their thoughts as they arise; this frees the person from the pressure of thinking they have to respond spontaneously at the time they are asked about whatever it is. Pictures can help the person indicate their preference, drawing what they want to say works for some, acting it out may work for others. Be as creative as may be required. An assessment by, or discussion with, a speech and language therapist (this is a professional with expertise in supporting communication for those who have difficulty) can be extremely valuable. Ask the person's GP, or specialist, about a referral.

Make sure you speak at an appropriate rate and volume, using words that will be understood by the person, using short sentences, not asking multiple questions. You cannot determine if the person is incapable of understanding if you have not communicated with them in a way in which they would understand.

A person may need more thinking time than previously, so be prepared to allow them this and do not harry them for a decision. Feeling pressured may hamper their ability to respond, leading you to conclude they are incapable when, given time, they would have come back to you with something.

You should not be tempted to complete sentences for the person, or fill silences. This is frustrating for them, and you cannot make an accurate judgement on their ability if you are filling the gaps for them.

Under this heading of communication, we should also consider the manner and structure of the person's communication. For example, if they ordinarily have an extensive vocabulary and use 'big words' for things and then you realise they have a reduced or changed language ability, this may offer you a marker on capacity.

The way in which the person talks may also be a marker. You should notice, for example, their tone, pitch or speed of talking compared to their norm, and raise any changes with the person in charge of their care, in case these changes are indicative of a need for professional attention.

The appropriateness of the person's responses is an indicator of capacity – do they give a relevant response to the question asked? However, do not assume that a bizarre response necessarily indicates incapacity.

> 'The other day I made a comment to my mum about a television quiz show we were watching; about how unpredictable the buzzer was [that the participants had to press to respond]. Her response was "Yes, the 26 is much more reliable" – what??
>
> On the face of it, it's a completely unrelated response; but she's not incapable, she just didn't have her hearing aid in! She thought I'd said "bus" not "buzzer" and "passengers" not "participants"; she had heard correctly the word "unpredictable" and from this had assumed I was talking about the local bus, which is unreliable, and hence her response that the 26 is much more reliable. All makes sense now. An entirely relevant response to the comment she thought I'd made.'

Communication is not just about the spoken word; you need also to assess the relevance of any non-verbal behaviours and what this may say about capacity.

> *'My dad, who has dementia, was struggling to the bathroom one night. Mum immediately got out of bed to help him; she caught her foot on the bedclothes and "launched" herself at him somewhat; he grabbed her wrist and was increasing his pressure the more she tried to free herself; he was hurting her, she was crying out. This woke me. On a very maternal command from me, he released her wrist but immediately ran behind me to hide, warning me against this danger-ous person in the room. My dad had never in his life hurt Mum, so this was aberrant behaviour, indicative of his lack of capacity as to who she was and that she was trying to help him, not harm him.'*

It is worth trying to think about what caused this reaction, and thus if anything would reduce the future likelihood of an abnormal behavioural response. In the case above, if the wife had not reacted so quickly, effectively startling her husband – especially if she had not tripped in the bedclothes and lunged towards him – the gentleman's reaction may have been differ-ent. So, to reduce the possibility of a recurrence, the bedclothes were better positioned, limiting too the likelihood of an accident. Thereafter the wife spoke to her husband before approaching him, for example to ask if he would like assistance; in this way he had forewarning of her coming towards him. Finally, low-level lighting was placed between the gentleman's bed and the toilet to increase his independence in navigating the route to the bathroom. In this case these steps all helped, and there was not another occurrence. However, such behavioural changes may be the result of a disease process rather than a capacity issue; so while it is worth considering whether anything can reduce the likelihood of aberrant non-verbal behaviour, don't feel too disappointed if nothing you try seems to change things.

To summarise, the questions relating to communication which you need to ask yourself are:

● Can the person communicate their decision to me? Do I need to do anything to ensure they are able to do so?

● Am I speaking to them in a way which allows them to understand?

● Have I given them enough thinking time, or am I rushing them?

● Am I letting them speak for themselves, or am I completing their sentences or filling silences?

● Are they structuring sentences as I would normally expect them to do?

● Are their tone, pitch, speed of response all as I would expect them to be?

● Are their actual responses appropriate? If not, is there any other reason for this?

● Is there anything one can/should infer from their non-verbal responses?

Taking action

Finally, in this section on assessing capacity we need to consider whether the person is capable of enacting or commissioning their decision.

> *Agnes had decided she wanted to grant a PoA to her son. She'd heard all about it on her favourite daytime TV programme; she mentioned it to her son, who thought it was a good idea. Sometime later he asked her whether she had now done the PoA; she hadn't. He asked whether she had changed her mind. She said, no, she was still sure this was a good idea, but she had no idea how to go about it. Her son researched the options and explained these to Agnes, who decided she would like to use a solicitor. Her son offered to find a solicitor nearby who could do this, make an appointment and take Agnes along. Agnes was pleased that this was getting sorted. A few weeks later the PoA was completed.*

You will see from this example that an otherwise capable person may not be able to commission the decision they have made without additional support. It is advisable, therefore, to check with the person that they are 'good to go' once they have decided how they wish to proceed with something, or whether, as in Agnes's case, you need to facilitate something for them.

Final pieces of advice

The very final thing to consider before you arrive at your decision regarding capability is: have I missed anything? Just do a final 'once-over' in your mind to make sure you have not omitted something which you ought really to have considered.

When you have reached your decision, you should ensure you keep a record. I talk about the importance of record-keeping in Chapter 10, but I'll make a brief mention here. It is important to make notes of the capacity-assessing process you went through – what you considered, your rationale for your conclusions – whether this was to conclude that the person was capable and could make an independent decision, or that they were capable but needed your support with the decision they themselves then made, or whether it was to conclude that they were incapable, and if so how you went about making a best-interpretation decision (see Chapter 7).

This concludes the chapter on capacity and incapacity. You can see how complex it is and why whole books have been written on the subject. I mentioned at the outset that capacity-assessing is not easy, but it is critical in deciding whether and when you can lawfully intervene for the person you are supporting; so it's something which is vital that you practise and become confident with.

Chapter 9

The legal principles that everyone must respect

Alongside supported decision-making and the consideration of capacity, there is one more fundamental framework you need to understand in order to administer a PoA effectively. This is the legal framework within which an attorney is required to operate – indeed, which anyone who is supporting a person with incapacity has to respect.

I've mentioned that a PoA is a legal document: it has to be granted in accordance with the law and the attorney has to act as the law requires. In this chapter we will consider what this means. Don't let your heart sink: I offer this information in easy-to-understand terms and you won't need a law degree.

It is important that you know about the legal principles, to avoid finding yourself in breach of the law. It is important too that you know about the Code of Practice, which I will touch on at the close of this chapter. I think it's also worth knowing the official titles of the Acts which govern PoAs so that you feel familiar with these if they are referred to, and, as they set out the law, you know where to look if you find yourself wanting to check the legal position on something.

The law which governs PoA in England and Wales is called the Mental Capacity Act 2005 (referred to in this book as the MCA); in Northern Ireland it is the Mental Capacity (Northern Ireland) Act 2016 and in Scotland the Adults with Incapacity (Scotland) Act 2000 (referred to as the AWI).

Within this chapter we look at the principles as they are set out in the law, then consider how they apply in practice, i.e. how you act in accordance with them; and we conclude with some deliberation as to how you manage when the principles may conflict with each other.

The legal principles (England and Wales)

There are five principles, set out in Section 1 of the MCA, which anyone operating under the MCA (this includes attorneys) is required to respect. Later in this chapter we will consider how an attorney respects these principles in practice; for now we will just look at the five principles:

Principle 1: presumption of capacity

A person must be assumed to have capacity unless it is established that they lack capacity.

The starting point is that a person has capacity to make a given decision, on any matter, for themselves. Only once it is established that the person lacks capacity in relation to the particular matter can the attorney become active in respect of that matter. There is information in Chapter 10 on how an attorney decides when to act.

Principle 2: offer support

A person is not to be treated as unable to make a decision unless all practicable steps to help them to do so have been taken without success.

Every support must be given to assist the person to make their own decision before one can make that decision on their behalf. In Chapter 7, we considered what it means to offer support with a person's decision-making.

Principle 3: right to make an unwise decision

A person is not to be treated as unable to make a decision merely because they make an unwise decision.

Just because a person makes a decision that seems unwise, or is contrary to what most other people might consider usual, does not mean that person is necessarily incapable.

Principle 4: best interests

An act done, or decision made, under this Act for, or on behalf of, a person who lacks capacity must be done, or made, in their best interests.

If someone is required to act on behalf of a person with incapacity, the decision they make must be in that person's best interest, even if the decision maker would themselves have made a different decision.

Principle 5: least restrictive

Before the act is done, or the decision is made, regard must be had as to whether the purpose for which the act or decision is needed can be as effectively achieved in a way that is less restrictive of the person's rights and freedom of action.

'Freedom' doesn't just relate to physical freedom, freedom of movement, being able to go wherever one may wish – it refers to freedom in any sense, for instance freedom of expression, of will, of not being controlled. Freedom has to be interpreted widely.

Although the principle requires one to take the least restrictive action, a heavily limiting, or restrictive, option may nonetheless be the least restrictive *if* it is the only way of achieving whatever is necessary. An example here may be the appointment of a deputy (in the absence of a previously agreed PoA). In legal terms the appointment of a deputy is a heavily restrictive option, since it give rights to another person over certain areas of the incapable person's life; it requires a court to make this decision (rather than the person themselves) and is covered by all sorts of rules and procedures. But if there is no alternative to this, because the individual needs someone to administer matters for them and there has been no PoA granted, then the appointment of a deputy becomes the least restrictive option, as it is the only way of achieving what is necessary.

The legal principles (Scotland)

The Adults with Incapacity (Scotland) Act 2000 (AWI), also in its very first Section, contains a similar set of five principles that anyone interacting with a person who lacks capacity is required to respect.

Later in this chapter we will consider how an attorney respects these principles in practice, but for now we will just look at the five principles.

Principle 1: benefit

Every action has to benefit the incapable person and cannot reasonably be achieved without the intervention.

'Intervention' is the legal term used, but it is easier to replace this in your thinking with the word 'action'. There are two parts to this requirement: 1) that the action must benefit the person, and 2) that one cannot achieve the result without the action.

Benefit is not defined in the Act, so it can be direct or indirect, physical or emotional, for instance.

Occasionally it is not possible to discern a positive benefit, in which case it can be helpful to look at it from another angle; it may be possible to see a detriment *without* the intervention. If you can avoid that detrimental effect by taking whatever the action is, therein lies the benefit of the action.

Example of an indirect benefit: an elderly lady with incapacity is cared for at home by her daughter; this impacts on the amount of time and attention the daughter can give to her young children. Once a year the elderly lady goes into respite care while the daughter goes on holiday with her family, which is paid for out of Mum's money. The family holiday does not benefit Mum directly, so why should she pay for it? The benefit is that, without some quality rest and relaxation with her family, the daughter may get 'burnt out' and no longer be able to care for Mum at home, which would mean long-term care for Mum, which is not only less preferable for her but is also much more expensive than paying for an annual family holiday for her loved ones.

You may have noticed that in Scotland the principle is one of 'benefit', whereas in England and Wales the equivalent principle is one of 'best interests'. You may have heard that these are different; perhaps the best way of trying to describe the difference is that 'best interests' naturally leads you to consider what is best for the person, it is your view of what is in their interests. The AWI preferred the emphasis to be on respecting the person's own wishes, so chose to use 'benefit' as an alternative. Legal academics and indeed some cases examine the subtleties of the difference, but in practice it doesn't really matter as long as you place the individual at the centre of your consideration, when acting under either law.

Principle 2: least restrictive

The action has to be the least restrictive option in relation to the freedoms of the person, consistent with the purpose of the intervention.

This has the same meaning as principle 5 of the MCA: see p. 187.

Principle 3: take account of the present and past wishes and feelings of the person, as far as these can be ascertained

Before taking any action you *must* take account of the wishes and feelings, past or present, of the person with incapacity and respect these in your decision-making. The Act requires you to take steps, if required, to ascertain these wishes and feelings, e.g. by the use of drawings or communication aids. It is not sufficient simply to say that the person cannot relay their wishes, and so you don't have to regard this principle. You must make every effort to discover those wishes.

Principle 4: take account of the views of relevant others, as far as is reasonable and practicable

You must take account of the views of relevant others – but only in so far as it is reasonable and practicable to do so. The Act stipulates some persons whose views you should seek, such as the nearest relative, the named person and the primary carer. But it is safer to think in broader terms, and to include anyone who you think might be able to offer a view, especially if they can offer an alternative view to your own, so you can be sure you have considered things from all angles.

The relevant other should be advised that they must offer a view on what they think the individual themselves would have wanted, or on what they feel would be for the person's benefit; they are not offering their own personal view per se.

Principle 5: encourage participation

You must encourage the individual to participate by exercising whatever skills they do still have, as well as encouraging them to develop new skills; this is aimed at facilitating the individual to make their own decisions wherever possible.

The legal principles (Northern Ireland)

The MCA for Northern Ireland has two overarching principles, which may sound simpler, but they require all the same considerations as those for the other two jurisdictions.

The first principle is that of capacity, which we will talk about more in the next section.

The second principle is that of acting in the person's best interests. In order to achieve this, you must have special regard to the following, in so far as they are reasonably ascertainable:

- the incapable person's past and present wishes and feelings
- any relevant written statement made by the person when they had capacity
- the person's beliefs and values that would be likely to influence the person's decision if they had had capacity
- other factors that the person would be likely to consider if able to do so.

You should:

- consult the relevant people about what would be in the person's best interests
- take into account the views of those people (so far as ascertained from that consultation or otherwise) about what would be in the person's best interests
- in relation to any act or decision that is being considered, you must have regard to whether the same purpose can be as effectively achieved in a way that is less restrictive of the incapable person's rights and freedom of action
- in relation to any act that is being considered, you must have regard to whether failure to do the act is likely to result in

harm to other persons with resulting harm to the incapable person.

You will see that, although worded differently, the principles in each of the jurisdictions fundamentally set out a very similar value base, which, as I mentioned, anyone supporting an incapable person is obliged to respect. Let us now consider, therefore, how you, as an attorney, should act to be in accordance with them.

Acting in accordance with the principles

Anyone acting with or for a person with incapacity is obliged to respect the principles; these will allow you to challenge yourself on your decisions. If you find your decisions or actions challenged by someone else, you should be able to show that you had regard to the principles in making your decisions – this grounding will give a robustness to your actions.

First, it's worth saying that the principles, in any of the Acts, are all equally as important as one another; you are obliged to respect them all; it is not sufficient to think that because you meet one you do not need to consider the rest.

Let us think more about what this means in practice. In the following paragraphs, we will consider how you might go about applying the principles: the principles themselves are underlined in italics. You'll notice that many of the principles are covered by things we've already discussed, and that there is some overlap between the principles and supporting decision-making or respecting rights, will and preferences.

In Chapter 7, I spoke about supporting the person's own decision-making. The principles have a similar requirement: within the legal principles we are obliged to *offer support to encourage their participation*. This means doing whatever is possible to permit and encourage the person to take part, or to improve their ability to take part, in making the decision. We spoke about how you can do this in Chapter 7. Here, I will just reiterate: if the person can make a decision for themselves, even if it requires a significant amount of support, then you should not be making the decision for them, even if you have powers to do so.

Assuming that you *do* need to make the decision on behalf of the person, and you have powers to do so, then we'll look at the next principles.

You are obliged to *act in the best interests* of (England and Wales and Northern Ireland), or *for the benefit* of (Scotland) the person with incapacity. These terms are not defined in the Acts. Best interests/benefits may vary from person to person and by circumstance. What may be of benefit for one person may not be for another, or what may be in their best interests at one time may not be at another time. Nonetheless, as an attorney, or as a person supporting someone with incapacity, you have to consider, in respect of each decision, whether this decision is in the person's best interests/for their benefit.

As there is no definition of these terms, you will have to decide on this in the circumstances at that time. Here are some examples:

> *A person needs a motorised wheelchair; they have funds to pay for this privately, so you wish to spend some of their money on it. This will promote their independence.*

This purchase would appear to be in the person's best interest/for their benefit.

> *An elderly lady with dementia lives with her daughter and her family; the family need a new car, which will allow them to take Mum out. Her daughter is her financial attorney and decides to pay for the car from her mum's money.*

Is the purchase of the car for Mum's benefit/in her best interest? To answer this would require more background information, for example what sort of car is to be purchased, how much would it cost, how much money the mother has, how often it would be used to take her out; is this the primary purpose or is the family getting the primary benefit? On balance, on the bare facts we have, it does not sound like the purchase would be sufficiently in the person's interests to make this a justifiable spend.

You are obliged to ensure the decision offers the *least restrictive alternative*. Let's use the examples above to think about this.

The purchase of the family car: the outcome for the lady in this example appears to be more outdoor time/time with her family. But is the purchase of a family car required to achieve this? Can it be achieved in a different way? Maybe paying for taxis on the occasions when the family wishes to go out, as costly as this may be, may actually be less than the price of a family car.

The motorised wheelchair: the outcome in this example is for the man to be more independent. If this can be achieved other than with the significant cost of a motorised wheelchair, then spending money on a motorised wheelchair is not the least restrictive way of achieving the outcome of independence.

It may not be the least restrictive alternative, but you may think, nonetheless, that it is the best decision. We will talk below about what to do when the principles create such conflict.

You can see from these examples how critical it is that you

identify the outcome of the decision, the reason for the decision, and what it is you are trying to achieve. If you feel you are struggling in making a decision, double-check that you are clear about what it is you are seeking to achieve. A lack of clarity on this can lead to an erred judgement on the decision.

In respecting the principles, you are obliged to *respect the person's past or present wishes and feelings*. We have spoken about this in the rights, will and preferences section of Chapter 7.

A person's wishes and feelings may be, or may have been, expressed verbally, in writing or through behaviour or habits. They may have religious, cultural, moral or political beliefs and values that may influence a decision; there may be other factors too. If you know the person well, then you will know their past behaviour and values; it is harder if you are supporting someone less well known to you. This is when a Statement of Wishes and Feelings, if there is one, can be valuable (see Chapter 5). Their bank statements may help you determine what they were spending money on, or their will, if you have access to this, may offer an indication of their views.

Seeking the view of others is one of the principles and can assist you in determining what the person's own wishes may have been. Even if you are a relative you may think you know these, but we all speak to different people about our feelings in different ways, so others may know of something, or an angle on something, of which you are not aware.

You are the daughter of, and attorney for, your mum Peg, who is now incapable. You have a brother, Peter, with whom you and your mum are estranged; you have not seen or heard from Peter for about twenty years, and you and Mum never mention him. Peter has heard that his mother is in the final stages of dementia and has asked to come to see her. Mum is unable to offer her own view on this.   →

> *You have power to decide whether Peter may visit, and you decide that you should refuse this as your mum would not have wanted to see him. However, you ask the view of your mum's best friend, Mavis; they have been friends for sixty-five years, and even now still see each other every week. Mavis tells you that Peg talked about Peter often; she wished the family would talk about him more. She forgave him for the issue that created the estrangement and she could understand why he had not been in touch but wished he had been; she would love to see him. Mavis says that Peg never mentioned these feelings to you because she knew how upset this would make you; she knew how emotional you were about all that went on. Mavis tells you how much your mum loved and respected you for all the support you gave her and that she did not want to cause you any more hurt by suggesting she would love to see Peter again. Mavis is sure Peg would love to know that she was reconciled with Peter, even if she isn't aware of it – but who knows, maybe she would be aware of it.*

Against what would have been her better judgement, after *taking account of the views of others* and *respecting Peg's now-known wishes and feelings*, the attorney took the decision to allow Peter to visit.

Consequently, if it is practical and appropriate to do so, consult other people for their views on the matter; do they have any information about the person's wishes and feelings, beliefs and values that they would see as relevant to the decision in hand?

People you should try to consult are the carer (if this is not you), the next of kin (if this is not you or the carer), any other attorneys, any other family and friends who have contact with the person and thus may be able to offer you the person's view.

It is helpful to talk to people with differing relationships with the person. For example, if the person has three sons and a daughter, and you have spoken to all three sons and they agree their mother would wish x as the way forward, just double-check this with the daughter as she may have had different conversations with her mother than her brothers had, and may offer you an alternative view which it is only proper for you to bear in mind.

With any of these conversations, you should ensure that the people are offering you their thoughts on what the person would have wanted, not what they think is right for the person.

When having these conversations, remember that the incapable person has a right to privacy, so you may not wish to share the full details with everyone. A guide here is to think about what level of conversation the person themselves would likely have had with whomever you are talking to.

Your conversations with these people therefore have a dual purpose: to find out their opinion on what the incapable person's views may have been, and to ensure you have learnt from them about any alternative options that may present a lesser restrictive way of achieving things.

Here is an example of using all of the principles in practice.

John is health and welfare and property and finance attorney for his mother, Celia.

Celia lives in her own house but is struggling, desperately, to get upstairs. Her only toilet is upstairs. She needs the toilet with urgency sometimes, so is rushing on the stairs; she has fallen both up and down a number of stairs a few times. It also upsets John that sometimes his mother doesn't get to the toilet in time.

John thinks that it would be better all round for his mother to live downstairs. He is debating whether to spend a lot of his mother's money converting the ground floor of her house so she can live on a single level; this includes a small extension to put in a downstairs toilet and shower room. →

In making the decision about the financial spend on the extension John needs to respect the principles, so he has to ask himself:

a) *Is Mum capable of making, or being supported to input to, this decision?*

    John has tried to support his mother in making a decision on this but is satisfied she no longer has sufficient mental capacity. John knows that a best interpretation of his mother's wishes would be to stay in her own home as far as possible.

b) *Would spending this amount of money so Mum can live downstairs in her own home for longer be in her best interests/to her benefit?*

    This may seem most obviously a yes. But we have talked earlier about being clear what the outcome is: what it is that is to be achieved. In this case it is for Mum to live in her own home for as long as may be possible, but, more specifically, this has to be safely and with dignity (so she can have easier, and so more timely, access to the toilet).

c) *What are the views of others?*

    John talks to his mum's carers about his idea. They are not sure that it is as good an idea as John thinks. They think the exercise that Celia gets from walking around her home is of value; they comment that she enjoys looking out of her upstairs window, as she can see the comings and goings of the neighbourhood from there, which she cannot do from downstairs. They think she will be more isolated if she is confined downstairs. They think she will try and use the stairs anyway, so John would have to physically block her access, which they disagree with. They talk about the proposed downstairs toilet, which looks as if it will be quite narrow. Celia uses a walking frame. It may be wide enough to take the frame, but there is not enough space to allow Celia to turn round. Does she have to back in, or leave her walker at the door and walk in unaided? Neither of these are acceptable, and neither make going to the toilet any safer or quicker.

d) *What is the least restrictive way of achieving the outcome (of being safe and of getting more timely access to a toilet)?*

The carers say they don't need a downstairs shower room: they can assist Celia on the stairs to access her current bathroom. Without this, could the size of the downstairs toilet be increased? They also talk about other ways of achieving the outcomes.

They will check that Celia hasn't got a urine infection which is making her need to go with urgency. They will ask the carers who do lunch and dinner support to ensure they take her to the toilet as well. They talk about using technology such as smart assistants to offer a reminder to go to the toilet. Finally, they talk about stair lifts and suggest John takes specialist mobility access advice before simply going ahead with the extension.

It seems from this that there may well be a less restrictive way of achieving the desired outcome and in which case, to comply with the principles, John should explore these avenues first.

e) *John is obliged to take account of his mother's views.*

John thought he knew these (that Mum wanted to remain in her own home), but he hadn't realised that she enjoyed watching the coming and goings from her upstairs window. He spoke to his sister; she added that many of the people passing waved to Mum and that she also enjoyed looking from the side window in the other bedroom out to the fields where people walked their dogs and where there was a lot of wildlife. She said Mum even enjoyed looking out for 'Charlie the Crow', whom she could recognise from his lopsided walk when he landed in her garden. The proposed downstairs arrangement had no side windows, so would deprive Mum of all of these enjoyments.   ➔

> *One can see from this that there is a bigger picture to take account of. Yes, it is important that Celia lives safely and with dignity in her home, but there is also an element to the quality of her life which John had not appreciated until talking to others.*

You can see from this example how using the principles as John's guide in his decision-making was extremely valuable. John genuinely believed the extension was a good idea to resolve the issues, but had his use of Celia's money for this been challenged by anyone his decision would have lacked robustness; although he had done what he believed was right, he had not considered the issues comprehensively – and had not acted in line with the principles.

Conflicting principles

This all sounds straightforward so far, but there may be times when the principles conflict with each other. The next section considers how you manage when this happens.

The example above of the motorised wheelchair is an illustration of the principles being in conflict. We concluded that, on the limited facts available, it may not be the least restrictive alternative, but it is going to offer the man benefit/be in his best interests (in being independent). He may have a wish for a motorised chair, and others too may feel this is the best solution. In this case, a requirement to offer the least restrictive option is in conflict with all of the other principles, or so it seems.

Rather than the principles being in conflict with each other, it may be that you have a situation where one principle is in conflict with itself. A common example is when the current wishes of the person conflict with their past wishes. An example may be that a person, when capable, recognised and accepted that they may at some point need to be admitted to a care home; now, with a loss of capacity, they are adamant that they do not wish to be cared for anywhere other than at their own home. However, they can no longer be housed safely at home; everything possible has been tried to allow them to remain there, but there is genuinely nothing more that can be offered. In this situation the person's current wishes conflict with their past views.

Let's look at another common scenario, just to show how confusing it can get. In this example, one person believes that a care home is the only option for the now-incapable person, while another disagrees and thinks care at home is in the person's best interests. This may be a case of the principle of best interest being in conflict with that of taking account of the views of another; or it may be that the principle of best interest is in conflict with itself – because there is a difference of opinion as to what is in the person's best interest; then again, it may be that the principle of taking account of the views of others is in conflict with itself because there are differing views.

I offer these examples to show how common it is for the principles to conflict. There are likely to be situations when you cannot get all the principles to neatly 'marry up'. You will recognise a problematic situation, but may not recognise that this creates a conflict of the principles. Even if you do recognise it as a conflict of principles, you may not be able to work out just what is in conflict with what: do not worry about this. It is not unusual for a situation to create tension between the various principles. The decision as to which principle you respect and which you effectively have to ignore is down to you as the attorney; you will need to find a way of balancing the tensions and weigh up the pros and cons.

The following checklist may assist; it is very similar to the one in Chapter 7 when dealing with conflict of rights, will and preferences, so you may wish to review that one again too:

- Do I understand the circumstances properly?
- Have all the right factors been taken into account; have I missed anything?
- Have I involved the person as much as is possible?
- Do I know their current views?
- Do I know their past views? If not, can I learn of these from somewhere?
- Can I glean anything from current behaviours?
- Do I know sufficient about their beliefs and values?
- Is there a compromise option which would resolve the conflict?
- Do I need to involve an advocate to elicit the person's views, if possible? (There is information about the role of advocates in Chapter 7.)
- Is there anyone else who may have information to whom I have not already spoken?
- Do I need any more information/a second opinion?
- Are there any options I have not considered?
- Have I looked at this objectively?
- Have I given due weight (not too much and not too little) to relevant parties' opinions?
- Would a case conference assist – having all relevant parties speak together?
- Would mediation assist?
- Should I, or do I need to, speak to the local authority or OPG, for example, to get their advice?

- Do I need to take legal advice?
- Do I need formal direction from the court?

Despite every effort, sometimes it is just not possible to eliminate the conflict. Then it is a case of making sure you have a correct and comprehensive understanding of the full situation, from which you have to reach what you believe to be the right decision in the circumstances. Sometimes there is no perfect answer: you must just try your best. As attorney you have the responsibility for the decision and its consequences. Keeping notes on your decision-making process will help you and will allow you to show others how you came to that point. I have already mentioned the importance of comprehensive record-keeping in such instances; I cover it in more detail in Chapter 10.

The Code of Practice

Finally, in this chapter on the legal framework within which you should operate I should mention the Code of Practice.

There is a Code of Practice for England and Wales and a separate Code for Scotland. A Code of Practice is in development for Northern Ireland. A Code of Practice is a set of guidelines for anyone acting as an attorney which provide guidance to anyone who is working with and/or caring for people (specifically adults) who may lack capacity.

The MCA requires an attorney to have 'regard to' relevant guidance in the Code of Practice, but neither Act, the MCA or AWI, imposes a legal duty on anyone to 'comply' with the code – it should be viewed as guidance rather than instruction. But if a person has not followed relevant guidance contained in the code, then they may be expected to give good reasons why they have departed from it. The codes are too lengthy to include here, but you can find them by going on the respective Public Guardian's website.

As an attorney, it is important that you are aware that there is a Code of Practice and that as far as is possible you act in accordance with its guidance. I would urge you therefore to have a look through the code (ensure you are looking at the right one for the country you are in) to get a sense of what sort of information it includes. If at a later stage there is something you are unsure of, or you are being challenged about, then remember the code, and have a specific read of the relevant section as it may well have information which is of assistance.

The codes cover such things as:

- when to act
- managing the person's finances
- paying for services
- obtaining specialist advice
- keeping records
- communicating
- dealing with conflicts of interest
- what to do where your powers are insufficient
- what if there is a complaint against you.

This book contains information on each of these topics, reflecting guidance that is in the code, but it should not be seen as a replacement for the code.

You now have all the information you need for a solid foundation as an effective attorney. The next chapters explain how to approach the administration of the powers with which you have been entrusted.

Chapter 10

Being an attorney

You may wonder why, in a book about PoAs, this chapter on actually being an attorney is so far into the book. In a way, this is an indication of how much there is to learn about how to be an effective attorney. If you have cut to the chase and come straight to this chapter, I would urge you to backtrack and at least read Chapters 6–9, as these put in context many of your responsibilities as an attorney. You will not be an effective attorney unless you are aware of the guidance in these earlier chapters. A lot of what follows in this chapter makes reference to the 'teachings' in these earlier chapters.

Now that we have covered not only the legal framework, but also the ethical guidelines for acting as an attorney, we will look at the 'the nuts and bolts' of being an attorney and how you can fulfil the role the way the person who granted it intended it to be. We will consider general things to prepare you for the role, then later in the chapter we will look at more specific information that will help you in the role, including a section on record-keeping.

Getting endorsed copies of the PoA

It is recommended that as soon as you know you have been appointed, and before you need to actually start using the PoA, you ask the donor/granter if they have endorsed some copies of the PoA document and, if not, you ask them to do so while they are still able, as this will ease things for you when you do need to start acting. There is more information on endorsed copies in the 'After registration' section of Chapter 5.

If you are using copies that have been endorsed by the granter, it is worth you knowing a bit about the lawful basis on which they can endorse copies.

Endorsed copies are equally as valid as the original, but some organisations don't know this and will insist on the original; or they will permit an endorsed copy only when it has been authenticated by a solicitor – because they do not appreciate that the granter is legally permitted to endorse the copies for themselves. You may therefore have to quote the law on occasions. Here it is.

The authority for the granter to validate a copy of the original PoA comes from Section 3 of the 1971 Power of Attorney Act, which Section remains in force notwithstanding the later Mental Capacity Act 2005 (England and Wales) or the Adults with Incapacity (Scotland) Act 2000. Section 3 of the 1971 Act states:

> *The contents of an instrument creating a power of attorney may be proved by means of a copy which is a reproduction of the original made with a photographic or other device for reproducing documents in facsimile and contains the following certificate or certificates signed by the donor (called a granter in Scotland) of the power or by a solicitor or stockbroker.*
>
>   *That is to say:*
>
> i) *a certificate at the end to the effect that the copy is a true and complete copy of the original; and*
>
> ii) *if the original consists of two or more pages, a certificate at the end of each page of the copy to the effect that it is a true and complete copy of the corresponding page of the original.*

So, if you have a copy, or number of copies, which has the above wording on each page, then you have a lawfully endorsed copy.

Deciding when to activate the PoA

Deciding that you need to start acting, officially, as attorney can be an emotionally testing time, as you may see it as a real indicator of the changing condition of a loved one, which can be hard to acknowledge.

It can make things easier if you remember that an attorney is not a person who just assumes all the decisions and responsibilities, restricting and controlling the life of the other person; by law, your role as attorney is primarily one of support, to enable the person to maximise their ability to participate in matters affecting them. There is much more about supporting decision-making in Chapter 7. For now, let us look at how you activate the PoA, having decided that this has now become necessary.

If the PoA is not already registered with the Office of the Public Guardian, you will need to do this before you can start operating on any of the powers. You can do this yourself or if, for instance, a solicitor was involved in the drawing up of the PoA, you can ask them to now proceed to register it. In which case, they will likely want evidence from you that the person is incapable and that it is therefore appropriate for the PoA to now be registered. A report from the person's doctor may be required, but speak to the solicitor first to see what they will accept.

If the PoA isn't already registered and you are now having to do this, you should plan ahead as the registration process can take some weeks; it is not a case of you submitting the PoA then being in a position to act a couple of days later. This time lapse can take people by surprise and has created difficulties for some in the intervening period. If you do need to start using the PoA with urgency, contact the respective OPG and ask if there is anything they can do to speed up the registration given your situation.

Assuming the PoA is already registered, there is nothing you have to do to 'activate' it per se; rather it is just a decision as to when you start operating as attorney, under the authority the PoA gives you. This will depend on what powers you need to act on: property and finance, or health and welfare.

Property and finance matters

You can start assisting the person with financial and property affairs as soon as the PoA is registered with the OPG, but while the person remains capable this should be under their instruction.

I would advise that you do not register the PoA with the bank or another financial institution before asking about their policy on registered PoAs. Do they take registration of a PoA to mean the person is incapable and so stop the person's own access to their account, or right to make their own decisions, thereafter?

If they adopt this approach, then defer registration of the document with the bank unless or until you need to use it actively. In the interim, you may wish to talk to the bank about how a third-party mandate works, which is an authority the account owner can give you that allows you to administer things with the bank on their behalf, but which still allows the person full access to their own matters too, as you are not operating under a PoA.

Health and welfare

Health and welfare powers do not commence unless or until the person is incapable – in relation to the decision or action to be taken.

You should first check whether the PoA requires you to get an independent opinion of the person's capacity; for instance whether you are required to get a doctor to advise you that the person is now incapable.

If this is the case, please ask the doctor to give written confirmation of their opinion, as you will need something for your records to demonstrate that you have indeed received the medical advice that was required.

If an independent opinion is not required, then you can make the decision yourself, as attorney, as to when you believe the person is incapable. But please read the section on assessing capacity, which starts on p. 170, to assist you with making a decision.

It's not a case of active or inactive

Even though you may have 'activated' the PoA and registered it with various organisations, you should only use it if and as required. If the person themselves is capable of making a particular decision, or of taking a particular action, then they should do so personally, or be supported to do so personally. The PoA, be it for property and finance or health and welfare, is only active as far as it is required to be. Even if you have started using the PoA for some decisions, this does not mean you then make all decisions, per se, or even all decisions of this type. The person's ability to make their own decisions, or be supported to do so, must be judged for each individual decision to be made.

Get familiar with the document and your powers

This is critical to the effective operation of a PoA. You will find that many organisations are not as familiar with the operation of a

PoA as you would assume they would be, and that in order for you to progress as you wish you will need, effectively, to steer them.

So, you need to know what you are permitted to do, and where to evidence this in the document. Spend some time, therefore, getting familiar with the content and layout of the document and what it all means. You need to know who else is appointed, if anyone, and if you are required to act jointly, or may each act independently. You may wish to read Chapter 3 if you haven't already done so, as this covers the appointment of attorneys in detail. Talk to one of the sources of advice listed on pp. 312–13, if this would put you in a greater position of strength.

The following example illustrates the critical importance of having a comprehensive knowledge about the PoA, its extent, limitations and the authority of your role.

'I was in a building society as I needed to close a savings account of my dad's. It had about £15,000 in it; we needed to transfer this to a current account as it was needed to pay for Dad's care. I am appointed financial attorney for my dad, jointly and severally with my brother; we have power to close the account. My brother and I had agreed on closing the account to release the monies we needed; as either of us could act, I went in to action our decision. The building society insisted that my brother must be present too. I challenged them: "Why, the PoA did not require this?" They could give no real explanation but remained adamant that my brother had to be present.

I reiterated my challenge; the PoA, which was an expression of my father's wishes, did not require us both to be present. Despite this, they remained insistent that both of us must be present, as my brother was named as an attorney. Yes, he was named as attorney, but we were appointed with joint and several authority; I showed them where in the PoA it said this and explained what this meant. ➔

> I then, very nicely, but assertively, said that if they remained insistent that my brother must attend, then I would take this as their company policy, as this was certainly not a requirement of the PoA; and unless they could show me where my father had agreed to this when agreeing to save with them, I would have no option but to charge them for my brother's attendance. I was not authorising this to be taken out of my father's estate when it appeared to be their requirement, not my father's; my father should not be penalised for their policy – unless, as mentioned, they could evidence to me where Dad had agreed to this.
>
> As my brother lived some 500 miles away and was self-employed, I calculated roughly the cost of travel and the loss of a day's income for him and advised them that I would be invoicing them for this cost.
>
> I suggested that they may wish to speak to their company's legal department about this. Their policy demanded joint action by attorneys, notwithstanding a PoA which permitted joint and several. Did they really have a policy which disrespected the wishes of a client, expressed in a lawful PoA? I commented that this was an erosion of a person's rights and was unlawful. Maybe they would prefer to review their policy before insisting on my brother attending and incurring the cost to their company that I was going to charge them for this.
>
> I don't know if they phoned their legal department, but they came back and said that "on this occasion" they would accept my authority alone!!' (Denise, attorney)

If you've started this book at this section, don't worry if you are confused by the above example; it uses a lot of terms that will be unfamiliar to you. I have done it deliberately to illustrate the importance of being prepared, of knowing what your PoA contains, where, within the layout, one would find things, who is authorised, how they are authorised to act and what this means. Denise was in an empowered position and was able, in the end, to enforce her position. Please ensure you are as prepared as Denise.

If you need assistance with clarifying any of the legal detail in the PoA, please do not hesitate to seek advice from one of the sources of support mentioned on pp. 312–13.

As well as knowing what your powers permit, it is also important to be aware of what they do not allow. The next section should help you decide whether you do, or do not, have power to authorise a particular action/decision.

Deciding whether you can act

For any decision that needs to be taken there is, in essence, a hierarchy in deciding when you should, or can, act. There is a series of questions you need to ask yourself:

1. *Can the donor/granter make their own decision on this matter?*
If this is the case, even if you consider that the PoA is in force, because you have been acting for them on other matters, the person must be permitted to make their own decision on the matter. Chapter 8 is all about assessing a person's capacity and Chapter 7 about supporting a person with their decision-making.

2. *Has the person been offered every support to make their own decision or offer their own view?*
If it seems the person is not able to make their own decision, before moving to make this decision on their behalf you should satisfy yourself that the person has been offered every support in enabling them to participate in the decision-making process as far as is possible (again, Chapter 7 covered this).

3. If I am to make this decision on the person's behalf, are there any exclusions within the PoA which preclude me making the decision? Or, put the other way, does the PoA have powers which permit me to make this decision or take this action?

You can only take decisions that the PoA gives you authority to take.

4. Do I know what the donor/granter's view on the matter would have been? Am I considering a decision that respects what would have been, or would likely have been, the person's views and preferences on the matter?

We talked about the legal requirement to respect the person's wishes in Chapter 9, and of respecting their rights, will and preferences in Chapter 7.

5. Does the law exclude me from making this decision/taking this action?

There are certain decisions, by law, which you are not permitted to make. See under 'Unlawful powers' in Chapter 2

6. Can I make this decision/take this action on my own, or do I need to do so jointly with a fellow attorney (assuming you are not a sole attorney)?

You cannot take a decision on your own if you are required to act jointly.

7. Even if I think I know the donor/granter's views on the matter, and even if I can make this decision on their behalf, is there anyone else who can possibly offer me a different angle to challenge any assumptions I am making? What are the views of relevant others?

No matter what the decision, you are theoretically required to consider the views of others. Although, this is clearly impractical for literally every decision.

> '*My brother and I are both appointed as Dad's health and welfare attorneys. We have power to decide on what Dad should wear. It's impractical to check with my brother what clothes I should dress Dad in each day; but there came a time when I thought it would be preferable to dress him in elasticated-waist tracksuit-type trousers, as this would maintain Dad's independence for longer, allowing him to access the toilet for himself and quickly. Dad was beyond being able to say whether he was OK with this, so I checked this decision with my brother, as Dad would ordinarily never had worn such casual wear. These trousers were such a departure from the norm for our father that I felt it necessary to seek the views of a relevant other before just proceeding with this.*'

I hope this gives you an example of when you should seek the views of others, even on practical everyday matters, and when you have to be pragmatic and just go with your own decision.

8. Can the same outcome be achieved in a way which is less impactful for the person? (The least restrictive option is also one of the legal principles which we covered in Chapter 9.)

Once you have completed this exercise, you will be in a position to know if you are able to act. As attorney the main things you will need to act on are decisions about financial matters, property and care; we will look at each of these in the next chapter, but there are a few other general things which are important for you to know as an attorney and which I need to touch on first.

Powers for you to take specific care over

There are some decisions which are more likely to give rise to challenges, for example whether and when the person should go into care, or whether you are going to stop certain people from seeing them. You may wish to look at Chapter 2, which raised these more difficult situations with the donor/granter and advised him or her to give them specific consideration. Chapter 11 offers more information on managing these difficult decisions.

What if my powers are insufficient?

What if you have conducted the exercise above and at point 3 found that you don't have power to do whatever it is that needs to be done; for example, maybe you need to sell the person's house but actually no power to sell a house has been granted to you, or power to sell the house is expressly excluded.

Occasions do arise where attorneys find their powers are not extensive enough to cover the matter which has arisen. Powers cannot be added, or amended, once the person has lost capacity. Powers are interpreted strictly and cannot be implied, but a legal interpretation may give the power a wider ambit than you had appreciated. A legal advisor may be able to find something in the interpretation of the powers that you had not seen at face value. You should therefore consider the merit of legal opinion; of course, this is a decision based on the cost of that advice versus the cost of not taking the action that you think is now necessary, so it is a judgement call for you in the given circumstances.

Keeping your decisions and actions under review

You should keep under regular review any decisions you make on behalf of the person, to ensure these remain appropriate.

In Chapter 9 we used the example of a motorised wheelchair

which would promote the independence of a person. Let us assume that initially you decided such an expense was not justified; you should review this decision from time to time to ensure, with the passage of time and any changes in the situation, that this remains the right decision.

As we covered in Chapter 8, capacity can fluctuate; so it may be that the person can today input to a decision which you originally took on their behalf when they were unable to input; if they are able to input today, you must afford them this opportunity.

Other things may change a situation: for example, you may have found out about a bank account, or a sum of money, which you did not know about previously; this may change the nature of a decision. Or you may have come across a friend of the person whom you did not know about and who can give you information on a matter or a fresh angle which you had not taken into account before.

It is important, therefore, that you do not get complacent or accepting of a situation and just act by habit: you should always be reviewing and reconsidering, even if you do then end back at the same decision.

Your role should not be purely reactive. You should not wait until an issue arises before deciding what to do. One way of ensuring that you keep the situation under review is to make it part of your calendar. Set a date to have a formal and proactive review of the whole situation, either annually or if/as circumstances change. The section on record-keeping below will give you a sense of what an annual review would look like on paper.

Feeling uncertain or confused?

It is not uncommon for an attorney to feel unsure about certain decisions, or confused as to whether they can take a decision or action or not. This may only happen occasionally, or can be a feeling you have most of the time – if this is you, don't worry; you are not alone.

Hopefully, this book will offer assistance if you are in this position; but if you remain worried about whether and how to progress with something or are anxious that things are going awry, do not keep battling on. If you are unsure about something, ask; there is a section on sources of advice at the end of the book. These sources of advice can offer you guidance, or direct you to where you may find it if they themselves cannot assist you. It is better to seek help and get the matter sorted early than keep going, only to find what you were doing was wrong and you have a lot of unpicking to do; or worse, that you are in trouble for something you have done, or not done, and especially if this exposes you to liability for this act or omission.

Taking specialist advice

You are not permitted to delegate your responsibility as attorney, i.e. hand it over to someone else who is not appointed as an attorney, but this is not the same as delegating authority to someone else who then acts under your instruction. This may seem a subtle difference, but it is fundamental; here are some examples which may help.

You are your mum's health and welfare attorney. Your mum cannot now make decisions about her diet; she needs food bought and carers to attend to cook the food and assist her with feeding. You retain responsibility for ensuring that there is a provision of food and that she is adequately nourished, but you can delegate the tasks of shopping, food preparation and feeding to others.

Another example may be:

> *You are your mum's financial attorney; you take independent financial advice (there is more about this in Chapter 11) which recommends investing a large sum of money with a portfolio-managed service. Using the principles and respecting your mum's preferences, you decide to follow this advice. You retain responsibility for this money, for deciding whether it should remain invested, whether the type of investment remains appropriate etc., even though you have delegated the administration to a company.*

If you are in this situation, ensure that you make a clear record of what you have asked the other person to do, how you are checking to ensure they do as you have asked, and that things remain appropriate. Record what you have done to amend things if they no longer seemed appropriate, so it is clear from your records that although someone else was delegated to undertake a role for you, you retained the responsibility and accountability as the attorney.

Which brings us neatly on to record-keeping.

Record-keeping

I've mentioned a number of times the importance of keeping records. Here we will look at what this means in practice: keeping specific records, for example over your financial decisions, as well as what sort of things you should consider making a note of by way of a general record.

You may think: 'Why bother keeping records, who's going to challenge me? I know what I did, I gave it full consideration and took all the necessary advice, so making a record of this is just a waste of time when I'm so busy anyway.' I can appreciate the temptation to skimp on records, but my only advice, drawn from years of experience, is expect the unexpected: you can never predict when someone may raise an issue. In these situations, those with comprehensive records win the day.

Bethan is an only child and sole attorney to her father, Sid. Sid had dementia. It became necessary for him to go into care. Bethan did an immense amount of research on what might be the right care home for him. She kept very full records on what she researched, whom she spoke to, her visits to several homes and her views on each and thus why she picked the one she did. Her father was very unhappy in care; he just wanted to be at home. His niece (Bethan's cousin), who visited him and saw how unhappy he was, complained about Bethan's actions as attorney. She felt that care in a home was not necessary, that the care home chosen was substandard, and that Bethan had not acted with due care and attention. The case ended in court for direction from a judge. The cousin was making a strong case for an alternative care arrangement, but Bethan won the case, she felt, on the strength of her records – which she had thought about not making. She was able to explain to the judge, in detail, just how much she had bent over backwards to get the right placement for her dad. She had all the paperwork she had printed off and reviewed, in folders and numbered, and could produce these for the judge. The judge ruled that Sid was in the right placement and should remain where he was. The judge even commented on Bethan's diligence (which was evident from her records).

This case today would require a deprivation of liberty consideration (there is more information about this in Chapter 11, in the section on 'Managing care decisions'), but it is given as an example of how important records and record-keeping proved to be to the outcome of the case – a case in which Bethan, as an only child and sole attorney, didn't think record-keeping was necessary, but was so grateful that she had made very full notes of everything.

You can retain records in whatever form you prefer; this may be in a notebook, in a diary, or on a spreadsheet, which would work especially well for financial matters; you can keep records in paper form or electronically. The key thing is that they are in an order, so that you can refer to them readily and draw out information if it is needed.

Specific record-keeping

You should ensure that you make a record of key matters. You may think of these as things which go beyond the day-to-day norms: for example, if you have made a decision on a large financial expenditure, or a significant care decision, or, as has already been mentioned, if you have dealt with a conflict of principles, and in respecting one principle had to disrespect another.

You should keep a record of everything that went into the decision-making. For example:

- what you considered
- to whom you spoke
- how you endeavoured to involve the person
- if the person couldn't participate, what you believed the best interpretation of their wishes would have been
- what your decision was
- how this aligns with the Acts' principles and the UNCRPD
- what were the pros and cons
- why you elected for this decision

● any ongoing consideration or further review you are going to give the matter.

This list is not exhaustive or prescriptive; I offer it to give you a flavour of the sort of things to include in your record-keeping. What you should take from it is that you can never be too detailed.

Financial record-keeping

You should maintain financial records in a structured way. What I mean by this is: know what accounts you are administering, where these are held, and keep any paperwork for them in date order and in dedicated folders (be these in paper form or electronically).

You should make a note of any major expenditure, typically when a single item is over £100, and put some narrative with this; ideally the narrative should reflect the principles of the Act and/or the requirements of supporting a person's decision-making and respecting their rights, will and preferences. For example:

> 20/12/19 *Mum increasingly struggling with mobility, even though using her stick. Discussed if a rollator walker would be better. Mum felt this would improve her independence. She tested a couple of models out, with guidance of the advisor in the specialist mobility shop. Purchased her preferred model, she felt steadier with four wheels, she liked the seat and preferred the front basket rather than the basket under the seat. Cost £130 (receipt no. 12); there were cheaper models (and dearer ones), but this was the cost of the one that Mum felt was right for her.*

What this entry tells us is that:

- having a rollator walker would be for her benefit/in her best interests
- she is already using a stick, so the rollator was likely the next least-restrictive way of achieving this assistance
- the mum was supported to make her own decision
- appropriate specialist advice was sought
- she expressed a preference on which model she wanted
- she was capable of this choice, because the matters which influenced the choice were all perfectly appropriate
- her preference was respected
- the selected model cost £130
- a receipt was retained
- the estate was being managed in a structured way – from the entry itself and from the reference to 'receipt no. 12'.

A relatively simple entry, therefore, using your own words, allows one to see a lot about the situation and that this attorney is complying with all their obligations and responsibilities. You don't need to use specific terms, or even lengthy explanations, to create clear, helpful records.

Receipts: you should keep receipts for larger purchases. You don't have to keep receipts for minor items. As with all financial records, it's helpful if you keep these receipts in a specific folder. Another suggestion is to photograph them (if you have a camera phone and this is easy), or scan them if this is available to you, to keep them in a digital file on your computer for easy retrieval. In this case, you would still also need to keep the physical receipts, but you may find it easier to refer to an image titled 'rollator receipt' than to rifle through a folder.

General record-keeping

General record-keeping covers those things which may become relevant at a later date. You may wonder how you know ahead what may become relevant later. In order to think about this in more depth, let's consider the following entries in a general record document.

19–27/12/19	*Mum with us over Christmas. She enjoyed her food. Train travel was a nightmare; ended up taking Mum home.*
24–26/01/20	*Howard and the kids spent weekend with Mum, took her to the garden centre for lunch and to the Mill shopping, she bought more stripy jumpers!!*
21–26/02/20	*Spent week with Mum, worked from her house but we went for a couple of meals out (Mum paid for one, me the other). Did a jigsaw, played cards. Great to spend a bit longer as had a chance to chat with Mum's neighbour, who is very good at looking in on her and also saw Mum's friend whom she sees each week.*
14–19/03/20	*Howard and I at Mum's for Mother's Day. Howard made a meal for us all (Mum insisted on paying for all the ingredients, she says it's worth it for his cooking). Howard took her car for service and sorted the insurance (from Mum's account) while I took Mum to doctors to have her knee checked out. She's struggling with pain, which is beginning to limit her mobility. Doctor explained arthritis to me.*

There were multiple entries of a like nature, over about five years; why are these entries relevant, or potentially so, and what do they tell us?

- they allow one to track the course of change when recorded over a period of time
- dates of the entries show the family were visiting monthly
- they enjoyed time with each other (meals, shopping, cards, jigsaw)
- the mum was enjoying food
- she was choosing to pay for certain items (jumpers/ ingredients)
- Howard (at least) was given permission to access her account (he paid for car service and insurance from her account)
- she was socialising – seeing a friend once a week
- there were neighbours who were looking in
- she was losing mobility
- she was happy for the maker of the notes to talk to the doctor about her medical issue and hear confidential information from the doctor about her.

Whether any of this will become relevant, one won't know; but this example of general day-to-day information can offer a good insight into the situation and relationship and may assist at some later point. If relationships sour between attorneys, or if anyone queries your judgements, or if something happens at a later date and you want to remember what you'd done in the past – in all these situations, having more general records will be helpful. Such records can help with reminding yourself, or demonstrating to others, what the person's past behaviour and general preferences were; we saw the importance of this in Chapter 7, in respecting the person's preferences, and in Chapter 9, in respecting the Acts' principles.

Since an attorney is required to keep records, it is good practice to get into this habit early. As you can see from the above example, the records can read like short diary entries, and may even be a pleasure to write and look back on.

That completes the section on record-keeping. There are a couple of other items that I need to touch on before closing this chapter on being an attorney.

Complaints about you as an attorney

You are not supervised in your role as an attorney, but people are entitled to complain to the Public Guardian or to the local authority if they have concerns about the way in which you are exercising your duties. The Public Guardian has authority to inquire into your actions as an attorney. If this happens, you are likely to feel upset and possibly offended, but if you have been acting properly and to the best of your ability you have nothing to fear. This is an occasion when good record-keeping will be to your advantage. Offer the OPG whatever you have and comply openly with their inquiry. If there is nothing to answer to, the complaint will not be upheld and nothing further will happen.

You may be keen to know who has complained about you, or to have your suspicions confirmed; but the complaint service, at this stage at least, is confidential, so the Public Guardian will not be able to tell who has complained or what the nature of the complaint is.

If the Public Guardian does find matters of concern, they will offer you advice on how to do things differently; for example, if they found that you were managing the person's money alongside your own in a single account, they would explain the importance of keeping the account in defined names and ask you to separate these, then check that you had done so before closing the case.

If there were matters of greater concern, the OPG may choose to supervise you for a period; you can agree to this voluntarily, or the Public Guardian is entitled to ask the court for an order to supervise you. An example of greater concern would be that you were stockpiling money rather than using it to support the person, and especially so if there was indication that the person was suffering as a result of being kept short of funds. The OPG would work with you for a longer period to ensure you had got the balance right between saving and spending, and that you were applying sufficient funds for the person's needs. There is much more about managing money in the next chapter; this information will assist you in exercising your duties properly.

If the concerns were such that the OPG felt that you were no longer able to act as attorney, they would apply to the court to have you removed. If you disagreed, you would have the opportunity to explain to the judge/sheriff why you felt you should remain.

I should close this section by putting these occurrences in perspective. There are some attorneys who mistreat the person, abuse their finances or otherwise take advantage of their position; these are the ones we hear about but they are, thankfully, very much in the minority. The vast majority of attorneys do a sterling job, often in difficult circumstances, with willingness and dedication.

Can I use the PoA in another country?

You are appointed under the PoA in one country, but now find you need to use it in another country. Most typically, this is because you, who live in Scotland, are appointed as attorney to your parent under a lasting PoA and your parent lives in England; as the parent ages, you decide to relocate them to Scotland to be closer to you. Does the lasting PoA still apply now that the donor is resident in another country – Scotland in this example, but it could equally be any other country; for example, if the person has made a lasting PoA while living in England but has retired to Spain. Can the lasting PoA be used in Spain?

There are various laws governing the cross-border use of PoAs between any country and the country of origin, even between England/Wales and Scotland, so you are advised to speak to the OPG, or equivalent regulatory authority, in the receiving country or state, as to what they will accept. You should also consider legal advice. You should not assume that the PoA you have cannot be used and incur unnecessary expense by seeking some other legal measure; but likewise, do not assume it will cover you and carry on without checking.

What about holidays abroad? It's a question which sometimes arises. For example, you are acting as attorney to your parent in the UK and decide that you will all go to Disneyland Paris for a family holiday. Can you use the PoA abroad, if it became necessary (or even in another UK country)? In preparation for the trip you should take care of every matter that is reasonably foreseeable so that you reduce the chance of needing to have to rely on the PoA. Emergency situations that arise abroad may not need you to invoke the PoA; the local medical team may be able to deal with these. But let us say that something has arisen and you feel you need to use your authority as PoA: you should not assume that this will be possible. It will depend on the relationship between the country in question and the UK. You may find that you need to engage solicitors in both countries to liaise with each other over the issue.

The sale of foreign properties is another common question. For example, you are acting under a UK PoA and your parent owns a villa abroad which you now need to sell. Will the authority of your PoA allow you to do this? Again, you should not assume that it will be possible as this too will depend on the relationship between the relevant country and the UK. In such situations you will probably find that you need to engage solicitors in both countries.

Court applications

The courts can offer guidance and direction to an attorney. This can be helpful, especially if there are divergent opinions, for example between you and a fellow attorney, or you and a healthcare professional, on how you should progress with something and you are at an impasse. You are entitled to seek the direction of the court, but you are advised to take legal advice about this. Going to court is not necessarily as costly as it sounds and can be worth the cost if it resolves, expeditiously and definitively, something that was becoming an entrenched stand-off. Talk to your legal advisor about the situation: is a court direction something worth considering, or is there another resolution they can suggest? If going to court is a feasible option, what is their advice about costs?

There is much more information in Chapter 12 about managing differences of opinion, which you should read; and refresh yourself on if differences do arise.

The end of a PoA

The PoA comes to a natural end on the death of the incapable person, at which point the powers of the executor of their estate commence. This may, or may not, also be yourself. If you are acting as both attorney and executor, ensure that your records demonstrate that you recognise a clear boundary. For example, in respect of financial records, don't just keep the same spreadsheet going. Show a closing balance under the PoA; this figure should then be the opening position under new executory records. If you are not the executor, ensure that your attorney records are up to date, particularly those relating to property and finance, so that you can hand over a clear position to the executor.

Taking care of yourself

Last, but absolutely no means least, I am closing this section with a message about taking care of yourself. This is critically important; being an attorney is a tough shift, made even harder if you are also the primary carer. There is a tendency to bend over backwards as an attorney, in addition to attending to your wider family, but to forget your own needs. You must consider how you are going to build 'me time' into the schedule; talking to others about how they have achieved this tricky balance may assist. Look for sources of support for carers. Many carers and attorneys feel guilty if they put themselves first; but you have to look after yourself to stay fit and so be able to give to others.

This chapter has got you started on being an attorney. The next chapter looks at the more specific decisions you are likely to have to make.

Chapter 11

Managing financial, property and care decisions

The information here goes to the heart of what you do as an attorney. It's important that you understand your obligations and how to do this properly on behalf of someone else.

The following points are things to keep in mind and to try to apply as part of your role. There is advice on a wide range of financial matters; some of it will be relevant to you, some may not apply in your situation. The subsequent section then addresses the management of property matters. If you are unsure about any aspect of managing an incapable person's finances or property, I suggest you seek advice from the respective Public Guardian (for England and Wales, or Scotland) or from the Office of Care and Protection in Northern Ireland. They would much rather you do this and keep yourself right than go on and find you have been doing something wrong.

Managing money

The simplest and most important piece of advice I can give you on how to manage someone else's money is to remember that it is *their* money and to keep it totally separate from your own.

> *Katie was looking after the financial affairs of her sister Kathy, who had a learning disability. Katie and Kathy had inherited about £300,000 each from their parents. Kathy was able to live largely independently thanks to the money and Katie's careful stewardship of it. Katie had two sons, aged eighteen and twenty. As she had separated from her husband, she made a will in which she bequeathed her whole estate, in equal share, to her two sons. Sadly, Katie was involved in a fatal road collision; when it came to sorting out her estate, it seemed she had upwards of £600,000.*
>
> *It transpired that she had kept Kathy's share of their inheritance in her own name; this had been the most pragmatic way of dealing with things. Now, with her death, this money, being in her name, formed part of her estate.*
>
> *The boys were delighted to gain such an inheritance, and despite being advised that actually about half of this was technically their Aunty Kathy's they didn't care. Legally it all showed as Katie's money. The boys chose to keep the full sum regardless of what this would mean for their aunt and how appalled their mother would likely have been.*

This may seem an extreme example, but sadly is not as uncommon as it may appear; it is based on a real case, but the names and exact situation have been changed. Here is another example based on a real case:

> *Don is married to Doreen, his second wife. Don manages financial matters for his son David, a child of his first marriage whom he has cared for since Don's first wife died when David was twenty. David has a learning disability and is now forty.*   →

Don managed David's money through his own bank account; he also held savings in his name which were technically David's. It had all seemed easier than trying to open an account in David's own name and had for many years worked perfectly fine, so much so that Don didn't even think too much about it.

Regrettably, Don and Doreen have decided to divorce; it is acrimonious. They are sorting out a financial settlement; as part of the calculations they are taking into account all of David's money, as this appears to be Don's. It looks like Doreen might get half of David's savings and income. Don is furious, explaining, vociferously, that these are not his finances but his disabled son's. It may be that he can prove the income is David's, as this is a monthly payment and can be traced back as belonging to David; but the savings are harder as they have sat for so long in Don's name.

These cases give a very salutary example of how important it is to keep a clear divide between your own money and that of the person you are supporting, no matter how pragmatic it may be to manage their money through your own account, no matter what their relation to you, or what plans you have in place to support them.

If the person already has their own account, then maintain this on their behalf; the PoA will ordinarily give you access to any necessary PIN or passwords that may be required. If this is not the case, make an appointment to speak to the fund holder (e.g. the bank) for their advice on how to proceed. There is a section below on dealing with banks.

If the person does not already have an account, or doesn't have a suitable account, then the PoA will ordinarily allow you to open one; ensure that this is opened in their name with you on their behalf as the PoA, rather than in your name.

Benefit entitlements

You should be sure to make a claim for any benefit to which the person is entitled or, more rarely, stop claiming any benefit to which they are no longer entitled.

Benefits could be things like universal credit, personal independence payment, tax credit, attendance allowance, pension credit or housing benefits. It isn't possible to offer definitive advice here about what benefits you, or the donor/granter, may be entitled to as these will vary depending on your situation. There is a full list on the GOV.UK website of the extensive range of benefits to which one may be entitled. You may find this a good starting point if you are not familiar with what benefits may be available.

Another good source of advice are benefits advisors. Various organisations offer a benefits advisory service, for example the Citizens Advice services, as well as many charities.

You should be alert to any other claim that it may be relevant to make, even if not a benefit per se: for example, a claim for mis-sold payment protection (PPI), had this still been an option.

Financial advice

You should consider whether it is prudent for you to seek financial advice. There is no rule which says you must do so in these circumstances but in other situations it's not required. You can be guided by what the person themselves would have done. If they were managing savings, with related financial advice, then, unless the situation is changing markedly, you should continue with this arrangement; offer the financial advisor all the relevant and updated information so they can advise you appropriately. Even if the person had never sought financial advice, you are managing their affairs in what is an unprecedented situation for them, so you should in any event consider taking such advice.

Spending v. saving

As for any of us, it is a case of achieving an appropriate balance between saving and spending. You are obliged to act wisely with the person's funds, hence why you may choose to take financial advice; but not to the detriment of the person's quality of life. You may become consumed by a need to save, especially if you are anxious about what the future may hold and how much you may need to spend on care; it is important to be prudent, but it is also your responsibility to ensure that you use the person's money for their enjoyment of life today.

Switching services

People often ask: 'If I can get better deals, e.g. on energy or phone services, by switching companies, am I obliged to do so?' If the person themselves switched providers to get the best deal, then be mindful of this and watch out for deals that may be of value; but it is not an absolute. If you are busy and cannot follow the market as frequently as they did do not fret, as long as you are managing appropriately the supplier and service that they do have.

Inheritance tax planning (IHT)

The advice here is very similar to financial planning generally: you should consider whether it is prudent for you to get specialist IHT advice. You may wish to be guided by what the person themselves would have done. If they have a will which they keep updated, then it is quite possible that they have considered, or taken advice on, IHT planning. When one is actively IHT planning it is appropriate to update one's advice and reconsider matters when there is a fundamental change in one's situation. You may feel that there is now a fundamental change in circumstances and that it is appropriate to update the IHT advice.

Shared expenses

You should not be using the person's funds to benefit yourself. It can be hard to know what this means, particularly when you live in the same property and have shared expenses. A rule of thumb is to share expenses proportionately.

> *Your mum comes to live with you; she is not capable of agreeing any financial arrangement with you. Your household expenses increase because of this, but you do not think you should take any money from your mum as it would be an abuse of your power as attorney to take her money for your own purposes.*

It is acceptable to reimburse your household for expenditure that your mum incurs; for example, if your heating and washing machine are on more and your electricity bill is higher, then you can be reimbursed for this. What is not appropriate is for you to use Mum's money disproportionately.

> *Mum comes to live with you, so you split all household expenses 50/50 and reimburse your household 'pot' to that value. However, living with you also is your partner and two teenage boys.*

This is a disproportionate use of Mum's funds as she is only one of five people in the household. Let us take the shopping bill, for example: even if Mum eats the same amount as the other people in the household, which may not be the case, she is only responsible for 20 per cent of the bill, not 50 per cent.

You may be wondering: what about going out to dinner? We always split the bill 50/50 even when there were five of us eating. It would be OK to continue to split such a bill 50/50 as this is a pattern of behaviour which the person was comfortable with and had agreed to when capable.

Using this same example, it may have been that on occasions the mother chose to pay the whole bill, for example as a thank you, or as a birthday treat; in which case, again, there is a pattern of behaviour that would make it permissible, on similar occasions and with a similar frequency, for you to pay the whole bill from your mother's funds.

If you are not sure how you should manage shared expenses, feel free to use the OPG helpline service for advice.

Funeral plans

Another question that comes up regularly is whether it is an appropriate use of the donor/granter's funds to purchase a funeral plan. This is something which is of value and which you may wish to consider. There are a range of such products on the market, so shop around; see what one offers over another for the cost being charged, so you can assess if there is a preferred product for your circumstances. If you then proceed with the purchase of a plan, you must consider what the person themselves would have wanted: for example whether their preference would be a small, inexpensive funeral or a more lavish affair.

Gifting

Routine gifts

Again, the guide is the previous behaviour of the person; continue gifting at a level which reflects the person's own habits and in the same pattern. For instance, if the person gave £100 at Christmas and birthdays to each grandchild, then continue with this. If they gave £200 to one grandchild and £100 to the others, continue with this, even if you do not agree with the fact that they treated one grandchild preferentially; that was their choice and you should act as they did, not substitute your own choice (we talked about this in Chapter 7) by changing the pattern of gifting.

Having said this, you should bear in mind the overall value of the person's estate, their income and outgoing commitments, and only maintain their pattern of gifting if it is financially viable.

A question that arises is whether, if the person bought carefully selected gifts, you have to do likewise, or can you give gift vouchers, for instance. It is the value that is important. Of course, if you feel able to select a gift and say this is from Gran, for instance, that's fine; but maybe you feel you don't know the recipient well enough and that it would be better if they choose their own. In this case offer them vouchers or money, but make it clear that it is a gift from the person concerned.

One-off gifts

Did the person give one-off gifts, or would they likely have done had the situation arisen – for example, a higher amount than usual for an eighteenth or twenty-first birthday? You can do this if there are sufficient funds, maintaining a level and pattern of gifting consistent with what the person was doing, or would have done.

What about a one-off gift of higher value? The usual discussion concerns weddings. Decisions on this will depend on the value of the proposed gift, the pattern of previous gifting, the value of the estate and the needs of the person for whom you are acting. The questions to ask yourself are:

- Can the person input to this decision at all?
- What would they likely have chosen to do?
- What was their pattern of gifting behaviour?
- Am I respecting this?
- Can the estate afford it – both now and in the future?
- Would it deprive the person of funds they themselves may need?
- Would it create a reduction in the estate value which may be to the disadvantage of potential beneficiaries? This is only relevant if this would be contrary to the wishes of the person.
- Is the gift of a value that would constitute a deliberate deprivation of assets? I discuss this concept below.

This latter point arises if you are considering a more sizeable gift in proportion to the overall estate value, and depends on the needs of the person.

A common gifting scenario

Particularly if there are sizeable care fees which are rapidly depleting the person's funds, there is a temptation to gift a generous amount of money to a grandchild, say, justifying this as 'his inheritance; Dad would rather he had it now than it go in care fees'. We all have things we would rather spend our money on, but if we did there would be consequences. I'd rather go on holiday this month than pay my mortgage but, regrettably, I don't have the luxury of choice on this one. A parallel can be drawn with payment of care fees, which have to be prioritised as essential expenditure above other things that you may well prefer to spend money on. Money gifted out of the estate to avoid necessary payments can be viewed as a deliberate deprivation of assets, which I talk about below.

We talked on p. 234 about the value of proper inheritance tax planning; you should be aware however that if you gift assets out of the estate to avoid payment of inheritance tax it is possible that this will be ineffective and inheritance tax may well be calculated as if the value of the asset were still in the estate.

Finally, in any gifting situation ensure you are not incurring, or creating, a tax implication for the donor/granter or the recipient; and if so, that this is managed properly.

University or school fees

Another question which comes up regularly is whether it is OK to pay university or school fees from the incapable person's funds – we assume here that the person can afford it and, let us say, had expressed a clear intention to cover these fees. On the face of it, this may sound permissible as you are respecting their wish, doing what they themselves would have done. However, their decision was based on their needs back then; if they have now lost capacity it is reasonably foreseeable that they will need care, and if they have sufficient funds to pay for education fees, then this care would need to be self-funded. Use of their funds for education may then be considered a deliberate deprivation of assets. There may also be tax implications which you need to consider.

Would the situation be different if the person was already funding the fees at the point when they lost capacity, and if you could not continue this the child would need to leave the school?

This makes a stronger argument for the payment to continue, and even more so if they are the signatory to the contract with the educational establishment to pay the fees; but you should not assume this or take this for granted.

Getting advice

Routine gifts such as birthday and Christmas presents are not likely to incur any challenge, particularly if you are respecting the person's own pattern of behaviour and spend, but without this, and especially for gifts of a more sizeable nature, you are advised to do your homework. You may wish to take financial or legal advice, or speak to the respective OPG before proceeding.

Deliberate deprivation of assets

This is a technical term and refers to a situation when someone intentionally reduces the amount in the estate to lower the overall value when it comes to a financial assessment for care-home fees. If, on assessment, your local council concludes that you have deliberately reduced the donor/granter's assets to avoid paying care-home fees, or to try to pay a lower contribution to care fees, they may calculate the fees due as if the person still owned the assets.

Examples of potential deliberate deprivation of assets are: divesting the estate of money, e.g. by giving unusually large sums to family members; making a large donation to a charity; moving money into a protected trust; selling a house and disseminating the proceeds; selling a house for substantially less than market value; or giving away items which could make reasonable sums of money if sold. This is not an exhaustive list. There are a wide range of things which could come into the category of deliberate deprivation of assets. If you are considering doing anything which will make a dent in the value of the estate, you are recommended to take legal, financial or OPG advice before proceeding.

Dealing with banks and like institutions

Many attorneys relay tales of woe about dealing with banks and similar institutions.

My advice here is to make an appointment to talk to the bank/institution about your situation. Do not just walk in expecting to have this conversation; this is a specific discussion and will take some time. When you attend the appointment, take with you (as well as the PoA) proof of your identity: something with your name and picture on it and a recent utility bill. You can ask when making the appointment what they will accept. They need this to prove you are who you say you are and that you are the person nominated on the PoA. Such proof of identity is required to meet the anti-money laundering regulations that financial establishments are legally obliged to comply with.

Make a list of the questions you want to ask. Here are some thoughts:

- What accounts are there, if you don't know?
- What are the 'rules' relating to these accounts?
- How have these been used over recent months?
- What may the bank require if you were to close or consolidate any of the accounts?
- How much notice do they need for any changes?
- What do they do when they have a registered PoA; do they still allow the person any access or not?
- Do you both want card access to the account; is this possible?
- Can there be a limit on the use of the donor/granter's card – if this is appropriate?

- Can you have online access; how is this regulated under a PoA?

Even once everything is up and running, if you need to do something specific do not expect to go into the bank and deal with the donor/granter's estate in the same way as you would your own. Plan ahead.

Make certain you are prepared for any conversation with the bank, or similar organisation. As has been said before, know the layout of the document, know what your powers are, know what you are permitted to do and not. Ensure you have the relevant paperwork. Take the principal PoA with you, in case the organisation wishes to make a copy, or take an endorsed copy. Do not assume that because you have provided a copy previously the organisation will necessarily have this to hand for your meeting. It's helpful too for you to have a copy or scanned image with you for your own use.

Plan ahead for any specific situations, especially where these are a one-off. For example, if you are selling the donor/granter's home, do not expect this to proceed as if you were selling your own. Ask the solicitor or agent for advice on what you need to prepare for, to avoid being caught out by delay.

In summary, the motto is 'be prepared'.

Let's now turn from managing finances to managing property.

Managing property

'Property' is not just a house, it refers to anything the donor/granter possesses, for example a car, works of art, or jewellery; even a social media account is your property. I've included a small section at the end on managing this sort of property, but as the majority of questions arise in respect of what is called heritable property, i.e. a house, most of this section addresses the manage-ment of this aspect of property.

Selling the house

It is common for attorneys to have to sell the person's home, for example when the person has moved to alternative accommoda-tion, most usually into care, and there is no prospect of them returning to the house. You may have to sell the house to release funds, but even if not you may prefer to sell it to avoid it incur-ring costs or falling into disrepair.

It is hard to give specific advice on decisions concerning the sale of a house as this will be determined by the circumstances. General advice is to gain a full understanding of the whole situ-ation before you make any decisions. Here are some questions which may help you decide whether to sell or retain the house:

- What are the views of the donor/granter, if they are able to offer them?

- Is there any steer from a Statement of Wishes and Feelings?

- Are you clear what the long-term care plan is for the donor/granter? If the intention is to rehabilitate the person and get them back to their home at some point, then of course it is pre-emptive to think about selling it.

- Do they own the house outright, or is there any mortgage or other debt, loan or security outstanding against it?

- Do they own the house in their sole name?

- Are any rights given to anybody over the house? For example, there may be a person living there who has been given a right to remain.

- What are the person's financial commitments at this point and for the foreseeable future?

- How much money is in the estate other than the house? Where and how is this held? I.e. do you actually need to sell the house at this point?

- Is there a will? What does this say about the house?

- If you sell the house, this changes the status of the value – from property to money; does this have any implications for the estate?

- What commitments does maintaining the house bring? For example, if it is old, empty and deteriorating and you cannot check on it regularly, then you may be more inclined to sell than if this was not the case.

- Can it be insured? You should make certain that the property is properly insured. You will need to advise the current insurer that the house is empty; they may no longer wish to offer insurance. You can get specialist insurance for empty properties, but if this proves difficult or expensive it may influence a decision on selling.

- Is it at risk of squatters or being vandalised? This may influence your decision on selling.

- Are there broader implications from the sale of the house? For example, the family all live distantly but can visit regularly as they have the house as a base; if it was sold, would it limit the family's ability to visit?

- What is the housing market doing? Would holding on to the house make financial sense, or is an early sale more advisable?

- What are the views of relevant others? There may be someone, another family member or close friend, who has a piece of information instrumental to the decision that you had not been aware of, or who can offer you an angle that you had not considered.

- Taking specialist advice. Do you need to take professional advice, for example from a lawyer, estate agent or financial advisor?

- Are you making an objective decision? This is particularly important if you decide to keep the house; are you doing so because this is the most appropriate decision, or because there is some sentimental attachment that makes selling too difficult?

Making a decision on the person's home is a significant one, and not one you should make without very careful and full consideration.

Value of sale

Once a decision has been made to sell the home, a question which often arises is: can we sell to a family member? And often: can we sell it at a reduced value to that family member?

There is nothing which says you cannot sell to a family member. It is advisable to check with other family members that they are OK with this. Even if you are selling to a family member you should do this through a legally contracted agreement, as you would with any third-party buyer, to avoid any suggestion that this was a gift, with its associated implications (see section on gifts and deliberate deprivation of assets).

As regards the sale price, if you are selling to a family member you are not having to market the property or potentially upgrade it for sale, so a reduction in price to reflect these savings is acceptable, but beyond this would potentially bring the transfer into the category of a gift, as well as potentially being seen as a deprivation of assets. You are advised therefore to obtain an official valuation and home (information) report so that you are treating the sale, albeit to a family member, as impartially as would be required to an independent third party. You can ask the advice of the OPG if you are unsure on any aspect.

Changing the name on the title deeds

What if you don't want to sell the house but you have decided to change the name on the title deeds to that of a family member, even yourself? This will class as a gift, will have tax implications and is very likely to be considered a deprivation of assets so should not be something you do without very clear advice.

Keeping the house

If, after careful consideration and discussion, you decide to keep the house, then you need to make sure it is looked after. You cannot just lock it up and ignore it, even if the person themselves didn't take much care of it; you have a duty not to let the property fall below its current value. Here are some things for you to consider:

- Does the heating need to be kept on, albeit at a low level?
- Does the water need to be switched off to prevent leaks and bursts?
- Are the windows and doors secured? Do they need boarding up?
- Is there an alarm? If so, the electricity supply to this needs to be kept on.
- If there isn't an alarm, would it be prudent to have one fitted?
- Are any other security measures needed?
- Ensure a regular check is made on the property – especially if there has been a period of bad weather or storms.
- Ensure any repairs are carried out in a timely manner.
- Keep the garden maintained – to give the house an

appearance of one that is lived in and cared for and not abandoned.

- What possessions do you wish to leave in or remove from the house?

- Do you need to tell neighbours, a neighbourhood watch scheme or even the local police that the property is empty? Ask them to keep a weather eye and give them a contact number.

- Home insurance – speak to the insurer of both the building and the contents to advise them of the situation. If you don't and there is reason for a claim, you may find this is not covered because the company were not aware the house was left unoccupied. The insurer may require specific protective measures which you should comply with to ensure that your insurance cover is not invalidated.

Renting the property

What if you decide to keep the property but wish to rent it out? You should give the same consideration to this as you would to renting out your own house. You need to be fully aware of the legal implications of renting, including that you, on behalf of the incapable person, become a landlord, with the stringent responsibilities this brings. Legal advice is therefore recommended. Assuming you decide to go ahead with renting, you should ensure that there is a legally enforceable lease agreement.

What if you want to rent to a family member? You may lease to a family member, but you should collect rent to a reasonable market value, to avoid being challenged that you are depriving the estate of an asset. You should also have a formal lease agreement, as disagreements can arise.

What if you want a family member to live there for free,

thinking 'payment' is their upkeep of the property? This will depend on how much upkeep is required versus how much market-value rent would be.

Scenario 1. Minimal upkeep is needed, the property is already well kept, is in a nice area and market-value rental income would be in the region of £1,000 per month, the value you would expect if this was leased to an independent party. For a family member to live their rent-free would deprive the incapable person of £1,000 pm income, which is unacceptable.

Scenario 2. The property requires major upgrading, say £30,000 of work, to get it to a marketable state. The family member will live there rent-free but will undertake to do this work, at their expense, in lieu of rent. This may now be acceptable.

The next question which often arises in this latter scenario is: when the property needs to be sold, what happens if the family member is interested in buying it? You may think of selling it to them at, say, £20,000 less than market value as they had paid for a lot of the work themselves; but they have done this work in lieu of rent, so to reduce the value of the house would effectively be to double-count their input.

The house can be sold to them at a marginally reduced market value to reflect not having to advertise, pay agents etc., but you cannot advantage a family member over the incapable person. Additionally, as was mentioned above, a transfer for significantly less than market value can create tax implications as it may be considered as a gift, or a deliberate deprivation of asset.

Remember that you can phone the Public Guardian for advice on how you fulfil your financial responsibilities or may wish to take independent legal advice. The Public Guardian cannot offer legal advice.

Let's now spend some time thinking about managing other types of property.

Managing other types of property

As was mentioned at the outset of this section, 'property' is anything the person owns, any of their possessions. The management of small items, for example a television or kitchen appliances, is rarely problematic. Even decisions about some larger items – for example, a car – tend to go smoothly. Challenges arise more frequently with items of value, for example expensive jewellery, works of art, family heirlooms, or with items which may have lower financial worth but where there is sentimental value.

You should use the principles and supported decision-making that were set out in Chapters 7 and 9 as a guide to informing decisions about the management of items of property. As an example, let us use a £10,000 diamond engagement ring which you are thinking of selling, assuming you have the power to do so. You need to establish:

- Is the person capable and able to make their own decision about this?
- Can they be supported to offer me their views?
- If you cannot get to an appreciation of their current view, do you know what their past views were?
- What may be a best interpretation of their view? Were they still wearing the ring on a regular basis, or has it been in a drawer for years? Do I know how much sentimental value attaches to this ring?
- Is there a will which may assist? They may have bequeathed this item specifically to someone, so to sell it, unless it is crucial to have to do so, would be to disrespect their preferences.
- Even if there is no will, is there any history which would assist me – for example that this ring is always passed to the first daughter?

- Is there a Statement of Wishes and Feelings which may offer the person's view, or from which you can draw a best interpretation?

- Is it in the best interest/for the benefit of the person to sell this ring? This will depend on the circumstances.

- The wider circumstances should also be part of your consideration: for example, if the ring, although valued at £10,000, is of an old-fashioned design it may be unlikely to sell, or may sell but for significantly less than its actual value, or may take a lot longer to sell than the time you have.

- You need, too, to consider whether this would amount to a deliberate deprivation of assets, depending on what is to happen to the sale proceeds, as £10,000 is a significant depletion of the estate value if the sale proceeds are not being put back into the estate.

- Is sale of the ring the least restrictive way of achieving the outcome? You need to ask yourself: why am I thinking I need to sell the ring? Can I achieve this without the sale?

- What are the views of relevant others? Circumstances may increase the importance of knowing their views; for example, if you are the child of a second marriage and this is the engagement ring from the person's first marriage which they have kept, albeit not worn, for many years, what do the children of the first marriage, if any, feel about the sale of the ring?

This systematic approach will enable you to arrive at an objective decision in what can be subjective circumstances. Once you have reached your conclusion, as I have said before, ensure that you make a clear record of the factors you considered.

This completes my advice on managing a lasting or continuing PoA, i.e. one which offers you property and finance authority. The other type of PoA, you will recall, is the one which offers health and welfare powers; let us now look at how to administer that properly.

Managing care decisions

Making decisions about the person's health and welfare can be among the most difficult, sensitive and upsetting; if you can approach these decisions objectively, even though this can seem dispassionate, it can help. Making a systematic assessment is the same as has been described above, i.e. using supported decision-making and the principles as your guide.

Let's use the issue of whether to move the person into care as an example, as this is often one of the toughest decisions a health and welfare attorney has to make. You would approach this by asking yourself a similar series of questions as you have seen in other sections of this book:

- Is the person capable and able to make their own decision about this?

- Can they be supported to offer me their views?

- Is the person free of undue pressure? Is the view being expressed by the person their unencumbered view, and are you sure they are not saying what they think they should say? Ensure that they are not being influenced by you, by someone else, or by the situation into thinking they have to say a certain thing.

- If it hasn't been possible to support the person to make their own decision, and thus you are going to rely on your power as attorney to make this decision on their behalf, you first have to check the PoA affords you this authority. There is a section on p. 215 in Chapter 10 that will help if your powers are insufficient.

- Assuming that you can go ahead with this decision on their behalf and that you cannot get to an appreciation of their current view, do you know what their past views were?

- What may be a best interpretation of their view? Is there a Statement of Wishes and Feelings which may offer their view, or from which you can draw a best interpretation?

- Is it in the best interest / for the benefit of the person to go into care?

- Is this the least restrictive option? Have you considered all other possible options? Is there a compromise position which may be more appropriate?

- Have you taken account of all relevant circumstances? Is there something which you have included that is actually a red herring, or have you left out anything which you should have included?

- What are the views of relevant others?

- Do you need to take professional advice?

- Is there anybody you need to tell?

This systematic approach will help you make an objective decision in what can be difficult, subjective, circumstances. Once you have reached your conclusion, as I have said before, ensure that you make a clear record of the factors you considered.

In both Chapter 9 on the principles and Chapter 7 in the section on rights, will and preferences I acknowledge that sometimes there is conflict; decisions on care are quite often when this arises. For example, the person may express a wish not to go into care, but this has to be done if you are to ensure their safety. Both chapters talked about managing such conflicts; look back at these sections if you find yourself with a challenging care decision to make.

Chapter 7 also touched on whether you can force treatment. It is worth considering this again here. Let us assume you have a situation where residential care is now required; it is the only option, you have done everything you can to avoid and then delay this, you have made a very objective decision about it and can genuinely see no alternative. But the person is adamant that they do not want to go and will not go. The PoA permits you to make decisions on care, but can you use this to force them to go into care?

This is a potential deprivation of liberty situation. I discussed this in Chapter 2; if you have not read that chapter I would certainly advise you look at the section on deprivation of liberty on pp. 32–3. It is unlawful for anyone to deprive a person of their liberty without due authority. Whether the PoA is classed as sufficient to give you that due authority may depend on exactly how it is worded, what the interpretation is of the donor / granter's intention and precisely what the situation is. Deprivation of liberty and how it applies to PoAs is a relatively new concept and the law in this area is ever evolving; consequently it's not possible for me to offer you a definitive position on it. The OPG websites, associated guidance and Codes of Practice will provide help; an internet search for 'liberty protection safeguards', 'deprivation of liberty safeguards' or similar wording will bring up several sites which will give you information on the position as at the time you are considering this. If you are facing a potential deprivation of liberty situation, I urge you to think about the value of legal advice rather than proceed unadvised and find yourself in breach of the law. Even if you have not had to consider a deprivation of liberty case, you will have undertaken a formal assessment of the whole situation before making a significant care decision; when you have done so you are advised to make a clear record of all the things you considered – the discussions had, actions taken and the rationale for your decision. There is more information on record-keeping in Chapter 10.

Chapter 12

Managing communication, confidentiality and conflict

In this chapter we are going to look at communication, confidentiality and conflict. I've chosen to put these three topics together, as one of the root causes of conflict is poor communication, which itself frequently arises from a lack of understanding of what is or is not confidential, so they are interrelated. We shall start by considering what level of communication is required of an attorney and how to get that right. We will then turn to confidentiality and how to decide what is or is not confidential. Handling these two issues correctly will reduce the possibility of conflict, but in the final section of the chapter we will discuss how one manages conflict nonetheless, as it can arise even with the best communication.

Communication

Good communication is a cornerstone of being an effective attorney as well as significantly reducing the possibility of a challenge or complaint about how you are fulfilling the role. Communication is a vast topic, which fills books by itself, so it's not possible here to give other than a very high-level overview. If you need more specific guidance on how best to communicate, do feel free to ask for this (see the sources of support and advice mentioned on pp. 312–13).

I'm going to touch on three areas of communication in this overview:

- How you communicate with the person concerned themselves, which can become increasingly challenging as their capacity becomes impaired.
- The importance of maintaining good communication with family and friends.
- Some hints and tips for communicating with the authorities, which many attorneys find very frustrating.

Communicating with the person

Communication with the person concerned is obviously one of the most important types of communication you can have as an attorney. There is more about this in Chapter 7, where I discuss supporting decision-making. Advice on communicating includes:

- communicate in a way the person is used to
- take time and make sure you use best time of day, if there is a best time
- use simple language with bite-sized chunks of information
- ensure appropriate speed, volume, pitch, tone
- use eye contact
- pause and check understanding
- repeat information, or the whole exercise, as may be required
- use verbal and non-verbal skills, and be cognisant of the person's verbal and non-verbal communication
- be aware of cultural, ethnic or religious factors that shape a person's way of thinking, behaviour or communication

- use aids if necessary, e.g. written symbols, drawings, pictures, picture boards
- Are mechanical devices such as voice synthesisers, keyboards or other computer equipment available to help?
- Would expert support assist, e.g. independent advocates or speech and language therapists?
- use qualified interpreters if necessary.

Here it is worth reiterating that communication is not just about discussing a decision in the moment, but also keeping in touch regularly with the person, so that you get a greater sense of their current habits, preferences and opinions. Also because it's good to stay in touch!

Communicating with friends and other family members

Many of the issues which end up before the Public Guardian or the courts arise from problems with communication, particularly where there is a long-standing divide in the family, or where different family members have differing views.

> We talked about the case of Sid and Bethan in Chapter 10 to illustrate how well Bethan had kept her records and how this was invaluable for her. This case is a good example of communication too. To recap, Sid had appointed his daughter, Bethan, as his sole attorney. Sid's dementia had progressed to a point he needed care in a home. Bethan did a lot of research to ensure she got the best home for her dad. She visited all the homes in the area and questioned the managers on their ethos of care, staff-to-resident ratios and a range of other things; she checked the official ratings for each home. She had welfare power to determine Sid's accommodation, so moved him →

to the home that she had ultimately selected as the most appropriate. Bethan did not speak to her cousins, but they still spoke to their uncle (Sid). They learnt, on the grapevine, that Sid was in care – which annoyed them. When they visited him in care, they felt Sid was really unhappy and that Bethan had just 'dumped' him there. They complained to the local authority and Public Guardian about Bethan's abuse of her PoA.

A formal investigation followed, which distressed Bethan as she had tried her very best for her dad and was upset about the whole situation as it was. The investigation was not upheld, the authorities recognised that a care home was the right place for Sid to receive the care he now needed, and that Bethan had been diligent in trying to make sure she got the right placement for him. (You will recall that this case ended up with a request for the court to make a decision, but this is not the focus for this illustration.)

In this case, lack of communication led to the complaint and investigation of Bethan's actions and decisions as an attorney, a complaint which you may see as unfair and unjustified given the lengths to which Bethan had gone to get the right care home. The complaint was eventually not upheld, but the inquiry and focus on her actions was nonetheless very upsetting for Bethan, in an already upsetting situation. In this case, the family's complaint was rooted in their own upset because they had not been kept up to date; they had no concept of how bad their uncle was getting and just how much care it was taking to look after him properly. Many of the complaints received by the respective Public Guardians about the practice of attorneys arise because of poor, or even absent, communication. You should think about whom you need to involve, even if this includes people who would not ordinarily be so involved.

Of course, communicating with family and friends is very much easier said than done, especially when there is a fracture in the family; but as an attorney you need to consider with whom you need to communicate, even if this is something you would rather ignore, or find awkward.

Communicating with the authorities

Another common complaint under the heading of communication is authorities' failure to communicate. I hear regularly from attorneys who say, for example, that the doctor would tell them nothing and would not let them be with Mum for example when he was talking to her. This is a situation where you have to know your rights as an attorney; if you haven't already done so, read the sections on 'Get familiar with the document and your powers' (p. 209) and 'Deciding whether you can act' (p. 212). Whether you are permitted to be with Mum on such occasions will depend on whether she is capable, whether you have her health and welfare PoA and whether it has relevant powers.

The table below gives you a quick reference guide.

1	Is the person capable of deciding whether I may be present?	Yes	Health and welfare PoA not active because person is capable (of this decision if not others).	Then I may be present if they wish this; they need to advise the doctor.
2		No	I have a relevant PoA and it allows me to support them with the matter in question.	Then I may be present. I need to ensure that the doctor is aware of the PoA and the powers it gives me.
3		No	I don't have a relevant PoA; or it doesn't have powers to allow me to support the person with the matter in question.	Then I have no right to be present.

The example I gave referred to doctors only because that is the most common scenario; but the table on the opposite page and the comments that follow apply equally to any professional who has a duty of confidentiality to their client, for example a solicitor, an employer or a bank official.

If you conclude that you are entitled to be present, or to have information shared with you, you need to ensure that the professional in question is made aware of this. It helps if you have a copy, or image, of the PoA available. Use your learning from this book to give you the confidence to insist on the professionals respecting the rights of the donor/granter of the PoA in allowing you to be involved in the conversations and decisions.

If the person is not capable and you do not have a relevant PoA, or don't have the necessary powers, then you have no right to be included. It does not matter if you are the person's next of kin and/or primary carer and you feel strongly that you should be involved in the conversations; as has been said many times in the earlier parts of this book, you have no automatic right to this. If a conversation between the professional and the donor/granter is confidential, then the professional may feel it a breach of her confidential duty if she has a conversation with you unless the person has given permission, or granted you legal authority, by way of a PoA.

That said, just because you do not have a right to be involved does not mean that the professional will not involve you. There may be wider duties that the professional has than that of confidentiality; in caring for an incapable person the professional too has to respect the MCA/AWI principles so, in order for her to decide what may be right for her client/patient in the given situation she may need or invite your involvement.

Knowing your rights, what you can insist on and what you have no authority for, is key to navigating these situations.

> 'My dad was admitted to care. I had his health and welfare PoA,
> which gave me powers to deal with medical matters. I asked the care-
> home manager when the patient-care meetings were so I could diary
> to be in attendance (I work full-time so wanted to plan ahead). She
> looked a bit blank; maybe I had used incorrect terminology. "When
> are the meetings at which you discuss the residents, patients, what-
> ever you call them, when you review their care package and decide
> if the care you are offering is right or needs adjusting?" She told me
> these happened each month, but relatives didn't attend!!!! What??? I
> challenged her on how the care team could possibly know what was
> right for my dad without hearing from people who could represent
> his opinion. I asked how she could take account of Dad's preferences
> on things when she had no idea what his preferences and values
> were. Anyhow, to cut a long story short I insisted that my mum and
> I were in attendance at any care meetings where Dad was discussed.'
> (Andrea, attorney)

You will see from this example how a) having her dad's health
and welfare PoA, b) with its relevant powers, and c) knowing
what this entitled her to meant that Andrea was able to enforce
these powers and insist on being involved as an advocate for her
father. This situation would have been different if any one of
these three elements had not been present.

Being prepared is most definitely the key.

In closing this section, I have to offer some balance. While
I hear from and of many disgruntled families, I hear too from
and of many families who are highly complimentary about their
relationship with the professionals and sing the praises of the
way in which care of their relative has been a partnership with
those professionals. It can be a positive and affirming experience.

Managing confidentiality

As has been mentioned, one of the largest causes of complaints to the OPG arises from lack of communication, the main sub-group of which is the attorney not telling a family member something which they wish to know or believe they have a right to know, with the attorney using 'It's confidential' as the reason for not sharing the required information. This section therefore focuses on what you should consider confidential, or what you can share with others.

Deciding what is confidential, or what may be shared, can be one of the hardest decisions an attorney has to make and, sadly, there is no easy answer. It's not a case of X information is confidential, so cannot be shared, whereas Y is not confidential and so can be shared.

The following offers some guidance to help you decide whether or not you should share information.

- Is the person capable? If so, they themselves must make, or be supported to make, the decision about sharing of information requested. Remember that capacity is decision-specific, so even if the person is otherwise incapable they may be able to express a view on whether they would wish this information to be shared.

- If the person is not able to be supported to make this decision, then you have to think: what would the person themselves have done or wanted? Is the information the sort of detail that the person would have shared with the person asking?

> *Martha treated her children Sam and Christine equally; both were aware of what finances she had. She was happy to be open with this information, as both supported her, ordered things online for her and the like. Sam (and his wife of some years, Irene) emigrated to Australia, so over time he became more removed from the current position, but nothing fundamental changed. Martha granted financial PoA to Christine, as this was easier as she still lived locally. Martha lost capacity. Some months later Sam asked Christine where the finances were up to; she declined to tell him. She said she was the attorney and that this was confidential information.*

The history is one of openness between Martha, Sam and Christine. Had Martha been asked the question, it is likely she would not have had an issue with updating Sam, so there was no reason for Christine to feel this was confidential.

> *The situation remains as above, with Sam and Irene in Australia. On Sam's behalf, Irene phones Christine to ask for an update on the finances.*

There is no indication that Martha shared her financial position with Irene – although Sam may well have done, but this is irrelevant. Christine should treat this information as confidential.

Christine could consider whether there is information she can share which would fall short of sharing confidential information.

> *Christine said she could not update Irene in detail but could tell her that Mum had the same accounts as previously, save for the one with ABC bank which she had had to close to release money to pay for Mum's care as she had been assessed as fully self-funding.*

Christine felt that, in the interests of cordial family relations, she could offer this high-level information and that her mum would have been comfortable with Irene knowing this non-specific detail about the current situation.

Sam and Irene have a child, Mick, now aged twenty-five. Christine received a call one day from Mick asking about his gran's finances. Christine took the view that she would say nothing; this was confidential. She was not even going to offer high-level information.

Christine was not aware that her mother and her grandson Mick had a relationship where any level of financial discussion would take place. She felt Mick could ask his parents for the information he wanted.

You will see from this series of examples that Christine took different decisions, with the same request, using what her mother would have done as the basis for her decisions.

● You should use the principles of the MCA/AWI to assist your decision. We will use Martha and Christine again as our example.

Martha has a colostomy and previously had had a sterilisation, which Christine had only learnt about from her aunty; her mother had never mentioned it herself. Martha is now incapable and is in care; Christine is having to decide what to tell the care home about her mother's past medical history. She must mention the colostomy, as this requires daily attention, but decides not to mention the sterilisation.

It was in Martha's best interests/to her benefit to mention

the colostomy. In order to achieve the outcome of advising the home of Martha's relevant medical history, it was not necessary to mention the sterilisation, as it isn't relevant to her current situation and care. Additionally, Martha herself had never told Christine about the sterilisation, so to withhold this information respected Martha's past wishes.

Christine used the principles of the MCA/AWI to help her decide the level of information she should offer.

- You should consider whether you have a legal obligation or duty.

> Martha has been admitted to care. The local authority has approached Christine to ask about Martha's financial situation, so that they can determine if Martha is due to pay care fees, and if so at what level.

In this situation Christine has a legal duty (what would technically be called a fiduciary responsibility) as an attorney to have an open and honest conversation with the local authority in order that they can determine Martha's care-fee contribution.

- Does the other person have a duty of confidentiality? It may be easier for you to decide to give a higher level of information if the person to whom you are giving it is obliged to keep that information confidential, for example under their professional code or legal duty.
- Does the other person have a statutory authority? If the person asking you for information which you consider confidential has a legal right to this information, then you cannot use confidentiality as a reason for not disclosing it.

For example, the local authority is legally entitled to the financial detail to calculate possible care costs. The Public Guardian has a legal entitlement to information where they are fulfilling their statutory function. A court may have ordered you to give over certain information, in which case you would be in breach of the order to decline to do so, even if you believed this information to be confidential.

At some point, disclosing information, or not, will be a decision you have to make. It isn't an easy one. You will need to, and should, give it careful consideration. Do not automatically take the easy route and claim 'It's confidential', as this may place you in breach of your duty as an attorney. Use the guidance above to work through the thought process. Keep records of your thought process and conclusion (see Chapter 10). It is a case of balancing what is to be achieved by sharing against the harm that could result from not sharing. If you are not sure what you should do, feel free to speak to the sources of advice that are there for your support (see pp. 312–13).

Managing conflict

We have already covered, in Chapters 7 and 8, dealing with the principles and will and preferences when they conflict with each other. This chapter is focused on managing personal conflict.

As I have said, a lot of the conflict which arises stems from poor communication or failure to share information that you could offer; but even with every effort conflicts can arise anyway. The following section considers how to manage these.

I am going to review the conflicts in three categories, as they are three most common scenarios where issues arise:

- managing conflict of personal interest

- managing differences of opinion – between you and someone else
- managing conflicts with an organisation.

Managing a conflict of personal interest

There may be decisions which create a conflict of personal interest for you; these can be particularly problematic.

> *You are financial attorney to your father. Each time you have needed a new car, since you learnt to drive and while your dad was entirely capable, he has loaned you the money. He much prefers to do this than have you borrow on finance, and he can afford to do it. You have repaid him at an agreed market rate per month over a two-to-three-year period. It equates to having a loan but without the interest. Dad has now lost capacity; you need a new car but it will cost about £10,000 and you cannot afford it. You gave up work to look after Dad, so don't have that much income, but you can't do without a car as you need it to do a lot of running around, taking Dad to appointments etc. You will have to get a finance loan but you're not sure how you are going to repay this. Your brother suggests you take the money from Dad's account – he has plenty to cover this – and that you agree a repayment plan. He suggests £200 per month, which will mean you repay over five years, which is longer than you would have taken previously but is at a level you can afford. He is positive Dad would have approved of this decision.*

This situation creates a conflict of personal interest: to borrow the money from your father is a conflict of your duties as attorney but to avoid the conflict you would need to take a bank loan and so disadvantage yourself.

Of relevance here also is the fact that, yes, you are the

attorney, but you are still your dad's daughter; if the attorney was someone else, what decision would they make if asked by the daughter if she may borrow £10,000?

You should act in accordance with the principles: we know that Dad's view would be to loan you the money and there is a clear history of this. Is it for his benefit/in his best interests?

The views of others (one of the legal principles) are helpful here; what is their take on your borrowing the money? This is an occasion when an independent advocate may assist, someone who can offer an impartial view on what the incapable person's views may have been. In this case, it is the brother who is suggesting his sister loans herself the money.

Of course any decision has to be placed in context: if the father was in care and had limited means, to borrow £10,000 may be seen as a deliberate deprivation of his assets (see Chapter 11) and may not then be viable, even if it concurred with the principles and respected his preferences.

Remember, you have access to various sources of advice; it may be advantageous, where personal conflict of interest is concerned, to seek the views of the Public Guardian and if necessary, depending on the issue, even seek a direction from the court.

Detailed record-keeping is essential, whatever decision you reach; see Chapter 10.

Managing differences of opinion

Having covered conflicts of personal interest, let us now look at managing a situation where there are differences of opinion – for example with a fellow attorney, a family member or friend, another third party or one of the authorities. Opinions can differ on so many things, but typically they concern what care the person needs, what is the right thing to do/what is best for the person, or what money should be spent on.

It is testimony to the commitment of those involved in the care of a person with incapacity that there are not tensions; but if these do arise, it is in everybody's interests to settle them quickly and effectively, with minimal stress and cost.

The advice on dealing with differences of opinion is similar to information that has already been given, so forgive me if this feels a little repetitive, but I think it is worth including. You should ask yourself the following questions; they may not all apply to your situation, but they may serve as helpful prompts:

- Am I clear what the decision is we have the difference on?
- Is this the decision that needs to be made or have we created a red herring?
- Have I genuinely listened to and respected the third party's views?
- Can the person make their own decision?
- Am I sure they cannot?
- Have they been given every support?
- Would involvement of an independent advocate assist?
- Would explaining things differently help?
- Have I used the principles to guide my decision-making?
- Do I know the person's views on the matter – can we get to a best interpretation of what their decision would likely have been?
- Am I clear of their rights, will and preferences?
- Can I draw anything from current behaviours?
- Can I draw anything for their past decisions of a comparable nature?
- Have I taken account of all angles on the matter?

- Have I communicated comprehensively on all of these aspects to the third party?
- Is there anyone else who may be able to offer a view which may bring a compromise solution?
- Am I sure I am assessing things objectively and not projecting my own beliefs on to the matter? Likewise, is the third party assessing things objectively and not projecting their own view?
- What is the impact of doing versus not doing?
- Does it require a case conference/family meeting?
- Would mediation assist with this?
- Would allowing more time assist, if the matter is not urgent?
- Can one of the sources of advice assist, for example the local authority or the OPG?
- Do I need to take legal advice?
- Do I need to get a direction from the court?

You may have gone through all of these steps, and still you have not reached an agreed position, or one of compromise. Despite every effort, sometimes it is just not possible to eliminate the conflict. As the attorney you are responsible for the decision. If the difference of opinion is between two attorneys and you cannot reach mutual agreement, then ultimately you may need the direction of the court.

I have already mentioned in Chapter 10 the importance of comprehensive record-keeping over key matters; this is such an instance – even more so if you are going to make a decision with which you know others disagree.

Managing conflicts with an organisation

There are two matters to cover here:

1. Where there is a difference of opinion between you and an organisation – e.g. a hospital doctor advising that a particular treatment is necessary and you disagreeing, or a local authority having assessed the person's funding for care and you disagreeing with their conclusions.

2. Where you are dissatisfied with the service delivered by an organisation.

To address the first of these, I am going to cover the worst-case scenario, which is a fundamental difference over the way in which your loved one is cared for. Such differences are extremely upsetting and can be very frustrating. It is easy for me to say, but you should try to remain objective and ensure you place the person's needs and what would have been their wishes at the centre of your consideration.

The list in the section on p. 268, for managing difference of opinion, will help you check that you have considered every aspect. Make a clear record against every aspect you consider. There is an additional point for you to consider, which is whether there is a more senior person to whom you can appeal or complain. You should ask what the process is – there is more about this in the next section.

A number of times now I have said that you as attorney have the responsibility for the decision. This is not clear-cut in such cases; the medical team may equally have a responsibility for the decision, be this by law, under their professional duty of care, or ethical code of conduct. If a mutually agreeable compromise cannot be reached, then this is a situation which will need a court decision. If you sense an impasse is likely, then I would advocate legal advice sooner rather than later.

If you have a difference of opinion with an organisation of a lesser magnitude, then using the list on the previous page and the information below will assist you in negotiating your way through this.

As an attorney, you will be interacting with many organisations on behalf of your donor/granter, from care homes to banks and utility companies. Occasionally, you may be unhappy about the service offered by one of them. It's not possible for me to give definitive guidance here about what you can do in these instances as there are too many variations that could arise. However, it is possible for me to give general advice:

- Be clear about your position, what the person themselves would be permitted to have, or not, what you can ask for, or not, what your PoA permits, or not. If this requires you to do some background research first, then complete this before raising any issue with the organisation. You need to be sure of your position before tackling the issue; you do not want to take a stance, albeit for what may seem a very legitimate reason, only to find you are faced with an embarrassing climbdown.

- As part of your research I would recommend you read Chapter 13, which is addressed to those organisations that you have to deal with; you can then assure yourself that you have considered things from their point of view.

- If you are progressing matters, ask the organisation for a copy of their complaints policy so you can find out the right person to report the issue to and the right channels and process for escalation of the matter. State your issue clearly, why you believe the matter is unsatisfactory and what you would wish as the outcome. Progress the matter in a courteous manner, step by step, to the top if necessary.

Try to give each person at every level along the way an opportunity to resolve the matter. Try to avoid jumping a level, i.e. going to someone's superior without giving that person an opportunity first. Find out if there is a regulator or regulatory body that you can report things to if this becomes necessary. You should give the organisation every opportunity of resolving your issue before going to a regulator; typically, a regulator will not review your concerns unless the organisation's complaints process has been exhausted.

- Remember, there are agencies who can offer you support. They recognise that such challenges between attorney and authorities can arise and will signpost you on what can be a difficult path. If your concern is about the care provided by a care home, you may wish to look at the sister book to this, *Care Homes: The One-Stop Guide* as it has a section on complaining about care.

- A final thing for you to consider is whether there is merit in changing provider, e.g. switching energy supplier or bank. If this is something which you are contemplating, I would suggest checking the policy of the potential new provider on the matter at issue before switching and finding out that things are no different. You should also check that there are no penalties for switching from the current provider, or if there are, that you believe it is worth incurring them in the circumstances.

Mediation

Before closing this chapter on conflict, I should touch on mediation. The suggestion of mediation has been mentioned a couple of times. Mediation is a recognised process that can be used to settle disputes in a whole range of situations. It involves an independent third party, the mediator, supporting the parties who have a difference of opinion to decide whether they can resolve things and what the most appropriate solution should be.

A mediator does not take sides or make judgements. You and the person with whom you are in disagreement both have an opportunity to explain your view and hear the other side. If you are unable to reach an agreement, you can still follow formal procedures such as complaints or a court action. If you do ultimately have to go to court it can reflect positively on you, as an attorney, that you have tried, or agreed to, what is a lesser restrictive intervention (in line with the principles) in an effort to resolve the disagreement.

You can ask the OPG or local authority about access to mediation, but it is likely that this will have to be sought and funded privately. If the PoA allows for it, you can pay the costs from the incapable person's estate.

Chapter 13

Working with an attorney

In the preceding chapters I have 'spoken' to those thinking of a granting a PoA, so they are clear what to include, whom to nominate and how to grant a robust a PoA. I have also 'spoken' to attorneys to allow them to fulfil this role with confidence. This chapter is dedicated to those of you working with attorneys. You may be a banking official, a care home, a social worker, a landlord, a utilities company; there are a wide range of institutions that may need to rely on a PoA, or more specifically on the authority given by the PoA to the attorney. This chapter is for you; that said, a lot of the other chapters will have information of relevance so I will draw your attention to these as we go along.

This chapter will also be useful if you are an attorney, or thinking of setting up a PoA – it's always good to know what is required of another's position. As an attorney, it will help you to understand what questions or challenges organisations face; and as someone setting up a PoA, you might be interested to see the different checks and balances that exist for attorneys.

This chapter comprises four sections:

- General information – which gives you a quick reference guide; this should be supplemented by a more detailed reading of the other chapters to which you are directed.
- Frequently asked questions – which responds to the

more common questions which arise when dealing with attorneys.

- Managing disagreements – which may be between you, the organisation, and an attorney, or between two attorneys; we look at how you manage their divergent views when these are impacting on the service you have to deliver.
- Reporting concerns about an attorney – which covers what to do if you have concerns about the way in which an attorney is fulfilling their role.

General information

Power of Attorney (PoA)

You should read Chapter 1, but in brief a PoA is a legal document which a person creates in order to grant to someone else the power to manage their affairs should they no longer be able to do so personally. A PoA can offer powers relating to finances, property and/or health and welfare matters.

Attorney

The attorney is the representative of the incapable person. Crucially, they should make a decision that the person themselves would have, or would likely have, made had they been able to do so personally. This can sometimes create a challenge when the attorney's view on the best or right course of action is different to the view the person themselves would have had.

You should find out whether your resident/client/patient has a PoA and who their nominated attorney is (see the FAQ section). Ideally, you need to develop an open and trusting relationship with that person, as you are both acting, in your respective ways, to support the person with incapacity.

Legal principles

There is a set of legal principles, covered in Chapter 9, with which you should make yourself familiar. Anyone exercising a function on behalf of an incapable adult is required to respect these principles. Thus, you need to ensure you are aware of them and respect them in your own dealings with an attorney on behalf of your incapable client/resident/patient.

Supporting decision-making

Chapter 7 covers the requirement to support an incapable person with their decision-making. You should read this chapter and become familiar with what this means as this requirement extends to you.

Respect for rights, will and preferences

Chapter 7 also covers the requirement to respect an incapable person's rights, their will on a given matter as well as their preferences. You should read the section on p. 137 so that you are familiar with what this means as this requirement also extends to you.

Code of Practice

The Code of Practice is mentioned in Chapters 2 and 9; it is a best-practice guide and can be a helpful reference document. If you are not sure how to progress with something it may well offer a steer. Consequently, as a person working with, or for, a person with incapacity it is important that you are aware of the Code of Practice and its content.

Frequently asked questions

This section addresses some of the more common questions which arise from organisations who are working with an attorney.

How do I know if the person is the attorney?

An attorney who is seeking to rely on a PoA will have a copy of it; you are perfectly entitled to ask to see this. Be wary of anyone who says they don't have a copy, can't find it, will bring it tomorrow but doesn't etc. In the majority of cases, the person will provide you with the PoA, on which you will see them named as the appointed attorney. If you have any uncertainty you can double-check with the public register (see below) where you will see the name of the attorney/s.

It is not uncommon for a person acting as a Department for Work and Pensions (DWP) appointee (someone appointed by the DWP to manage the person's DWP benefits) to refer to themselves as the attorney. This is usually a misunderstanding on their part about the differing roles of appointee and attorney, rather than any deliberate attempt to pass themselves off as the attorney.

Public register

You can check if a person has granted a PoA, and if so, who is appointed as attorney, in the public register. In order for a PoA to be valid it has to be registered with the relevant Office of the Public Guardian (OPG). You can check whether a PoA is registered, and a limited amount of other information, including who the attorney is, by telephoning the OPG (Scotland) or by making a request on the appropriate form to the OPG (England and Wales).* In due course you may find that the public register

---

* https://www.gov.uk/find-someones-attorney-deputy-or-guardian.

is available online; a review of the respective OPG website will then advise how you get access to the register.

How do I know what powers the attorney has?

It will depend on whether it is a property and finance or health and welfare PoA, which in Scotland can be combined in a single PoA.

In England and Wales, the donor will have decided what powers, if any, they do not wish the attorney to have; you should therefore check what exclusions, if any, there are. If there are no exclusions, then the attorney is authorised to take such decisions as the donor themselves would have been permitted to make (but see the next section).

In Scotland, the PoA deed will list the powers. There is also, in most cases, a catch-all power (called a plenary power), which tends to come before all the listed powers and which says something along the lines of 'everything I would otherwise have been able to do myself'.

So, to check whether the attorney is authorised to conduct the element of business in question, look within the listed powers to see if the attorney has an express power which would cover the matter, and if not check to see if they have a plenary power that they, and you, can rely on.

Chapter 2 tells you more about the powers that an attorney can have, and the first sections of Chapter 10 would be of value for you to read.

What if there is more than one attorney; can I deal with either, or any, of them?

Chapter 3 offers detail on how attorneys are appointed and what this means. In brief, if attorneys are appointed jointly, then you must deal with all of them; if they are appointed with individual authority, then you may deal with any of them. You should check the PoA to see how the attorneys are appointed as you may find yourself liable for actions taken on the say-so of only one of them if the authority of all of them, jointly, was required.

Can I accept a photocopy of the PoA?

Whether you can accept a photocopy will depend on your company policy but, by law, you can accept an authenticated copy of the original, i.e. you are not required to see or have the principal version. There are a number of ways in which a copy of the original can be authenticated formally as a true copy; the ones you will usually see are validated by the donor/granter themselves or by a solicitor.

There is a form of words that needs to be used to declare the copy a true copy of the original: see the Resources section at the back of this book.

Can an attorney with relevant power make whatever decision they want?

There is a process that an attorney must go through before they take a decision for the person, even if they have the power to make this decision.

1. Assessing capacity

Welfare powers only commence if the person is incapable in respect of the decision to be made; so if the decision is of a welfare nature, the first thing an attorney should do is satisfy themselves that the person is not capable of making this decision for themselves. Chapter 8 offers a comprehensive overview of how one determines capacity. You should become familiar with this yourself.

2. Supporting decision-making

Connected to this, before the attorney decides the person is incapable, they must first have offered all support that may be necessary to allow the person to make their own decision. See Chapter 7. This requirement applies to property and finance PoAs as well as health and welfare.

3. Respecting the rights, will and preferences of the person

In making a decision on behalf of the person the attorney is obliged to respect the rights, will and preferences of that person. The decision should be one the person themselves would have made had they been able to do so. See Chapter 7.

4. Complying with statutory principles

The legal principles should be respected in considering the appropriateness of a decision. See Chapter 9.

Do I have to comply with a decision of the attorney?

> *A common example is an attorney who wishes to deny access by other family members to a person who is now in care. The care home may feel it is preferable for their resident to have visits from their broader family but are aware that the attorney, who has the relevant authority, is opposing this. The care home do not agree with the attorney's decision but they feel their hands are tied. Does the care home have to comply with the decision of the attorney?*

Not without your own consideration of the matter. You will have your own duty of care to your resident/patient/client/customer/tenant. You may have professional standards/policies/

rules/codes that you are required to adhere to. Mere compliance with a decision of the attorney without your own consideration of the matter may place you in breach of your professional responsibilities, or even your industry or professional regulator.

You are legally obliged to follow the same steps outlined above. So, you must first satisfy yourself that the person is not capable of making the decision personally, having offered whatever support may be necessary to facilitate them to make their own decision. You must also consider their rights, will and preferences in respect of the matter. You are also required to act in accordance with the principles of the relevant Act.

So, if I don't necessarily have to comply with a decision of the attorney, can I just disregard the attorney?

No. When exercising any function for an incapable person you are obliged to adhere to the legal principles, one of which is respecting the incapable person's past wishes. The person, while capable, elected the attorney as their representative, so you must have regard to them. The attorney is effectively the voice of the person in that moment.

Another of the principles requires you to take account of the views of relevant others which, most definitely, would include an attorney.

We talk below about what you should do if you disagree with the decision of an attorney.

We have been discussing here how much notice you must take of an attorney, but the question applies equally the other way around: how much notice does an attorney have to take of your view?

To comply with the principles an attorney must take account

of the views of others (you in this case). The requirement is to *take account* of the views of others (you), i.e. your view must be given due consideration. It is not a gratuitous exercise; an attorney cannot take account of your view then simply disregard it because it does not accord with their own. They have to have justification for setting aside your views.

The level of regard the attorney should pay to your views will depend on your relationship with the incapable person and your level of expertise; so, for example, if you are the care home you are the primary carer, and have a statutory position and thus higher status than if you were simply a good friend. If you are the person's medical specialist you have a higher level of expertise so your views, on a relevant medical matter, must be given more weight than, say, the views of a friend on that same matter.

What are the attorney's responsibilities in respect of financial administration?

In short, an attorney has a fiduciary responsibility; this is a duty to manage money in a careful and proper manner, for the best interests/benefit of the person whose money they are managing. Chapter 11 provides a lot of detail about the attorney's responsibility for managing money.

I can see changes in patterns of money management; what should I do?

Changes in patterns of money management may be an indication of wider financial administrative shortcomings and should be reported (see the final section of this chapter).

Managing disagreements

You can see from the nature of many of these FAQs that organisations have the most anxiety when there is tension between them and an attorney, or when they are seemingly caught between two attorneys with divergent views. This next section looks at how an organisation may manage these situations.

Disagreement between you and an attorney

If you haven't already got one, you would be advised to have a policy on how you support your client/patient/resident/tenant to maintain their autonomy and independence. The policy should include how you treat capacity as decision-specific, and that you presume capacity as a starting point when seeking a person's input on matters affecting and relating to them. It should cover how you apply the legal principles, and how you respect the person's rights, their will and preferences in supporting the person in their autonomous decision-making. It should include how you will approach best-interpretation decision-making in the event that the person cannot make their own decision. This should include when you will involve independent advocacy, more of which below. Chapters 6–9 cover these various matters.

Specific to this section, this policy should also include how you manage disagreements with attorneys; this is more important if you too hold a statutory position, e.g. if you are the care home and so are the primary carer. You should offer this policy to all key persons involved in the life of a new resident/patient/client/tenant as part of the induction of the individual into your care.

In the event of a disagreement arising there is, effectively, an escalation process.

1. First, always review your communication. Chapter 12 stressed the importance of open and timely communication to avoid conflicts arising or escalating. If you sense tension, the first thing you should consider therefore is whether you should adjust the nature, style, frequency or format of your communication. This can often be sufficient in itself to resolve, or de-escalate, the situation.

2. Be clear that the person is incapable in respect of the decision to be made.

3. Be clear that you have done all that you can to support the person to offer their own view.

4. Arrange an early meeting with the attorney, acknowledge the issues and try to agree a mutually acceptable way forward.

At this meeting:

5. If the person can input to the decision, remind the attorney of your policy on this and the respect you will give to the person's own view.

6. If necessary, remind the attorney of the legal obligations that both you and they must fulfil – to respect the legal principles, to support the person's own decision-making, to respect the rights, will and preferences of the person; to act in accordance with your best interpretation of what would have been their will and preferences on the matter.

7. You may wish to take the advice of your organisation's legal department if you haven't already done so.

8. If you have not already done so, consider whether the expertise of an independent representative or advocate will allow the person to offer their own view. An advocate could represent the views of the person by way of non-instructed

advocacy if the person cannot offer their own opinion (there is more on this below).

9. Consider the involvement of others; who can assist? Another attorney, another relative, a long-standing friend, for example.

10. Arrange a case conference with all key parties invited, including the incapable person themselves, so that a comprehensive review of the way forward can be explored fully.

11. If you have reached an impasse you may wish to consider asking the court for direction. I offer this as an option, not to suggest that you have to go to court if you cannot resolve things any other way. You should take legal advice about what legal options may be available to you in your given circumstances.

Disagreement between two other parties

Sadly, this is not uncommon. Typically, as in the example above, one relative is the attorney and is denying another relative something to which that other relative feels they are entitled, or indeed may even be entitled. A common example is where the attorney who has powers to decide who can visit their elderly relative in care has decided that their sibling is not permitted. The sibling is aggrieved at not being able to visit their parent, on the whim of the attorney as they see it.

You may feel like you are expected to be the intermediary. Without seeming to take sides, you can signpost both as to where they can get additional support, e.g. the local authority social work department, the OPG, Citizens Advice, or suggest they review the Code of Practice.

If you wish to consider something more active, action is likely to follow the same pathway as that outlined immediately above.

If the matter is at impasse, and particularly if you feel the individual's views are not being considered or respected, then you may wish to report the matter to the local authority, OPG, or Mental Welfare Commission (in Scotland). You can decide whether you advise the attorney of this; you are not required to.

What should you do in the interim?

It is hard for me to be definitive about this as it will vary depending on who the parties to the disagreement are. For example, if it is a situation where two attorneys have diverging views, which one of them are you to accept instruction from? You can find yourself being pushed and pulled by their dispute. In these situations, easy as it is to say, you have to reach your own objective view based on all the things we have spoken about – the view of the person, best interpretation of their view, the rights, the principles, your policy on this etc. – and advise both attorneys that you are siding with neither of them per se, but for X, Y Z reasons, this is how you will be approaching the situation – which will probably be seen as siding with one of them; you will need to accept this. I have emphasised a number of times the importance of comprehensive record-keeping; Chapter 10 offers detail, and this is one such occasion when detailed records are crucial.

If the dispute is between the attorney and a third party, you may feel you have to respect the attorney's authority, even if you disagree with the line they are taking. The FAQs covered this scenario. You should not simply comply with the decision of an attorney, because they are the attorney, where this is damaging to the person. You have a duty at least to report this to the authorities.

In any dispute you should respect your organisation's protocol on management of disagreements, if they have one, and you should consider involving, or indeed may be obliged by any protocol to involve, your organisation's legal department.

Can we involve an independent (mental capacity) advocate if the attorney is refusing this?

The involvement of an independent advocate has been referred to a number of times; their role in supporting a person with incapacity is covered in Chapter 7.

The involvement of an advocate, an independent and impartial third party, can be extremely valuable where there is a divergence of views, be this between attorneys, or attorney and other parties, or even between the attorney and yourselves.

When such differences arise, the views of the incapable person can easily be lost sight of; you need to be alert to this. There is an obligation to support the person's autonomous decision-making, and to act in accordance with their will and preferences. If this has been overlooked in the fracture of the disputing parties, you should consider whether an advocate may be of value in reinstating focus on the views of the person.

You may find, however, that if you suggest advocacy involvement to the attorney they refuse. This leads to the frequently asked question: can I ask for an advocacy opinion even if the attorney is refusing this?

There is a subtlety which arises next. The answer is no, you cannot involve an advocate to represent the views of the person in the dispute if the attorney has declined this. Although of course you should try and persuade them to agree, reminding them of their responsibilities to take account of the wishes of the person.

However, you have a duty of care to your resident/client/patient and have all the same obligations to support that person's autonomous decision-making and respect their preferences; to fail to do so places you in breach of the law, as has been said. Consequently, if you feel the assistance of an independent advocate would help *you* to fulfil *your* obligations, then you should take legal advice about arranging this, whatever the view of the attorney.

You will appreciate that this needs caution; it can appear as if you are countermanding the authority of the attorney and involving an advocate anyway. If this is something you are contemplating, before proceeding I would advise you to take legal advice. The advice should direct you in two things: a) on the principle of you instructing an advocate and b) on just what your instructions to the independent advocate should be. The instructions to the advocate must focus on asking the advocate to establish things, if this proves possible, which allow *you* to fulfil *your* own statutory or regulatory compliance; it is not about the dispute per se, it is an advocacy opinion for you, to ensure you comply with your statutory requirements. Careful framing of the instruction is key.

You should advise the attorney that you are doing this. We talked earlier about a policy for managing conflicts; if you have one, then ensure you are acting in accordance with it. You should have advised the attorney, as part of your induction process, about your policy for managing conflicts, which makes it a lot easier now to tell them that you are instructing advocacy and that the advocacy is to advise you, to make sure you fulfil your duties and obligations and are thus acting lawfully.

So, in summary, you cannot countermand the authority of an attorney and invite an advocate to represent the views of the person directly in the disputed matter, but you can invite an advocate to represent the views of the person to you, so you can comply with your statutory obligation to take account of their views and respect their wishes. There is a subtle but fundamental difference.

Reporting concerns about an attorney

This section may seem to cast attorneys in a negative light. At the outset, therefore, please let me stress that the vast majority of attorneys take on onerous responsibilities, often in difficult circumstances, and do a sterling job, willingly, with dedication and without complaint. However, abuse of the vulnerable is more common than we may care to accept.

What is abuse?

Sometimes I wonder whether the word 'abuse' is so serious that it causes us to overlook more minor intransigencies that are nonetheless abuse. Perhaps we should think in terms of ab-use – i.e. improper use.

Abuse can occur in many forms; it can be physical, including by neglect, or it can be financial, verbal, psychological or sexual. It can be a single act, or a series of acts, of the same nature or different; it can arise from failures or omissions to do something that ought to have been attended to. There is often more than one form of abuse occurring: for example, a daughter who says she won't keep doing the shopping for her mother unless Mum pays her £20. Mum knows she needs her daughter's support so pays her the £20; here we have both psychological and financial abuse.

There aren't any statistics that tell us, reliably, how much abuse occurs and then, as a subset of this, how much is committed by attorneys, but abuse by attorneys does occur.

Recognising abuse

Below are some examples of factors that may place you on alert; but there are so many things that may present a red flag that an exhaustive list cannot be given. It is safest to remain open to the fact that attorney ab-use can arise; do not overlook a red flag thinking, 'No, it can't be, I must be mistaken or imagining.' If you have any concerns about the way in which an attorney is acting, then report this soonest (there is information on how to do this in the next section).

Some examples of abuse are:

- unexplained physical injury – for example, cuts, bruises, welts, burns, fractures (bearing in mind that any of these can occur purely accidentally, especially in older people, so do not of themselves suggest anything untoward)

- untreated injuries in various stages of healing or not properly treated

- poor hygiene (when this is unusual for the person)

- loss of weight

- soiled clothing; unkempt appearance

- missed medical/dental/optical appointments

- the person talking about things which suggest abuse

- changed or unusual spending habits

- unexplained financial transactions

- monies around the house vanishing

- possessions missing from their home

- rings or jewellery missing from their person

- a new best 'friend'

- legal documents being changed or disappearing

- unpaid bills, utilities that are shut off, or threats of eviction

- signatures that seem to be forged

- unexplained mood changes

- becoming overly talkative or under-talkative, being particularly defensive

- withdrawal from social groups
- unexpected changes to visiting pattern of relatives
- estranged relatives reconnecting.

Many of these alone may be perfectly innocent, or part of a natural disease progression, but when coupled with other factors may be indicative of a wider picture. As a single organisation you may only see one changed behaviour and so think nothing of it, but if you reported it the central agency would be aware that, in fact, they had several reports of changed behaviours from different organisations.

By way of example:

- *Mrs Smith attended a weekly lunch club. The organisers noticed her becoming depressed, then she stopped coming.*

- *Mrs Smith has a cleaner each week; Mrs Smith leaves money on the side for her. Several times recently there has been no money left, but the cleaner doesn't like to say anything as she is aware that Mrs Smith is getting a bit forgetful.*

- *Mrs Smith's neighbour has noticed that, unusually, her grandchildren are visiting regularly; on chatting to Mrs Smith about how happy she must be about this Mrs Smith starts crying and abruptly ends the conversation.*

- *Mrs Smith's good friend notices that she is no longer wearing her engagement ring; she would normally always have this on.*

Each of these, in isolation, may be indicative of a general deterioration in Mrs Smith's condition, but when grouped together may suggest an abuse that needs further inquiry; but if the lunch club, the cleaner, the friend and the neighbour all say nothing, because individually none of them have anything definitive to report, then the potential abuse can continue.

The message from this is: no matter how small your concern, and even if it turns out to be nothing to have been worried about, it is still better reported.

The focus so far has been on deliberate abuse; but abuse, especially by a family carer, can be unintentional. Being a carer is a relentless task; carers generally receive minimal support and often no respite, which can occasionally result in unacceptable behaviour by the carer towards the cared-for. This is not to excuse any maltreatment by a carer, but rather to put it in context and recognise that carers need help too. In reporting what appears to be a sign of abuse, you may obtain support for a fraught carer who did not know where to turn or may not even have realised how emotionally difficult the situation had become.

Up to this point we have talked about recognising the signs of abuse, but these can be very hard to spot: a person being abused may avoid conversation, have remarkably plausible explanations for things or put up a great shield of pretence, so you shouldn't feel any guilt if you learn that abuse was happening and you didn't recognise it.

I have deliberately called this section reporting 'concerns' rather than reporting abuse. There can be a tendency for people who have concerns to adopt a wait-and-see approach in order to try to satisfy themselves that there definitely is something of concern and that they're not just imagining things. If there is abuse, a wait-and-see approach allows it to continue, so you should report early anything which you are concerned about.

Before we consider this further, it is worth touching here on the supervision of attorneys or, more pertinently, the absence of this. Attorneys are not supervised routinely. The reason for this is that a PoA is a document granted by a person while capable, appointing, presumably, a person they trust to support them and act for them as may be necessary. It is seen as inappropriate for a state authority to supervise the person a capable individual has chosen to appoint. There is a reliance, therefore, on you reporting things where you have concerns. Let us consider this more.

Concerns about the way in which an attorney is operating can arise. Examples may be: an attorney apparently spending the now incapable person's money on themselves, or making decisions that seem not to be in the individual's best interests.

You should not worry about reporting concerns; no one will judge you for doing so. Do not worry whether it is something you can or should report, or not. Any concern can be reported; there is nothing off-limits. It is never too early to report something, but it can be too late. It is better to report something early, even if it turns out to be nothing, rather than leave it, report it late and find out you were right all along and wished you had done something sooner.

Concerns can be reported to a variety of people, including:

- to the attorney, if it is not the attorney themselves giving rise to the concern
- to a second attorney, if there is one, where you have concerns about one of them
- to the person's GP if it is a medical issue and you know who the GP is
- to the person's bank, if you have financial concerns and know who they bank with
- to the relevant local authority safeguarding services – you can report any concerns to them, no matter what form or how minor you feel they are

- to the Care Quality Commission (England): Care Inspectorate (Wales) or Care Inspectorate (Scotland) or Regulation and Quality Improvement Authority (Northern Ireland); these bodies are the regulators of care homes, so they would be keen to hear of any concerns you have about care
- to the respective OPG for welfare and financial matters in England and Wales, or for financial matters in Scotland
- to the Mental Welfare Commission (Scotland) for welfare or financial matters
- to a relevant charitable helpline, for example Hourglass (formerly Action on Elder Abuse)
- to the police, if you feel it is sufficiently serious.

There are so many possible agencies here that you may feel confused about who to raise your concern with. Don't worry about getting the right authority; they all know of each other so if you have approached the wrong one they will either accept your concern and refer it on or direct you to the correct agency.

The majority of the agencies prefer a written report of a concern and may have a form for you to complete. You should check the relevant website, where information on how to report a concern will be available, and any forms that you need can be completed or downloaded from there. If there is no form but they do require it in writing, you can email them via their contact-us button or send a typed or handwritten letter to their postal address. Some organisations accept reports verbally, via a telephone helpline or call centre; you may prefer to start with this route, if only to get information on how they prefer you to progress your concern.

You don't need hard evidence or proof before you can report

something; for example, you don't need a copy of a bank statement to evidence financial misconduct. You will rarely find the hard evidence or be entitled to access it, and waiting to see if it materialises may mean a delay in which further abuse arises. An explanation of the circumstances which have given rise to the concern are sufficient.

Let's look at an example.

> *You are Agnes's home help. You visit each week. You notice that a picture of Susie, Agnes's daughter, which was always on the shelf, has disappeared; you ask about this and Agnes is at first evasive, then makes up an excuse which holds no water. The next week you make a drink for Agnes and notice her fridge is empty and she has no biscuits, which is unusual as you know she enjoys one with her tea. When you talk to Agnes about this she gets angry with you; you've never seen her like this before. This same month, the monthly bank transfer to you for your support to Agnes, arranged by Susie as her mum's attorney, is not made. You speak to Susie; she apologises profusely and says she will rectify this but takes no action. You contact Susie again but cannot get hold of her.*

There are a number of red flags in this example:

- the picture of Susie has been removed
- Agnes is evasive about this then makes an excuse that holds no water
- the fridge is empty
- Agnes does not have her usual biscuit treats
- Agnes gets angry when you mention this
- Susie misses your payment

- this is not remedied even though you have raised this with her
- you then cannot get hold of Susie.

Any of these alone may be nothing, but when combined are sufficient for a referral to be made to one of the safeguarding agencies mentioned above. You have no hard evidence of anything untoward, but you can use the factors above, which have prompted the alert, in support of the concern you raise. Once submitted, the agency can then decide what they do with the information you have given them. If they need anything more from you, they will come back to you.

You do not have to tell anyone you are reporting a concern. For example, in the Agnes / Susie scenario above, the home help may wish to report her concerns about Susie – the flags that have alerted her and caused her to become concerned. She does not have to tell Agnes or Susie that she is doing so, or has done so.

Confidentiality

Many people worry about confidentiality if they decide to report a concern; will the person being complained about find out who made the complaint? In principle complaints are confidential; so, for example, in the Agnes / Susie scenario if this has been reported to the OPG, they would not go to Susie and say, 'We've had a complaint from your mum's home help about a number of things that have given her cause for concern.' However, absolute confidentiality cannot be guaranteed. What this means, using the example of the Public Guardian again, is that if your complaint results in a report to the police or to the courts, the Public Guardian will be obliged to say from whom the complaint originated; if the matter progresses the person being complained about will ultimately find out who made the complaint.

If you raise a concern, you may want to know the outcome; but confidentiality applies here too. You should not expect to find out the full (or maybe even any of the) outcome. The organisations and professionals involved are bound by an ethical code and duty of confidentiality so there will be certain things they are not permitted to tell you, even if you are the person who went to them in the first place. This can be frustrating, but please do not let this put you off raising concerns in the first place.

I should finish by reiterating that it is only a minority of attorneys whose actions give cause for concern; the vast majority of attorneys work committedly, often in difficult situations, and their only focus is to do their utmost for their loved one. Organisations which work with attorneys should develop their skill and expertise in order that they can identify, as early as is possible, those attorneys whose actions do require challenging and have the confidence to do so.

Resources and helpful organisations

Useful terminology

Acts	Refers to the Acts of Parliament governing the field of incapacity. In England and Wales this is the Mental Capacity Act 2005 and in Scotland the Adults with Incapacity (Scotland) Act 2000.
adult	In Scotland, the term that is used in the AWI to refer to a person who has lost mental capacity.
attorney	The general name for someone appointed under a PoA to act on behalf of a person who is no longer mentally able to do so personally.
AWI	Adults with Incapacity (Scotland) Act 2000
continuing power of attorney	In Scotland, a property and financial PoA which continues after the person has lost capacity.

deputy	In England and Wales, the name of the person appointed by the court to manage the affairs of a now incapable person where no prior attorney has been appointed, or no attorney with relevant powers.
donor	In England and Wales, the person who has executed (made) the PoA.
DWP	Department of Work and Pensions
granter	In Scotland, the person who has executed (made) the PoA.
guardian	In Scotland, the person appointed by the court to manage the affairs of a now incapable person where no prior attorney has been appointed, or no attorney with relevant powers.
jurisdiction	The word has a range of meanings, but in this case it refers to a legal territory. There are three separate jurisdictions for adult incapacity matters in the UK: England and Wales, Scotland and Northern Ireland.
Lasting Power of Attorney (LPA)	In England and Wales, a PoA which lasts beyond the person's incapacity and gives property and financial powers.
LPA health and welfare	In England and Wales, a PoA which commences on the person's incapacity and gives health and welfare powers.
MCA	Mental Capacity Act 2005 (England and Wales)

Office of the Public Guardian	See OPG.
OPG	The Office of the Public Guardian. The body established in England and Wales by the Mental Capacity Act 2005 and in Scotland by the Adults with Incapacity (Scotland) Act 2000. In respect of attorneys the OPG register PoAs and support and supervise attorneys as may be required. They have an investigatory function which allows them to inquire into the actions of an attorney where concerns have been reported.
ordinary PoA	A PoA that offers financial authority which ceases on incapacity, i.e. does not last or continue into incapacity.
'P'	In England and Wales, the term that is used in the MCA to refer to a person who has lost mental capacity.
PoA	The legal document which appoints and authorises an attorney to act on your behalf if you are no longer mentally able to do so personally.
Power of Attorney	
the principles	The values which underpin the actions of anyone working with or for a person with incapacity. They appear in Section 1 of the respective Acts.
Public Guardian	The head of the OPG, the official charged with ensuring the OPG fulfils its statutory function.

RWP	Rights, will and preferences
sole attorney	A person appointed as the only attorney on a PoA
SDM	Supported decision-making
UNCRPD	United Nations Convention on the Rights of Persons with Disabilities
welfare power of attorney	In Scotland, a PoA which commences on the person's incapacity and gives health and welfare powers.

Example of Typical PoA Powers

These examples are not exhaustive, nor are they legally worded. It is insufficient for you to cut and paste these into a blank PoA document.

Financial and Property Powers

You can offer powers over such things as:

- bank accounts
- pensions, benefits, allowances and the like
- deeds, documents, contracts
- investment and tax planning. Payment of tax
- access to financial and other relevant confidential information
- household expenses, common repairs
- insurance
- buying, selling, leasing property
- medical care and residential care costs

- debts
- legal action
- gifts
- payment for holidays or respite care
- cars
- employment of others
- access to social media

Welfare Powers

You can give authority to someone to make decisions on your behalf about such things as:

- care and accommodation
- deprivation of liberty powers
- access to medical and other relevant confidential information
- consent, or refusal of consent, to medical treatments
- dress, diet and personal appearance
- social and cultural activities
- who may visit, or not
- work, education or training
- holidays or respite care

Endorsing a PoA

We talked in Chapters 5 and 10 about endorsed copies of PoAs and how valuable these can be.

An endorsed copy is a confirmation that a copy of the original PoA is a true copy, or representation, of the original. The donor/granter of the PoA can endorse their own copies. I explain below how you do this and the wording which must be included on each page of the copy for it to be classified as an officially endorsed copy.

1. Scan or photocopy the original, i.e. produce a replica of it. Make as many copies as you think you need.

2. You, the donor/granter, must sign and date each page (apart from the last page) with the words: *I declare this is a true and complete copy of the corresponding page of the original.*

3. You must sign and date the final page with the words: *I declare this is a true and complete copy of the original.*

4. Someone else can write all the words: you can just sign and date it. I would advocate signing in blue ink (or a colour other than black), as this gives rise to less challenge about whether it is a photocopy.

You *cannot* just put the declaration and signature on one copy and photocopy that as many times as you wish as this secondary photocopy is not an image of the original, but rather is an image of a copy of the original, which is not acceptable as an endorsed copy.

Endorsing a copy is best done as soon as the PoA is returned to you, so there can be no later challenge as to your capacity to have made this declaration.

Creating a Statement of Wishes and Feelings

An attorney is required to respect the wishes, feelings, will and preferences of the donor/granter; for these to be 'spelled out' in a Statement of Wishes and Feelings can be extremely valuable in facilitating the attorney to respect the donor/granter's views.

There are no rules about what a Statement of Wishes and Feelings should, or should not, include; it can include anything that is important to you. The following information will offer you a guide.

The headings below are my suggestions as to how you might divide the information in your Statement. Using headings will help people to navigate the text and find things quickly. However, since this is not a legal document and is intended to reflect your wishes, you should feel free to structure it as you see fit.

Preferences

On pp. 99–100 I offered an example of the type of things you may wish to include in a list of preferences in a Statement of Wishes and Feelings. There is no limit to what you can specify; cover anything which you wish to bring to the attention of people who will be using the Statement at a later date to guide decisions they make for you, should this become necessary.

Factual information

As well as your preferences, it is helpful to include some factual information, e.g.:

- the name of your doctor and address of the medical practice
- any relevant past medical history
- medications that you are on
- any allergies you may have
- any aids you may need for your mobility
- the name of your dentist and address of the dental practice
- if you have false teeth, a dental plate or crowns

- the name of your optician
- if you wear distance or reading glasses, or contact lenses
- if you wear a hearing aid and where you have your hearing tests
- any family history that your attorney needs to know
- family that you would wish to remain in contact with, or prefer not to see
- where you bank
- where personal papers can be found
- if you have made a PoA, and where this can be found
- anything about your pensions that your attorney may need
- any other financial information they may need
- who your financial advisor is, if you have one
- who your solicitor is, if you have one
- who holds title deeds to your house, if you have one
- where a copy of your will can be found, if you have one
- which church you worship at, if you do
- any social groups you attend
- if you donate to any charities, or would not wish donations to certain charities
- which hairdresser you use, if you do
- any other factual information about you that your attorney may not know or that you would want your attorney to know.

Special instructions

If there are particular instructions, include these in the Statement. For example:

*'I wish my daughter Beth to continue to live in the house, even
if I have to go into care. This is her home.'*

*'I do not wish you to sell the diamond necklace in my jewellery
box as this is gifted to Beth in my will.'*

You need to be aware that the attorney is obliged to respect
your wishes, but it may not always be possible to give effect to
these; for example, if you make it clear that you do not wish
your house to be sold, but this becomes necessary, your attorney may be left with no option but to sell, notwithstanding your
preferences.

Explanatory information

Some of the things you have requested above may be news to the
person now caring for you or may come as a surprise to them.
If you think this is likely to be the case, it can be helpful to offer
some explanatory information; this helps your loved ones understand your position and thus makes it more likely that they will
respect it. An example may be:

*'I would like my grandson Adam to take over the running of my
business if I am not able to do so personally. This may come as
a surprise to some of you, as he is fresh out of college, but I see
him as an extremely bright young man who will go far in the
business world. We have had many a long conversation about
his aspirations and he shows a natural aptitude for the business.
He is enthusiastic and can be hands-on, when I know the rest
of you already have your own families and work to look after.
Adam: Sally, my very trusty secretary, has all the information
you need to hit the ground running. Use her wisely Dear Boy
and treat her well. Good luck, have fun, be happy and do me
proud. I have every faith.'*

Information on family and friends

This section is particularly important if you have a more complex family situation. It is quite common for long-lost family to get in touch when they hear a relative is ill. It can be hard for those caring for you to know whether they should allow a particular individual, or certain people, to visit you.

Offering them some guidance within your Statement of Wishes and Feelings about whom you would wish to see, or maybe whom you would not wish to see no matter what, can be extremely helpful.

If there is a good friend with whom you have shared many confidences it can be helpful to name this person in your Statement. This person would potentially be able to offer your family information about you that maybe they themselves do not know.

Confidentiality

It can be hard for your loved ones to know what information to share with others, particularly other family members. This is often the cause of family upsets, where one family member thinks information is being deliberately withheld from them but the other family member is only trying to respect your confidentiality. Consequently, it can be helpful to include something in your Statement of Wishes and Feelings about what information you are happy to be shared with whom, or not, as the case may be.

Expressions of love, affection and appreciation

Some people choose to include in their Statement of Wishes and Feelings an expression of their love, affection or appreciation to family and friends; this is especially relevant if they have struggled to find the right words while able to do so.

It is important for any person close to you to hear of your love, affection or appreciation if they haven't already, but it may be particularly important if you have a family member who has become estranged:

> *'To Paul, I know we fell out a long time ago but I want you to know that I have thought about you every day and no matter what happened you will always be my son and I will always love you.'*

If including such statements is not for you, just omit this.

Style

A Statement of Wishes and Feelings does not have to be a dull list of instructions. It can leave a legacy for your family showing your personality. There is no set format, so draft it however it seems right for you. The comment to Adam under **Explanatory information** above is an illustration of how a Statement can show personality.

Thanks/close

It can be nice to offer thanks to the person now taking care of all your wishes.

> *'These are my wishes and feelings. I am aware that this is not a legally binding document, but if I lose the capacity to make decisions personally, I wish for this document to be used by others to guide how I should be cared for and how my affairs should be administered.*
>
> *I thank, most sincerely, those who are now, as far as is possible, trying to respect these. Your efforts for me are very much appreciated.'*

Then remember to sign and date this.

Keep it somewhere safe and tell key people where it is.

If you have a PoA, give a copy to you nominated attorney/s.

If you have a solicitor, you may wish to give a copy to them.

You should give a copy to your doctor for filing in your medical records.

Anticipatory care plan

A Statement of Wishes and Feelings can complement an anticipatory care plan.

Anticipatory care planning helps you make informed choices about what, how and where you want to be treated and supported in the future. For example, if you have a chronic illness you can work with your health and social-care team to anticipate the likely disease pathway and so advise them on how you would wish this to be managed. This becomes your anticipatory care plan. Hopefully, you can see from this how it complements a statement of your wishes and feelings.

If an anticipatory care plan is something which you think would be of benefit for you, a web search will bring up several sites which give you all the relevant information; alternatively, speak to your doctor about this

A life story book?

Some people wish to do a life story book in addition to a Statement of Wishes and Feelings. This can be helpful too as it shows 'you' to people caring for you at a later stage who may not have known the younger you. A life story book is like an album, with pictures, souvenirs and mementos which accompany the story of your life. There is no set format; include whatever makes you who you are. Examples may be:

- where you were born
- the names of your parents and any siblings
- where you lived as a child
- any pets you had
- where you were schooled
- what qualifications you obtained
- any memories that stay with from your young days
- any higher education
- your working life
- things you have achieved/are proud of
- when and how you met your partner
- the birth dates and names of any children
- hobbies/volunteering
- family holidays
- times with good friends
- things you have enjoyed in retirement
- anything else which you feel makes you who you are.

Include with the commentary, if you wish, the likes of photographs, press cuttings, certificates, badges, souvenirs – anything which brings your story to life. If you think doing this is too much for you, many of the charities have volunteers who can support you with the writing or typing-up and with the collation of your mementos.

There is no set format for a life story book. Dementia UK have a resource with ideas and a template, but you could buy a large photo or wedding album and fill it with any memorabilia you have; or you may choose to use a treasure/memory box rather than an album, filling it with treasured possessions. You can put photograph collages on the outside of such a box; let your creative side loose. It's all personal choice.

If you are an attorney for a loved one and there is no life story book, you may wish to think about making one; work with the person on this, drawing insights into their life into one album. Using stories and pictures from the person's history will give a valuable insight to others as to who they are. Often you find you learn things about the person, which can assist you with identifying where their values sit and so what their likely preferences on a matter would be should this become necessary. Putting such a life story together can assist the person's own recall and can offer many happy times, both in its creation and in looking through it over the months to come.

Advance Directive (living will)

An Advance Directive offers your views on your care in the final stage of life, about treatments you want or may wish to refuse. A Statement of Wishes and Feelings does not replace an Advance Directive. You may still wish to complete an Advance Directive; a web search will bring up several highly reputable sites which give you all the relevant information.

Sources of support and advice

The local authority social work department in the area in which the person resides. You can find a number for them by searching online for the relevant council. Their home page will usually link you to the social work department, which will contain the contact details.

The Office of the Public Guardian: the statutory authority for supporting attorneys as well as receiving complaints and investigating concerns about attorneys. Contact details are below.

Citizens Advice Bureaux: the national citizens' advisory service is a valuable source of support, or signposting. You can find a local service by an online search for Citizens Advice in your area.

Voluntary organisations, e.g. Age UK/Age Scotland, Alzheimer Society/Scotland.

There are a large range of voluntary and charitable organisations, some of which are listed below. Most will have websites; many facilitate social media chat for people in a similar position; some have face-to-face group meetings in some areas. You may be surprised how much is happening in your area that you had not been aware of. If you feel there is a lack of voluntary support, why not think about starting a group yourself?

Independent banking/financial/mortgage advisors. An online search will bring names of independent advisors in your area.

Legal advisors: most solicitors are familiar with PoAs and would be able to offer you advice to ensure you are acting properly on a given matter.

Government websites: there is a lot of information on the respective government websites. Contact details can be found over the page.

Useful organisations

Offices of the Public Guardian

Office of the Public Guardian (England and Wales)
PO Box 16185
Birmingham
B2 2WH
Telephone: 0300 466 0300

Office of the Public Guardian (Scotland)
Hadrian House
Callendar Business Park
Callendar Road
Falkirk
FK1 1XR
01324 678300

Office of Care and Protection (Northern Ireland)
Room 2.2A
Second Floor
Royal Courts of Justice
Chichester Street
Belfast
BT1 3JF
Telephone: 0300 200 7812
Email: OCP@courtsni.gov.uk

Financial contacts

British Banking Association
www.bba.org.uk
Telephone: 020 7216 8800

Financial Conduct Authority
www.fca.org.uk

Medical and clinical contacts

British Medical Association
www.bma.org.uk
telephone: 020 7387 4499

British Psychological Society
www.bps.org.uk
Telephone: 0116 254 9568

Mental Welfare Commission (Scotland)
www.mwcscot.org.uk
Advice line: 0800 389 6809

Care inspectors and regulators

The independent bodies responsible for monitoring and inspecting the availability and quality of care home services and encouraging improvements in the quality of those services.

Care Quality Commission (England)
Telephone: 03000 616161
Email: enquiries@cqc.org.uk

Care Inspectorate (Scotland)
enquiries@careinspectorate.gov.scot.
0345 600 9527

Care Inspectorate Wales
www.careinspectorate.wales
Helpline: 0300 7900 126

Regulation and Quality Improvement Authority
www.rqia.org.uk
Contact: 028 9536 1111

Government departments

Department of Work and Pensions
www.gov.uk/contact-jobcentre-plus
Find your local council: www.gov.uk/find-local-council

All government departments for England and Wales
www.gov.uk

Adult incapacity government site in Scotland
www.gov.scot/collections/adults-with-incapacity-
forms-and-guidance/

For PoA information in Northern Ireland
www.nidirect.gov.uk/articles/managing-your-affairs-and-
enduring-power-attorney

Mediation services

Family Mediation Council (England and Wales)
www.familymediationcouncil.org.uk
Telephone: 01707 594055

Scottish Mediation
www.scottishmediation.org.uk
Helpline: 0131 556 8118

Legal services

To find a solicitor:
Law Society (for England and Wales)
www.lawsociety.org.uk

Law Society of Scotland
www.lawscot.org.uk

Law Society of Northern Ireland
www.lawsoc-ni.org

Charities

Age UK
www.ageuk.org.uk
Advice line: 0800 055 6112

Age Scotland
www.ageuk.org.uk/scotland
0800 12 44 222

Age Wales
www.ageuk.org.uk/cymru
08000 223 444

Age Northern Ireland
www.ageuk.org.uk/northern-ireland
0808 808 7575

Alcohol Related Brain Damage
www.arbdcare.co.uk
01934 422 822

Alzheimer's Society
www.alzheimers.org.uk
Support line: 0333 150 3456
(This is the same web address and support line for Wales and Northern Ireland.)

Alzheimer Scotland
www.alzscot.org
Helpline: 0808 808 3000

Carers UK
www.carersuk.org
Contact their helpline by filling in the form which is on this website.

Citizens Advice Bureau
www.citizensadvice.org.uk
You will be directed from this home page to CABs in your
nation and from there you can find a local service.

Headway
For support with traumatic brain injury
www.headway.org.uk
Telephone: 08088002244

Lewy Body Society
For information on Lewy Body dementia
www.lewybody.org
Information line: 01942 914000
Helpline: 0800 888 6678 (manned by Admiral Nurses)

Mind
Support with learning disability and mental health
www.mind.org.uk
Support line: 0208 215 2243

Stroke Association
www.stroke.org.uk
Stroke Helpline: 0303 3033 100
Supporter Care: 0300 3300 740

We Are Hourglass
Dedicated to calling time on the harm and abuse of older
people
wearehourglass.org
From here you will get links to We Are Hourglass in Scotland,
Wales and Northern Ireland.
Helpline: 0808 808 8141

Acknowledgements

I wish to express my thanks for the support of the Offices of the Public Guardian in Scotland and England and Wales, both professionally over the years and specifically with information provided for this book. An amazing team of dedicated staff.

I have worked with many solicitors, social workers, doctors and civil servants, all of whom share a commitment to supporting some of our most vulnerable citizens. I have learned much from them – as well as from the many people who have shared their personal experiences with me in the hope of improving things for others.

I would like to acknowledge Adrian Ward for his expert guidance and support over so many years and to thank him for his professional feedback on the draft manuscript. Adrian is so well known in this area of law, especially in Scotland that, like Kylie and Cher, he doesn't actually need a surname but I've included it.

I would like to thank Professor June Andrews for suggesting I should write a book on PoAs. Although I have cursed her at various points along the way, as those who have felt the pain of writing a book will appreciate.

My husband and brother are worthy of awards for their patience, interest (even if feigned) and their willingness to listen – in some cases again and again as I went over various sections. Particular recognition has to go to my mum, Muriel Leach, for her dedication to my father over sixty-two years of marriage and most notably for her devoted care of him in his latter six years as he battled dementia. Her insights have helped to give this book a whole different dimension as I am able to relay the personal impact as well as the professional advice.

Last, but by no means least, my thanks to Louisa Dunnigan, Linden Lawson and Graeme Hall at Profile Books for providing me with many useful comments and suggestions from the perspective of independent readers.

Index

PoA indicates Power of Attorney.